Viva Kennedy

Number Twelve:

TEXAS A&M SOUTHWESTERN STUDIES

Robert A. Calvert and María Cristina García, General Editors

IGNACIO M. GARCÍA

Kennedy

Mexican Americans in Search of Camelot

Texas A&M University Press   College Station

Manufactured in the United States of America
FIRST EDITION

The paper used in this book meets the minimum
requirements of the American National Standard for
Permanence of Paper for Printed Library Materials,
z39.48-1984.
Binding materials have been chosen for durability.

Library of Congress Cataloging-in-Publication Data

García, Ignacio M.
    Viva Kennedy : Mexican Americans in search of
Camelot / Ignacio M. García.
        p.   cm. — Texas A&M Southwestern Studies:
no. 12)
    Includes bibliographical references (p.   ) and
index.
    ISBN 0-89096-917-5 (cloth)
    1. Mexican Americans—Politics and government.
2. Mexican Americans—Societies, etc.
3. Kennedy, John F. (John Fitzgerald), 1917–
1963—Relations with Mexican Americans.
4. Presidents—United States—Election—1960.
5. United States—Politics and government—
1961–1963.   I. Title,   II. Series.
E184.M5G367   2000
324.973′0926′0896872—dc21   99-37706
                                                      CIP

This book is dedicated to the men and women of the Viva Kennedy Clubs, the individuals such as Hector P. García, Albert Peña, Jr., Edward R. Roybal, Henry B. González, Carlos McCormick, Ed Idar, Jr., María C. Urquides, Bob Sánchez, Henry "Hank" López, José Alvarado, Cleotilde García, Raul Castro, and many others who gave of themselves to improve the lives of their people. *Camelot* may not have been what we needed, but your efforts kept the fires burning in the souls of those who have always fought for *la raza*.

Contents

Illustrations

Acknowledgments

This book began as an interesting project and ended as a labor of love. In the process, I came to appreciate once more the constant struggle of my people to overcome the burdens with which they have been saddled for the last 150 years. I did not believe, when I was writing my two books on the Chicano Movement, that I would write about a generation of Mexican Americans who had chosen to struggle in a less radical fashion. Both my own experience as a social activist and the time spent researching and writing my first two books had convinced me that the Chicano Movement would be the measuring stick in assessing any twentieth-century effort by Mexican Americans to free themselves of poverty, political powerlessness, and discrimination. Writing this book has helped me again to appreciate the fact that while our struggle has been constant, our methods have been diverse. Talking to former Viva Kennedy Club members and reading their documents has been quite educational and enjoyable. Thus it is the Viva Kennedy people that I first have to acknowledge as being very responsible for this book. I am quite sure that many of them have a different perspective on the thesis of this book, but I hope that they will realize that there is a great deal of respect for them on my part.

One of the first people responsible for my doing this work is Robert Wooster of Texas A&M University in Corpus Christi, Texas. Rob was one of the first people with whom I spoke about doing something on Viva Kennedy. He was quite enthusiastic about the project and saw great validity in it. Since he is an excellent and productive scholar and was my mentor at Texas A&M, his encouragement meant a lot to me. Once the project ensued, I was very fortunate to have some outstanding research assistants. José Luis Montoya, Melanie Hall, and Wendy Butler did many of the website searches and ordered the microfilmed newspapers and documents necessary to tell the story. They provided input and kept asking questions that made me rethink my project several times. Adriana Ayala, at the University of Texas, and Magdalena Prado, at UCLA, were helpful in researching archival material for me in those two universities. They served as my eyes and ears in those two institutions. I found them to be excellent doctoral students who are bound to contribute much when they finish their studies. Veronica Guzmán-Hays conducted several interviews with former Viva Kennedy Club members in Corpus Christi, Texas. These interviews were particularly important in understanding the Texas contingency of the Viva Kennedy effort. Veronica remains one of the two most talented students that I have ever had the privilege to teach.

Two other people were extremely important in seeing the project become a reality. One of them is Tom Kreneck, director of the special collections at Texas A&M University in Corpus Christi. Tom introduced me to the Dr. Hector P. García Papers and convinced me that there was enough material available to write a good book. The fact that I had the director on my side facilitated my work in the archives. Over the last several years, he has remained one of the most faithful supporters of the project, often providing me cost-free materials that were invaluable. Thanks, Tom!

The other person, and the one to whom I owe the most for the completion of this book is Grace Charles, one of the assistant archivists at Corpus Christi. When I spoke to her about the project, she became as enthusiastic about the book as I was. And she probably did more work initially than I did. Her knowledge of the García papers was extremely helpful. If anyone knows the life and times of Dr. Hector P. García, one of the founders of the Viva Kennedy Clubs, it is Grace. I was continually amazed at her tenacity in finding me new material. I would unexpectedly get envelopes from her periodically with new material that she had located both in the García papers and in other collections there in Corpus Christi. When I had questions about the Viva Kennedy Clubs, Dr. García, South Texas, or other similar topics, I would grab the telephone and call her. Sometimes I felt like telling her that she should write the book because she knew more about it than I did. Grace confirmed a valuable lesson that I try to share with my graduate students constantly: you are nothing without a good archivist on your side. To Grace, *con todo cariño,* I say, *gracias, muchas gracias.*

Of course there is never a book without a good press and good editors. Here, I also have two people to thank. The first is Mary Lenn Dixon, Managing Editor of the Texas A&M University Press. I met Mary Lenn in Sacramento at a conference of the National Association for Chicana/Chicano Studies. She heard me say something about Viva Kennedy in a presentation I made, and she quickly set up a meeting with me. We talked for about two hours on Viva Kennedy and she offered me a book contract. And for almost two years, she remained enthusiastic and supportive. This project became a reality because she believed that it would be a significant contribution to Mexican American history. The other person who has made this a good manuscript is Maureen C. Bemko, the manuscript editor. Her editing has made this manuscript much better. She asked tough questions and helped me refine the work.

There are many others who contributed. To all of them, I say thank you. As always, my wife Alejandra and my children (and now my grandchildren) have contributed to my desire to write Mexican American history. Writing history has always been a very personal endeavor and having someone to share it with makes all the hard work worth it.

Viva Kennedy

Introduction

In the mid-1970s, Albert Peña, Jr., an old-time liberal politician, responded to a question of political affiliation by declaring, "I'm a Kennedy Democrat." The term would fascinate me for years. I had been too young to remember many of the details of the John F. Kennedy race for the presidency. But I do remember once having turned on the television and seeing two men debate each other. I did not understand what they were talking about, but I do remember that my brother and I took sides, as most young boys do whenever they witness a competition. For no particular reason, I chose Richard M. Nixon. My older brother, who would turn out to be politically neutral in his adult life, sided with the more youthful and energetic Kennedy. Years later, while doing research for my first book, I came across the article describing Peña's self-designation. I was fascinated by the implication that the user seemed to give the term

"Kennedy Democrat," but at the time I was not interested in looking at Mexican American politics in the pre-Movement years of the 1960s.

After completing two books on Chicano politics, I decided to go back and pick up the story of John F. Kennedy and Mexican Americans. During the long interval between rooting for Nixon and my work on *Chicanismo,* I had run across numerous indications that Kennedy had become an important, though small, part of the *mexicano* political and cultural folklore. It was not uncommon for me to see in the homes of friends or acquaintances old newspaper pictures of Kennedy prominently displayed alongside those of *la virgen de Guadalupe,* or of other family pictures. Even my mother had one in our living room. I also discovered that a number of *corridos,* or border ballads, had been written about his life and death. And I would remember that during my high-school years, one of the dreaded football rivals was a predominantly Chicano school that had been named after the president—one day before he was killed.

In my research on Chicano politics, I had also come across tidbits of information which indicated that some Mexican American politicians and reformers had become politically active as a result of the Kennedy presidential campaign. Finally, and most important, my first teaching job took me to Texas A&M University–Corpus Christi, whose library held the Hector P. García Papers. It consisted of several hundred boxes of documents, letters, and newspaper and magazine clippings, many of which deal with the Kennedy campaign. García, as it turns out, was one of the national coordinators of the Viva Kennedy Clubs. I seemed destined to write this book.

But as is often the case with destiny, what I started out to do turned into something quite different. I had planned more of a cultural history of the Kennedy phenomenon, a quest to ascertain why Mexican Americans had been so attracted to him and how nostalgia had become history after his martyrdom, which transformed him from a mildly popular president among Mexican Americans to a status almost that of a saint. Even today, old-timers speak reverently of him and are more than willing to tell you how different things would be in the barrio if he had lived. Shortly into my research, however, I realized that the focus of the book had to change. Most of the nostalgia on Kennedy, I found, was rather shallow in details—especially those dealing with actual policies favorable to Mexican Americans. The Kennedy myth, while widespread, was more the result of rumor and repetition than of any real action. Trained as a historian and not as an anthropologist or folklorist, I decided to write a political history. In this area, I would find much more substance.

The real story, then, is about a group of Mexican American reformers and politicians who came together to support the John F. Kennedy presidential campaign. They came together from the traditional Southwest but also from the Midwest, East Coast, and Northwest. Some were experienced reformers, while others began their political career with the Kennedy campaign. This effort led Mexican Americans to come out in record numbers to vote for president of the United States. This mass movement to support the candidate from Massachusetts was spurred on by hundreds of political clubs known as the Viva Kennedy Clubs, which arose in many Mexican American communities nationwide. They were an official arm of the Kennedy presidential campaign, though they functioned mostly on their own; Mexican American leaders wanted to prove that they could do it on their own, and they wanted to remain independent of the state Democratic Party committees. The original purpose of the clubs was simply to gain support among Latinos for the Kennedy campaign, but the founders of these clubs soon had more than a presidential election in mind. They worked hard to introduce Mexican Americans to the electoral process by promoting Kennedy as a true friend of the community, someone well aware of the barrio's problems. They also pushed to make their own reform agenda part of the liberal agenda that Kennedy promoted. After the election and through the mid-1960s, these elites constructed a view of American society that included Mexican Americans at the highest levels of government and promised them access to all the benefits of a prosperous postwar society.

While a number of scholars have written about Mexican Americans in the 1940s and 1950s, few have ever given much more than a cursory treatment of Mexican Americans at the beginning of the 1960s. This generation of Mexican Americans, of which there are a number of rather prominent men and women, has been lumped together with that which the historian Mario T. García calls the Mexican American Generation. This generation he describes as being reform-oriented, much more integrated in its politics, and possessed of a generational mindset that gave them a sense of commonality in their philosophical outlook. They worked hard to overturn de jure segregation and to bring Mexican Americans under the protection of the fourteenth amendment. They challenged discrimination at all levels, yet they remained optimistic that American society was fundamentally fair.

While agreeing with many aspects of this description, I believe that the Mexican American leaders who were active in the political arena in the late 1950s and early 1960s differ from those that García relegates to the time period of the 1930s to the 1960s. For one, this group sought to express its activism in the political arena and not in desegregation of schools or public facilities, or in fighting discrimination per se. That is not to say that they were not interested in integrated public facilities or the elimination of racist and ethnic stereotypes. They were interested, and many had gotten their first activist experience in those arenas. But this group of men and women saw the electoral arena as a place where Mexican Americans could have the greater impact. They believed that they were now ready to assume positions of leadership in their community. The fact that their community had grown tremendously made election to office a real possibility.

The Kennedy Democrats would politicize the Mexican American reform agenda and shift emphasis from educational and social reform to political and electoral participation. Inherent in this shift was the belief that they could introduce the Mexican American community to the electoral process and integrate their reform agenda into the larger liberal agenda. Three assumptions arose in the minds of these elites. One was that the enthusiastic support for the Kennedy campaign provided legitimate access to political power at the highest level. This access would translate into high-level appointments in the executive branch and jobs for their constituency in the federal and state bureaucracies. It also assumed strong support for Mexican American candidates and platforms.

Another assumption purported that as Mexican Americans participated in electoral campaigns, they would become attracted to the American political system, thus committing them to political activity from then on. Mexican American elites constantly worried about the lack of electoral participation among their people. Many Mexican Americans did not pay their poll tax to register, and others, having registered, did not vote. A third assumption professed that the Viva Kennedy Clubs movement would bring diverse groups and individuals together into a political confederation that would become a powerful advocate for Mexican American interests. The leaders of the Viva Kennedy Clubs hoped that a national political organization could circumvent petty divisions at the local and regional levels.

These assumptions would prove to be only partially right. Nonetheless, the Kennedy campaign caused a shift in the emphasis of many Mexican Americans from social reform to political participation. Voting and holding political office became the new avenue by which to continue reform activity. This participation in the national campaign would also shift—in the minds of Mexican American elites—the center of power from the local and state levels to the national level. More and more Mexican American reformers looked toward the federal government and the national Democratic leadership for the resolution of problems affecting the barrios. This new political perception magnified the detachment of the Mexican American middle class from the working-class community. Political participation, unlike social reform, required citizenship, English proficiency (before bilingual ballots), some education, and Anglo American empathy.

This period signaled a significant shift in the ideology and thought of Mexican Americans. Before, there was a community struggling with traditional civil rights matters. Its leaders were concerned with their role as Americans of Mexican descent. They desired to be good Americans, to find a balance between their Americanism and their Mexicanism. The label of Mexican American served as a collective label, a collective idea that united them from different regions, and made them not Mexicans, not strictly Americans, but Mexican Americans. This Kennedy contingent also searched for an identity, but a less ideological one. There was no concern with identifying, discussing, or philosophizing about being an American of Mexican descent. An earlier generation had gone through that. This generation accepted that their identity resulted from the bonding that Mexican American leaders of the past had sought. Their main concern now went beyond just being good citizens. While they saw many of the same problems that past reformers had fought against, they also accepted that many of them were anxious for a greater role in American society.

Their militancy developed as they sought to practice the rhetoric of progress in areas of strong conservatism. Their own personal conservatism made the early 1960s liberal agenda seem much bolder than it really was. What they wanted were opportunities to serve the nation through appointments and through elected office. They saw themselves as the bridge to Latin America and the ones who could save the nations to the south from communism. They also believed that the United States could not remain a beacon of democracy for the world if the problems of the Mexican American remained unresolved in the eyes of the world.

Leaders of this generation were relatively successful in Anglo America. Some had already proven their ability to win elected office or to win major legal cases against discrimination. They led in their own organizations and communities, and some had significant Anglo American support in their efforts. Though few in numbers, they were well established, well educated, and committed to integration. They were Americans who happened to be *mexicanos*. Mexico had begun fading in their hearts and minds. Since they rarely acknowledged discrimination personally—with a few exceptions—there was no permanent scarring. They were liberal in orientation, and they were optimists in outlook. Kennedy gave them hope because he recognized them, and recognition was something they sought fervently. They believed that the greatest dilemma that Mexican Americans faced revolved around their invisibility to most Americans. While most would have been content with being seen as American, most also understood that U.S. society seemed unwilling to grant them that wish. They were also sincerely concerned that their *raza* suffered discrimination, segregation, and violence. And they believed wholeheartedly that when Mexican Americans voted in large numbers and got themselves elected to public office, these problems would fade.

This group of reformers and politicians would become the most politically successful group in Mexican American history. They would capture two congressional seats, one governorship, and a number of local elected offices. While failing to attain their own political Camelot, they did hold on to power and open the door for thousands of other Mexican Americans to participate in American politics. Only now, almost forty years later, has this generation relinquished leadership to a newer Hispanic generation. My interest in this generation of reformers, however, is not to extol their triumphs or lament their losses—of which there were many of both—but rather to look at what their existence meant to the Mexican American barrios and what it revealed about the American political system.

The story of the Kennedy Democrats is a story of political mainstreaming and why it has not worked as a collective effort. At this stage it might well be worth repeating the comments by José Angel Gutiérrez, who said about American society: "It is willing to allow individual upward mobility, but it will never allow a collective rise of our people." While this is no ingenious discovery, it was, in part, for the Viva Kennedy leaders, who really believed that a new age would arrive for barrios across the nation. They were not so much naive as they were hopeful and committed to that outcome. They did all of what they believed could be expected of them. They played by the rules, they participated politically, they registered, they voted, they negotiated with power, and they never questioned the fairness and legitimacy of the American political and economic system—as others before had done and others after would continue doing—and yet they did not accomplish much of their collective agenda. As individuals they were quite successful, but their organizations would unravel without the major victories they had envisioned.

While this work seeks to provide an ample look at these Kennedy Democrats, it has certain limitations. It does not provide an in-depth biography on any of the Viva Kennedy reformers, it says very little about Kennedy himself, it concentrates more on Texas than other parts of the nation, and it covers only the period between 1960 and 1964. I consider these parameters to be appropriate for several reasons. There are no major biographies on any of the prominent men or women in the Viva Kennedy effort. There was even a lack of readily available biographical sketches or articles on most. To have done a biographical sketch on only a few would have meant crisscrossing the nation from archive to archive, plus interviewing numerous individuals whose "memories" would have had to be corroborated through more research. This is a process that should be done, but the work for future Chicano biographers will be difficult and beyond the scope of my scholarly agenda.

Concentrating on Kennedy was, as mentioned before, a temptation, but the magnitude of the myth would have overshadowed the real story. Kennedy himself was a small part of the story, as few of the Viva Kennedy leaders actually knew him personally or even had thorough knowledge of his political agenda. While more could have been done on his "constructed" image and its influence on the Viva Kennedy leaders and Mexican Americans in general, I leave that to future scholars. There is much more about the Kennedy image in the Mexican American mind than what is covered in this work.

In the latter portion of my book, I concentrate on Texas because it is there where the Kennedy campaign had the most effect. It is the Texas contingency that called itself Kennedy Democrats and where the most significant offshoot of the Kennedy Clubs arises. It is from Texas where the few major appointees to the federal government come. It is also there where Mexican Americans are strong enough to present a threat to the established political order. This threat, I believe, ended by 1964, and so my story ends there. Much more happens in the succeeding years, but by then there is another force coming into the Mexican American landscape, and I chose not to tie the two together, though there were some important links. I decided, however, that the Viva Kennedy people deserved to be seen, at least initially, on their own. After all, we do not even know their story well. What has been written has been a rather summarized and concise version of a very important period in the history of Mexican Americans. For many of the Viva Kennedy leaders, the presidential campaign and its immediate aftermath were crucial in their political development. To link their story to the Chicano Movement is to steal their political time and space and to lump them together with a political movement that some of them resisted and fought against. It would also make them victims of an analysis that would unfairly malign them as not being radical or militant enough. Their own time and space will serve as the context for their place in history.

The story of the Viva Kennedy Clubs is a fascinating tale that can teach us much about Mexican American history, especially about those individuals who yearn profoundly to be seen as American. It may also tell us what might be the outcome of a politics of accommodation that does not undertake a profound analysis of whether American political institutions can simply absorb Mexican Americans into the American dream. It may also cause us think whether being Americanized *mexicanos* allows us to offer something new to American society. After all, if we offer nothing new to American society, or particularly to our own community, why should we emphasize our ethnic distinction?

At this juncture I wish to make one methodological note. In the text I present an analysis that is often hard to substantiate by one or several citations. Since there are no secondary works on the Viva Kennedy Clubs and not one of the surviving members could provide a complete view of the organization, there was much reconstruction to be done. While there were some very good documents, there were no extensive narratives on organizational activities or even organizational philosophy other than a couple of open letters to the public and a declaration of principle from the Texas Viva Kennedy group. Also, Carlos McCormick, national director of the Clubs and the only man who was in a position to see both the inner workings and the national activities, has not been heard from for many years. His family, while initially open to assisting with the project, never did provide any of his documents or his unpublished memoirs. Given these limitations, some of my analysis may seem to overstep the bounds of my knowledge. However, I believe that my interviews with participants, my extensive research of primary documents, my knowledge of the secondary sources, and my profound cogitation on the period and the individuals' actions after Viva Kennedy have provided me the intellectual depth to make the assertions that are a key part of this work. I believe that time and more research will confirm that my conclusions are legitimate even if not the only ones that could be made.

It is worth noting that I engaged in an extensive search for documents in all the major archives, among numerous personal collections, and I sought to interview as many Viva Kennedy people as possible. It was disappointing, however, to find that beyond the García Papers in Corpus Christi few had much on the Viva Kennedy Clubs. Even those Mexican American reformers who were leaders in the presidential effort had little in their collections about this time period and their participation. The John F. Kennedy Presidential Library provided almost no information on the Viva Kennedy Clubs, its archivist admitting that the library did not even have a category for them. The library's thousands of stored and unprocessed documents may yet shed light on the Clubs, but they will have to wait for further cataloging and research.

I interviewed a number of Viva Kennedy Club leaders but found that beyond a small core of them, most knew little about the inner workings of the movement or its efforts beyond their own localities. While their stories are valid and can contribute much to the story of the Mexican people in the United States, they are beyond the scope of this work. It is unfortunate that Sen. Dennis Chávez of Arizona, Rep. Joseph Montoya of New Mexico, Prof. George I. Sánchez, and numerous other important leaders had died even before this work was conceived. Hector P. García was too ill to be interviewed and never recovered, and Henry B. González was also ill and his staff chose not to set up any interviews. While it is always possible to do more, I feel confident that the research done is more than sufficient to tell such an important story. No doubt, the story of these valiant and tenacious men and women will spur many other such stories.

1. The Fifties: No Happy Days for Mexicans

 To understand the Kennedy Democrats and their search for an American Camelot, it is important to understand the Mexican American community during the postwar years. The contradictions of poverty amid plenty were nowhere more prevalent than in the barrios. For most Americans, the postwar years were a time of prosperity and optimism. The end of World War II brought not only peace but also a rise in the standard of living, a new prominence in world affairs, and a renewed American ethnocentrism that had been badly shaken by the Depression. Issues of ideology, class, and equality were pushed into the background. American liberals who had questioned their society's ability to provide for the disadvantaged became concerned with communism, with controlling an affluent society, and with the growing influence of the "mass-man," the human specimen devoid of individuality. For many of them who had

flirted with leftist and communist ideologies, America was now a country of affluence. In their minds, the quest to end poverty had ended. Wrote the editors of *Life* magazine, "[Americans] have now virtually eliminated one of the chief drives behind all human effort, namely the fear of poverty."[1] While they would still be concerned with the issue of civil rights for blacks, few would look elsewhere for a new crusade against poverty and injustice. They were more concerned that communism and conformity were making America soft and undermining its role in world affairs. For those liberals who were distraught by poverty, the issue was white affluence and black misery, white racism and black exploitation. There were also those like Michael Harrington who decried white poverty and the neglect of the elderly.

For these liberals, the "colors" of the issue rarely deviated from black and white. In this kind of environment, the plight of the Mexican American occupied no portion of the American mindset. While social scientists had documented the poverty, illiteracy, poor health, and horrid educational conditions of Mexican Americans, few Anglo American sympathizers had come to the forefront to help alleviate the situation.[2] Mexican Americans seemed not to inspire any great social crusades, nor did their problems spur any intellectual debates. Anglo Americans in the Southwest, and consequently nationally, did not know what to make of the Americans of Mexican descent. So they ignored them.

This indifference reflected the distance both geographically and intellectually between Mexican Americans and the centers of power in the United States. Mexican Americans were simply too far removed from the decision-makers to warrant serious consideration.[3] The people of the Southwest were also historically far from the American mind. The war with Mexico occupied a very small part of the American historical conscience, and most students received less than a day's lecture on the ramifications of the war. Despite the size of the conquered territory, most students knew much less about Mexico's lost land than they did about the Louisiana Purchase. What little information students received about California, Texas, Arizona, New Mexico, Utah, and Colorado included only cowboys, Indians, forty-niners, Mormons, and pioneers.

A lack of national or regional voice compounded the situation. For years, the language of concern, protest, and reform had been Spanish. Though as early as the late 1920s Mexican American reformers had begun to use a rhetoric of reform in English, the voice often seemed fragmented and regionalized. Having been kept isolated from each other, Mexican Americans often spoke as Californios, Tejanos, Hispanos, and Spanish Americans. Shifting to English often meant putting deeply held concerns into a new linguistic culture. While much study still has to be done to understand this shift, here it suffices to say that as English became the language of reform, the idea of citizenship and constitutional rights replaced the notions of Mexicanness and workers' rights. The new reformers would no longer demand to be respected as Mexican workers but rather to have their rights as citizens respected. This new language became restricted by citizenship, place of birth, loyalty, voter participation, and a host of other qualifiers. The English language also created a dilemma of identity. Chicano activist Carlos Guerra wrote many years later that Mexican Americans only confronted identity problems when they spoke in English. In Spanish they were all *mexicanos,* but in English they became Spanish American, Latin American, Spanish-speaking, American of Mexican descent, and a host of other linguistically constructed individuals.[4]

Having no national voice to provide a sense of direction compounded the problem of language. The attempts to form organizations that transcended regions and localities had rarely proved fruitful. Organizations such as the League of United Latin American Citizens (LULAC), Alianza Hispano-Americana, and later the American G.I. Forum represented more a conglomeration of chapters than the creation of national entities. There were no headquarters, no funds, and little influence beyond the limits of each chapter's social geography. While the voices coming from these reformers were often articulate and profound, no medium existed to disseminate them beyond their localities. With no national magazine, no national leadership, and no national consensus they lacked a voice to speak to the problems of the community.

Geography was one problem, and poverty was the bigger problem. The economic gap between white Americans and Mexican Americans grew in the postwar years. While a small but significant middle class arose in the barrio, the majority of Mexican Americans continued to live in poverty, with high unemployment, high incidence of disease, and children receiving inadequate education in segregated schools.[5] Yet Mexican Americans were anything but passive, waging sustained campaigns against bad schooling, segregation, law enforcement violence, poor housing, and a host of other ills they faced. They wrote literature, got college degrees, ran for office, and formed labor unions and middle class reform organizations.[6] They grew in numbers, too, through a high birth rate and through large migrations from Mexico, attracted by the promises of high-paying jobs. But while many individual Mexican Americans found elbow room to benefit from the postwar prosperity, the community as a whole suffered under the burden of reactionary politics and conformist social norms of the 1950s.

The Cold War had an impact on Mexican Americans, as it did on most other Americans. Radical unionism and other forms of leftist activity would suffer under a climate of suspicion and rigid political conformism. Unions had acted as a voice for Mexican Americans in the mines, fields, packing plants, slaughterhouses, and sweatshops throughout the first part of the twentieth century. Most of the time, unions which worked with Mexicans were those that were Mexicanized—founded by Mexican and Mexican American workers. The 1920s and 1930s, in particular, were times of much union activity in the Southwest. Large armies of native and foreign-born Mexicans were recruited to work in the fields of the Southwest, Midwest, and Northwest. The mines of Arizona, Nevada, New Mexico, and Utah recruited thousands with promises of high wages and good working conditions. With this movement came the urbanization of Mexican and Mexican American workers who saw no alternative but to settle in the urban centers nearest to the promised jobs.[7]

The Depression initially increased rather than decreased union activity among Mexican Americans. Mexican workers came together to fight a dual-wage system, exploitative work conditions, and rampant discrimination. They joined unions in mass numbers and revitalized the union movement in the Southwest. They challenged the national unions to adapt their efforts to the changing labor demographics and to become concerned with issues beyond those of collective bargaining.[8] Where unions were not possible, Mexican and Mexican American workers established workers' associations, unity leagues, and mutual-aid societies to protect their rights. While some of these organizations were strictly interested in labor issues, others were interested in combating discrimination, housing segregation, police brutality, and a host of other problems confronting the workers' families. Given the nature of the oppression faced, most early twentieth-century unionists were either fervent nationalists or militant leftists. Few were in step with the emerging national union leadership.

During the 1950s, the union movement among Mexicans and Mexican Americans suffered a drastic decline. Their challenge to the more conservative union leadership and the red-baiting of the Cold War set government, business, and labor against them. By the mid-1950s, the National Farm Labor Union; the National Agricultural Workers Union; the United Cannery, Agricultural, Packing, and Allied Workers of America; the International Union of Mine, Mill, and Smelter Workers; and numerous other agricultural and industrial unions that recruited Mexicans were in decline or had disappeared altogether. Yet, while the working class fervently fought labor bosses, agribusiness, mine executives, and factory owners, Mexican Americans in the middle class learned to conform to the restrictive society of the 1950s even as they waged campaigns to reform it.[9]

There were three aspects to the Mexican American experience that made middle-class Mexican Americans conform to the cultural and political parameters of the Cold War. Their experiences as soldiers or fervent civilian supporters of the World War II and Korean War mobilizations had imbued in many a fierce loyalty to American institutions, particularly government. For many of them the military had provided an opportunity to be "American," while the wars had permitted them an arena in which to show their valor and demonstrate their skills. As soldiers and now veterans, they had been recognized by their government—if not the general populace—through medals, the G.I. Bill, and numerous jobs in the public sector.[10] This recognition and reward bonded them to a federal government whose harmful domestic policies seemed far away from them. Unlike the governmental hostilities at the local or state levels, the federal government seemed friendly to many. As war veterans they had been socialized into American foreign policy. Lacking national leaders who could define and interpret national policy, many accepted the federal attitude of harsh anti-communism. National or regional dialogue among middle-class Mexican Americans that sought to understand the dynamics of the Cold War was nonexistent beyond a few leftist organizations.[11]

Not all veterans were middle class or became so. There were many who returned to the barrio and found few things had changed. Some were willing to fight for change, others simply took advantage of whatever their veteran status provided them, and still others became resentful. But as American veterans few of them came home to join radical organizations or even nationalistic ones. Most accepted World War II as a sort of rite of passage into American society, allowing a new breed of more Americanized Mexicans to become the leaders in the barrio. They also chose to concentrate on finding an economic and social stability that had eluded them before the war. Without a major ideological alternative or leaders and organizations to articulate a national response to American racism, most veterans either embraced, tolerated, or ignored American foreign and domestic policies. In this, they were like most American veterans.[12]

Catholicism was another characteristic of the Mexican American experience that promoted conformity in the 1950s. The American Catholic Church of the 1950s was staunchly anti-communist and fervently conformist. Catholic leaders such as Fulton J. Sheen constantly denounced communists and fellow-travelers in their sermons and urged Catholics to be good Americans.[13] Sheen's radio broadcasts were translated into Spanish and became a daily staple of the Spanish-language radio. Catholic priests were usually Anglo American, often with Irish or Eastern European roots, thus adding a cultural dynamic to this anti-communism. Assimilation resounded from the pulpit and in the catechism. The Catholic Youth Organization promoted American ideals to Mexican children, and the lay organizations did the same for the adults. While the Catholic Church may have been unintentionally responsible for maintaining Mexican culture, it did, however, seek patriotism and acculturation in its Mexican American members.[14]

Most of the middle-class reformers to arise in the 1950s were devout, or at least practicing, Catholics. The parameters of their desired reforms were well within those espoused by their religious beliefs in order, respectability, and appropriateness. The church, which provided spiritual guidance, monetary assistance, a building for social and cultural events, and sometimes protection from blatant prejudices, also promoted respect, accommodation, and loyalty to American institutions. The church discouraged ethnic nationalism, radical unionism, and any other -ism that might disrupt Mexican American conformity with American society.[15]

The third characteristic of the Mexican American experience revolved around the issue of cultural and racial inferiority. For many Mexican Americans, their culture and history represented backwardness and inferiority. The proximity to the border re-emphasized to many the failures of Mexican values. Mexico's struggles with poverty and governmental corruption reminded many Mexican Americans how lucky they were to be Americans. The constant migration of farm workers and unskilled laborers from Mexico reminded them of how far they had come. The immigrants and the poor barrios seemed such a weak premise on which to base racial pride or solidarity. These difficult circumstances also threatened to subsume all the progress they had made. After all, for many Anglo Americans, a Mexican was a Mexican. This perceived threat pushed Mexican Americans to emphasize their Americanism and to cling to national policy. For some reformers anti-communism may have been distasteful, but preoccupation with their place in the pecking order subsumed the issues of political and civil liberties at the national level. Middle-class Mexican Americans would face red-baiting, but aside from federal surveillance they would suffer much less than the few militant working-class groups that had survived the 1940s.[16] For many of them, the worst part of their experience was their political and social isolation from the mainstream. Detached from working-class nationalism and attracted to American postwar ethnocentricity, they were very concerned with their place in society. They saw themselves as successful despite the odds and felt good about their future.[17]

Yet inferiority always lurked just beneath Mexican American optimism, made possible by the lack of historical importance, by political powerlessness, and the seeming backwardness of their culture. These middle-class individuals had no Mexican American heroes from the past, they could not get elected to office except in the border region, and they felt uncomfortable with some aspects of Mexican culture. This inferiority continued to be reinforced by the literature and the media of the times. There seemed to be no reprieve from constant stereotyping or even sympathetic condescension. The literature of the 1940s through the early 1950s would highlight Mexican fatalism, alcoholism, machismo, eroticism, alienation, illiteracy, and poverty. Another version of condescension was the romanticization of the Mexican peon who lived in simplicity, rejecting all progress and maintaining centuries-old values and traditions. Both depictions, however, trapped the Mexican character in a world in which he—and much less she—had little control, and which could be upset without warning or provocation.

Anglo American writers, often sympathetic, still wrote condescending fiction in which Mexican Americans were depicted as being weighed down with almost insurmountable problems. Oftentimes, Anglo American heroes came to the rescue of the less fortunate Mexicans, but in reality little significant change could be made in their lives. Hart Stilwell's *Border City* chronicles an Anglo American journalist's attempt to help a

Mexican American community gain control of political power. His efforts fail when the Mexican vote, manipulated by a barrio politician, goes to a rival slate. In *Wetback,* by Claud Garner, Dionisio Jesús Moreno, an undocumented bastard son of a Mexican mother and an American father, desperately seeks to be an American. Deported and exploited numerous times, he finally marries and makes money through smart farming techniques. With that success comes residency and acceptance from an appreciative Anglo society. The book is disparaging toward Mexico and is full of stereotypes even as it romanticizes those like Dionisio who seek the "American way." Other novels, such as *Trial, Giant, Square Trap,* and *The Shadows of the Images,* while seeking to be sympathetic, provide a picture of a community with little resiliency, no political capital, and limited intellectual independence.[18]

Mexican Americans fared no better with Mexican American writers such as Mario Suarez, Antonio Villarreal, and John Richey, whose mother was Mexican. Whoever read their works would be reminded of language deficiencies, promiscuous lifestyles, unsanitary habits, laziness, and fatalistic religiosity. Those Mexican Americans who wrote literature were either apologetic, angry, or apolitical. Suarez, while angered by Anglo American racism, often wrote of barrios with numerous problems, wayward residents, and little hope beyond making it in the Anglo world. Villarreal spoke from the angle of the emerging middle class. While his characters were working class, their obsession with escaping the misery and incivility of the barrio separated them from the thousands who seemed happy living in proximity to other Mexicans. Richey wrote from within the barrio but as a spectator rather than a participant. His work chronicles *la raza* but did little to provide a positive picture of the community, as his own ambivalence about being Mexican but not Mexicanized kept him preoccupied with the oddities of Mexican American society.

The 1950s, with the renewed prosperity and optimism, magnified the plight of the barrio experience. While often critical of American society, these Mexican American writers could not articulate a separate vision for their community. Their own alienation from the community trapped them into constructing an uncomplimentary view of their own people. American racism and discrimination was emphasized through the depiction of vulgarity, violence, and frustration in the barrio. But victimization served only to highlight how dependent these writers were on Anglo

American sympathy and justice. Success, identity and happiness seemed contingent on becoming Americanized.[19]

Unlike the Chicano writers who sought to provide meaning to the plight of the Mexican American by looking inward, Mexican American writers could see no final redemption within the Mexican soul. They lashed out at American complicity in their tragedy, but they could not formulate an alternative vision of themselves and their people. Their language—English—seemed not to offer them the rhetorical power to escape victimization. There were those who wrote in Spanish. Their message may well have been more critical and yet their visions more positive, but their language was fading as the language of reform in the barrio. Their words smacked of separatism, and of Mexico, and so it became a private rather than a public language.[20]

Mexican Americans fared no better in the popular nonfiction literature; they were continually portrayed as having problems which could be remedied only by their acculturation or by assistance from the outside. There were numerous articles on Anglo Americans who raised food, money, and clothing for poor Mexicans.[21] These poor Mexicans were seen as people constantly in need of assistance and incapable of helping themselves. There were also articles like "Let Juan Do It for You," written by an Anglo American woman describing her Mexican carpenter. She details his constant tardiness, his excessive work breaks, his bad temper, and his propensity toward inoffensive dishonesty. Yet "he was a good carpenter," she wrote, and the type of Mexican worker any good Anglo American family could utilize if they were willing to put up with his idiosyncrasies.[22] While written to show the value of the Mexican skilled worker, it came across as condescending and paternalistic.

Scholars who sought to write sympathetically nonetheless pointed out that the problems of the barrios rested primarily on the shoulders of the Mexican Americans unwilling to assimilate into American society. Language limitations were cited as the major reasons for the problems of the barrio. If Mexican Americans learned English, they would communicate more effectively, get better jobs, understand the political issues, become better citizens, and get along better with Anglo American neighbors. Notwithstanding their own admission that poverty and discrimination were factors in the conditions of the barrio, they continued to prescribe integration as the panacea. They seemed quite able and willing to minimize the factors keeping Mexican Americans poor, powerless, and segregated.[23]

Anglo American scholars approached the problems of the Mexican American within an ahistorical context; thus, they saw the Mexican American experience as a reflection of cultural limitations, clannishness, and contemporary discrimination—racism was seldom used to describe prejudicial feelings. Most of the works were sociological and anthropological in nature, and most lacked any historical perspective. Mexican Americans simply had no history. Anglo American scholarship, though often written to discover these hyphenated Americans and garner sympathy for them, painted a community in disarray.[24] Mexican American scholars like Carlos Castañeda, George I. Sánchez, Arthur Campa, and others fought this depiction with their scholarship but were unable to overcome the onslaught of prejudicial writings, and they sometimes contributed to the stereotypes because they had their own misgivings about their people.[25]

For those who did not read literature or scholarly works, radio, television, and film became the medium by which they learned what it meant to be an American. American television in the 1950s had joined the war against communism and for patriotism. This circumstance meant that controversy rarely raised its head in the programming and that diversity meant different game shows and soap operas, and not different skin colors or foreign accents. In his classic work *The Culture of the Cold War*, Stephen J. Whitfield argues that television created an ideology of conformism: "Game shows demonstrated that ordinary people could seize the fabulous economic opportunities that capitalism promised; situation comedies and soap operas showed that personal problems could be resolved with laughs and love . . . and the stalwart cops and detectives who . . . captured thugs in twenty-eight minutes . . . fortified confidence in an infallible criminal justice system."[26]

Nowhere on the television screen were Mexican Americans or other Latinos depicted as more than servants, peons, buffoons, or law breakers. Films provided no better role models. *Bandidos,* unkempt cowboys, Latina spitfires, Latin lovers, and gay *caballeros* were the stock characters of movies on the West. There were also films on wetbacks and exploited workers, and the most sensitivity Mexican Americans could expect was a sympathetic cowboy or a kind border patrolman.[27]

Radio would be the one medium in which Mexican Americans had an influence. English-language radio stations ignored them and their music, but Spanish-language radio flourished in the barrio. Having been around since the early 1920s, Spanish-language radio by 1956 accounted for two-thirds of all foreign-language broadcasting in the United States. More so than on other foreign-language stations, programming on Spanish-language radio was nationalistic, concentrating on music from Mexico and news on that country.[28] But the Spanish-language stations also promoted the local by announcing community activities such as dances, church gatherings, club meetings, letter exchanges, and civic functions. Since much of the programming was personality-based—that is, the disc jockey was the most important element of the broadcast—radio's connection to the community depended on the on-air personality. Some took a personal interest in what occurred in the Mexican American community, others were simply interested in their popularity, or their profits from advertising or serving as masters of ceremonies in the numerous functions in the barrio.

Regardless of Spanish-language radio's relationship with the community, the goals of most stations seemed the same. They sought to facilitate the integration of the Mexican and Mexican American communities to the larger community. Listeners were encouraged to register with the appropriate authorities, to go to night school, vote, pay their taxes, and stay out of trouble. They were constantly reminded to be good citizens. Wrote researcher Robert Graham, "Listening to these broadcasts, one realizes that the station, while selling goods and services in Spanish, is also projecting American life in a language most acceptable to its listeners. It is, so to speak, an agent of acculturation even though this was never its conscious purpose."[29] This acculturation would shift the leadership of the Mexican American community away from the mutual-aid society, union, and other working-class organizations.

In this vacuum would rise to prominence, almost unchallenged, the middle-class organizations that had long existed in the barrios. As early as the 1920s, precursor organizations to the League of United Latin American Citizens (LULAC) had been working on a variety of self-help projects, encouraging citizens to pay the poll tax and fighting segregation, for example. By the middle of the 1950s, though, most legal restrictions to integration had been eliminated. LULAC lawyers and those of the American G.I. Forum had successfully challenged legal and institutional segregation in the school systems of the Southwest. School districts would find ways to circumvent the law, but they could not claim the support of the legal system. Mexican American reformers had also won for their people protection under the fourteenth amendment. Compared to the rigid segregation of the past, the late 1940s and the early 1950s provided openings for Mexican Americans to enter the schools in larger numbers and even go on to college. The G.I. Bill also allowed veterans to go to school, get vocational training, buy homes, and start businesses.

The returning veterans and the beneficiaries of the prosperity of the postwar era joined the small pre-war middle class to form a much more Americanized community. At least up until the 1950s, native-borns made up the majority of the population within the Mexican community, and their outlook diverged from that of the immigrants. The constant exhortation to integrate that had been heard in the barrios from as early as the late 1890s had begun to pay off for this generation.[30]

Vicki L. Ruiz, in her work on Mexican American women and acculturation, posits that powerful forces of acculturation entered the barrio from the 1920s to the 1950s. The first and foremost influential force was the public education that Mexican Americans received. In schools, they were forbidden to speak their language, their history was ignored, and they were saturated with American values and history.[31] They also became acquainted with American literature, holidays, heroes, and the like. In segregated environments, acculturation for Mexican American students sometimes occurred at an even faster pace than in integrated schools. Segregated schools provided Mexican American students an opportunity to be in student councils, clubs, and athletic teams. The more they became involved in these activities, the more they reflected American values. As students vied to be the best in their schools, they were, in actuality, vying to be the most acculturated. The system rewarded those who stayed in school. The fact that there were many who dropped out or became engaged in delinquency only strengthened the status of those who stayed in school and out of trouble. School, particularly high school, became an important space for Mexican American students on the road to acculturation.

In some places like San Antonio, unaffiliated social clubs brought high-school graduates back to the campus for school festivals, homecoming games, and fund-raising activities. This extension of high-school activities continued the Americanization process for those working-class graduates who remained within the confines of the barrio. In some barrios, there were several generations of graduates from the same high school.

Each generation took one more step in the assimilation process. Ironically, as the larger society retrenched in its de facto resistance to integration and Mexican American reform activity, Mexican American youth praised American political and social virtues in civic, speech, history and government classes, as well as in plays, readings, homework assignments, and holiday celebrations.[32]

The contrast between their homes and their schools worked to create a duality of thought and action among Mexican American students. Their familial and social experience outside the school taught them that there were limitations to their educational opportunities, geographic mobility, and employment possibilities. They had a prescribed role in society and they were to play it to avoid conflict with the larger society. Yet their schoolteachers taught them that America was the land of opportunity where everyone had only themselves to blame for their limitations and where equality, liberty, and the pursuit of happiness were guaranteed to all. They were thus free to succeed.

Many could not deal with this contradiction and lost the necessary desire to overcome linguistic difficulties, bad schooling, and poverty. They subsequently dropped out of school. Others, however, learned to compartmentalize their lives. They were Mexicans at home and Americans in the school. With time, for many of the more successful students, their Americanism won out, but it did so within the confines of the barrio. They became Americans intellectually while remaining Mexicans geographically. English became their public language and Spanish their home language.[33] Their civic participation became an expression of their Americanism while their social life became a recognition of their heritage.

Employment, particularly in the urban centers, also served to promote American ideals to Mexican Americans. American businesses had, by the 1950s, begun to dominate work culture.[34] American capitalism promised benefits from a job well done. In a time of prosperity, the promise seemed genuine. Here again, upward mobility meant acquiring good language skills, avoiding union membership, and being loyal to the company. Following this path did not bring rewards to most people, but it did to a few. As factory workers, custodians, mechanics, drivers, and skilled laborers in a host of other positions, Mexican Americans were enjoying a standard of living that was much better than that of their parents. These jobs provided stability, which barrio residents valued highly. Economic stability brought with it more voter participation, better English skills, more participation in civic affairs, and a greater identification with American capitalism. Anything posing a threat to that stability represented an attack on their Americanism. These lucky few in the barrio that benefited from American prosperity were part of the growing skilled-worker class that, together with the middle class, was forming the new Americanized sector in the barrios.[35]

The media also facilitated acculturation. We have already discussed radio, television, and the film industry. We can add that, beyond public service announcements, the media created an appetite for consumer goods. Writes Vicki Ruiz, "The Mexican community was not immune to the orchestration of desire, and there appeared a propensity toward consumerism among second-generation women."[36] This consumerism seemed to vindicate American capitalism's claim of a better society. Mexican Americans, like other Americans, interpreted the accumulation of goods and services as a sign of a fair and just society. The fact that Spanish-language media had by the 1950s become a conduit for sending corporate products to the barrio accelerated the process of Americanization even more. Juan Gómez-Quiñones argues that the Spanish media, while sympathetic to the community, nonetheless reflected the editorial philosophy of its Anglo counterparts.[37] Competing against nationalist feelings in the barrios of the 1950s were theaters, newspapers, beauty pageants, veterans' groups, and businesses promoting American values, products, and services. These promoters of assimilation created a "barrio Americanism," an illusion that Mexican Americans could and were enjoying the fruits of a prosperous and egalitarian society even as they were confined to live their lives in the barrio because they felt unwelcome by the larger society.[38]

The U.S.-Mexico border stood as another major factor in the creation of barrio Americanism. No greater symbol of American superiority, prosperity, and progress was as vivid as the two thousand–mile–plus stretch of imaginary division. Border dwellers and others who frequented the border were constantly reminded of how lucky they were to live on the northern side of the Rio Grande. A trip down south meant visiting relatives or friends in greater poverty, confronting corrupt customs officials, and acknowledging an undemocratic political system.[39] The decade of the 1950s was a period of state capitalist accommodation in Mexico and the breakdown of the revolutionary nationalism of the Mexican elite. Mexico, rapidly descending toward capitalism, created among its citizenry a desire for consumer goods and a longing for American lifestyles.[40] For the

Mexican American coming back from Mexico or the border, things were much better in the United States.

The barrio Americanist philosophy that many Mexican Americans acquired provided an imagery of inclusion even within the confines of a segregated barrio. America had come to the barrio without letting Mexicans out of it, except in small numbers. Mexican Americans could interject themselves into movie plots, magazine short stories, and novels to become the beautiful blond heroines, the handsome suitors, the brave cowboys, the talented musicians, and any other character that represented the best of American society. These Mexican Americans—and they were a sizable minority—could live the American dream vicariously. Ironically, the production quality of the earliest movies filmed in color was so poor that characters on screen looked more like white-skinned Mexicans than they did blond, blue-eyed Anglo Americans. The fact that movie characters also reflected a conservatism of lifestyle that was fading among Anglo American youth also reinforced the notion that these characters were "like us."[41]

Beyond those barrio residents who felt mostly American, there were those who could lay claim to having lived the American dream. For the most part, those who would lead the reform movements of the late 1940s and 1950s could proudly claim a Horatio Alger experience. The few biographical works on men like Ernesto Galarza, Bert Corona, Carlos Castañeda, George I. Sánchez, Edward Roybal, Henry B. González, Albert Peña, Jr., Hector P. García, and the few women such as María Urquides and Jovita González-Mireles depict a story of good grades, stable homes, leadership opportunities, Anglo American friends, and for the most part good jobs or careers. More will be said about them later, but it is important to note here that these individuals believed that American society was fundamentally good. Their own efforts on behalf of their community seemed an attempt to give their fellow people an experience such as theirs and to convince the larger society that there were many more like them in the barrios waiting for the same opportunities.

Notwithstanding their love of American society, or because of it, Mexican Americans of the late 1940s and 1950s were not content on hoping that things would get better. As has been well documented, Mexican American reformers were quite active in defending their rights, challenging segregation, and promoting self-help within the barrio. According to Guadalupe San Miguel, these reformers redefined the "Mexican problem." Rather than accept that Mexican Americans were a monolithic group of nonachievers with a backward culture and limited language skills, these reformers described their community as diverse culturally, linguistically, and philosophically.[42] As native-born Americans, they were also much more interested in gaining the benefits of American society than going back to Mexico as some immigrants in their community would eventually do. These reformers also shifted some of the blame for barrio conditions to discrimination, segregation, and Anglo American antipathy. But unlike the Chicano activists of a later period, they would refrain from challenging the fundamental ideals of American society.

Anglo Americans' feeling of superiority seemed to be the most reprehensible aspect of American society to these reformers. This superiority complex continued to devalue Mexican American patriotism and any economic or social gains they made. The reformers believed that Anglo American feelings of superiority were responsible for humiliating depictions of Mexicans in the media, the history books, and in advertising.[43] To combat this attitude, Mexican American reformers fought on two fronts. First, they challenged the view that Mexican Americans were inferior by constantly reminding American society of their patriotism, their help in developing the West, and the fact that they were no different than other Americans. Carlos Castañeda wrote a complementary history that fit American values and ideas; George Sánchez challenged the whole field of intelligence testing of schoolchildren;[44] Ernesto Galarza sought to organize farm workers, an unorganizable mass, according to most union leaders;[45] Hector P. García fought for the end of de facto segregation and the hiring of more Mexican American teachers; and Edward R. Roybal led efforts to register voters and groom candidates for office. All these efforts, beyond their immediate goals, had the intention of proving to Anglo Americans that Mexican Americans were good citizens.

The second approach of the reformers centered on convincing Mexican Americans to live up to their citizenship. They constantly reminded Mexican Americans that they did not pay their poll taxes, did not vote, did not protest segregation enough, did not attend PTA meetings, and were too content with their low-level jobs. These reformers also wondered why Mexican Americans were where they were. Asked García, "Why can't we organize?"[46] As early as the 1940s, one reformer remarked, "We have concluded that our Mexican youth are not meeting the social and intellectual requirements of our highly progressive American civilization."[47] Many of the reformers were conscious of the obstacles that discrimination, segregation, and poverty represented to the community. But because they developed no ideology beyond a liberal capitalism, they could provide no solutions besides staying in school, voting, and learning English. No matter how aggressive their reform, they offered no fundamental critique of American institutions, and their solutions required no structural changes in American society.

This conclusion should in no way imply that their criticism lacked passion or substance. As early as 1947, García, subsequent founder of the American G.I. Forum, had vehemently blamed the segregation of the public schools as being responsible for Mexican American casualties in war. "[I] wonder if some of those lives might not have been lost if those [Mexican] American soldiers had had a better education," he wrote in an open letter to the citizens of Corpus Christi. "Perhaps those soldiers would have learned more and . . . would have been better equipped and trained to defend themselves . . . they firmly believed in the ideals of democracy . . . today they return [dead] to the same land where they were discriminated against and where their brothers, sisters, and their children are still segregated."[48]

In Houston, the Civic Action Committee declared in its newsletter, "The way some of our people are discriminated against, you would think that we don't pay taxes; that we didn't help pioneer, settle and build this great state with our sweat, our brains, and our sacrifices."[49] In an article in the liberal *Texas Observer*, George I. Sánchez, professor of education at the University of Texas, accused some of his colleagues of perpetuating segregation and stereotypes by opposing integrationist state policies. "I am shocked when a colleague here and there serves as the instigator of differential treatment not based on any of the accepted tenets of the profession, but on pre-judgment alone."[50]

Going beyond individual protest, Mexican American reformers founded a number of organizations. In fact, a study done by John R. Martínez in the early 1960s found that Mexican American elites usually tended to participate in more than one organization at a time. Organizational affiliation provided status and gave them strength in negotiating with those in power.[51] These organizations were not mass-member groups but small circles of relatively well-educated, well-situated individuals.

Only LULAC, the American G.I. Forum, and a few other regional groups sought large constituencies. Even those large organizations usually depended on a small core of reformers to do most of the work.

The rise of these organizations shifted Mexican American activism from bread-and-butter issues, which had been the prime focus of labor groups, to issues of segregation and civil rights. These new reformers were concerned about the poverty in their communities, but as middle-class pseudo-capitalists they believed that the American economic system would resolve those problems if only discrimination could be terminated. They believed that discrimination would end when Mexican Americans participated fully in the political system.

To this end, Mexican Americans became active in pursuing political office, though in the early 1950s, this political activity was undertaken as an individualistic endeavor. While these candidates usually promoted themselves as the Mexican candidates in the barrio, they articulated no political philosophy beyond extending American services and "rights" to the Mexican American community. There were numerous campaigns throughout the Southwest for local, regional, and statewide offices as Mexican Americans entered new political arenas. The most significant politicians to come out of the postwar years as elected officials were Edward R. Roybal of California, Dennis Chávez and Joseph Montoya of New Mexico, and Henry B. González of Texas. The four represented Mexican American politicians who could win by attracting significant non–Mexican American voters. Of course, none of them could have won without a strong base of support in the Mexican American barrios.

The Mexican American population had grown to the extent that its voting strength promised some success for officeholders. Though there were many Mexicans who were not citizens and others who were not even legal residents, the numbers of those who were eligible to vote provided a sense of strength. The census reports of 1950 showed that in the five major Southwestern states, native-born persons of Mexican descent made up 85 percent of the counted Spanish-speaking population. In Texas, 81.8 percent of Mexicans were native-born; in New Mexico, 95 percent were; in Colorado, 95.8 percent; in Arizona, 81.9; and in California, 78 percent. Fifty percent of all native-borns had parents who were themselves of native birth. These individuals were scattered throughout the Southwest in a way in which they formed a significant voting bloc in a number of states. By 1960, they made up 14.8 percent of the Texas population; 28.3 percent of New Mexicans; 14.9 percent of Arizonans; 9 percent of Colorado's residents; 9.1 percent of Californians; and nearly 12 percent of the total Southwestern population.[52]

The major collective participation of Mexican Americans in the John F. Kennedy presidential campaign did not develop overnight. In fact, the coalescing of political links in the barrios nationally only magnified the efforts of individuals and organizations to gain political power. Already, there existed several prominent Mexican Americans who had exhibited an ability to win elective office and retain it in spite of the fact that the times had not been conducive to Mexican American electoral efforts. Only in New Mexico did Mexican Americans have significant voters that participated persistently, though even there the numbers had declined by the late 1950s. Still, Dennis Chávez, who had been elected to the U.S. Senate in 1933, continued to play a dominant political role as the only Mexican American senator at the time and the first of only two ever to reach such a lofty national position. Chávez, a strong supporter of New Deal policies, was a firm promoter of Mexican American politics, continually urging his fellow *manitos* to run for office and to vote.

In Los Angeles, Edward R. Roybal had been elected to the city council in 1949, becoming the first person of Mexican descent to be part of that body since the U.S.-Mexico War. Roybal had shown an ability to create coalitions of minority voters, labor people, and liberals that would sustain him in office through the 1960s. From his position in the council, he had run for lieutenant governor and encouraged others to run for regional and statewide office. By 1959, he had also helped formed the Mexican American Political Association (MAPA), a political rather than social reformist organization that distinguished itself by its militancy and its mass participation approach to decision-making.[53]

Henry B. González of Texas duplicated Roybal's and Chávez's winning strategies en route to the Texas state legislature. A strong liberal like his aforementioned counterparts, he continually won re-election through tenacious campaigning and an immaculate record on civil rights, housing, labor, and constituency services. In 1958, he even ran for governor, falling slightly short of making the run-off against the incumbent.[54] There were others less well known but still significant in their ability to win office when the Mexican American vote was less than the majority. These individuals had found the cracks in a closed society. But while they lamented the difficulty of others like them to do the same, the very fact that they had won elected office made them believers in the system.

These individuals had learned the political process well. They were mainstream, though slightly liberal, in their politics. Some had been aroused politically by the New Deal, while others had come back from World War II anxious to be leaders in their communities. As well-educated and articulate individuals, they quickly rose to the top in their communities. These men, as well as those that followed them, were joiners of organizations and seemed willing to become involved in constant crusades. They were, however, different from the *mutualistas* and other reformers of the pre–world war era who worked within the context of an organization. While these men were joiners, they retained their political and social independence. The organizations were a vehicle for their politics and their reform activities but provided no restriction on their personal ideology. Even the American G.I. Forum, a national organization for veterans, had a loose confederation of local chapters acting as a constituency. This personal independence was tempered by the conformism of the 1950s and by the politics of the Cold War. The lack of ideology did not mean that they had no vision for their community. They did, but it did not initially differ significantly from that of Anglo American liberals.

By the beginning of 1960, Mexican American reformers were anxious to have a greater impact on their communities as well as the nation as a whole. The presidential election seemed the kind of event where they could have an influence. Individually and collectively, these reformers had now been involved in politics since the end of World War II and had found varying degrees of success. In what appeared to be a wide-open election—at least initially in the Democratic primaries—they believed that they could influence the candidates on particular issues. There was as yet no collective mindset on which candidate was better, nor even on the idea of a national Mexican American campaign effort. There was only a belief among numerous individuals that 1960 was a good time to become involved nationally.

2. Organizing the Viva Kennedy Clubs

The national Democratic Party convention held in Los Angeles in July, 1960, attracted a number of Mexican American elected officials and reformers interested in influencing the party's presidential nominee. The three major interests of these elites were the creation of a pro-nominee electoral effort among and by Mexican Americans, a strong push for a civil-rights plank in the platform, and recognition of the plight of the Mexican American. It appears that these three efforts were unconnected in that no consensus existed among Mexican American attendees, and no prior meeting had taken place to plan strategy. It is doubtful that most Mexican American delegates had any prior knowledge of who else was going. But it is certain that those three interests had support among Mexican Americans at the convention.

The effort at the Democratic Party convention reflected a maturing of

political activism for Mexican Americans. While there is little information on Mexican American participation at national political conventions,
it seems apparent that the 1960 meeting in Los Angeles attracted the largest contingent of Mexican American delegates and spectators up to that
time. California sent a number of elected officials as did New Mexico and
Arizona. Texas sent only one delegate but several other observers. The
fact that the convention took place in California provided accessibility to
more Mexican Americans than those conventions normally held on the
East Coast or in the Midwest. The fact that these delegates came with
agendas signified that some were ready to try practicing politics at the national level. But at this stage they came as individuals.

Coming into the convention no one candidate held the loyalty of all
the major Mexican American organizational leaders and politicians.
While John F. Kennedy may have had the largest group of supporters because he was the front runner and the most organized, there were a number of prominent Mexican Americans who were for either U.S. Senator
Lyndon Baines Johnson or former candidate Adlai Stevenson. Up to this
moment, no significant campaign effort had been conducted among Mexican American voters. Most Mexican American politicians and leaders
of organizations had been contacted individually or had become involved
through personal preference.

Democrats at the national level had rarely sought to galvanize Mexican Americans into a voting bloc. They either took them for granted or
saw them as simply another part of the Democratic coalition. While Stevenson had attracted large enthusiastic crowds in the barrio and tenacious
support among some leaders, the support had not developed into an organizational effort. Only Henry Wallace in 1948 had developed a Mexican
American component to his campaign. Amigos de Wallace groups had
appeared mostly in California and a few isolated communities in the
Southwest.[1] The Republicans, on the other hand, had made greater efforts
among Mexican American voters. Dwight D. Eisenhower was the first
Republican to receive organizational help, and it served him well in his two
campaigns. The Latin American Veterans and Volunteers for Eisenhower-
Nixon organization targeted Mexican American veterans, middle-class
voters, and uncommitted voters. This California-based effort remained
mostly at the county and local levels because there were few Republican
Mexican American leaders outside of California.[2] The Republican strategy of organizing Mexican American voters has remained in use to the

present. Ironically, Richard M. Nixon first discouraged this kind of effort on his behalf, feeling uncomfortable about an "ethnic" angle to his campaign. He would change his mind only after seeing the Democratic success among Mexican Americans and African Americans.

By the time of the convention, there were those Mexican American leaders who believed that political participation represented the best option for solving the problems of the barrio. Elected officials represented a voice that had become more distinct and articulate in the 1950s. Even nonpartisan organizations such as LULAC and the American G.I. Forum saw the need for a stronger role in the political arena. With Mexican American union activity in decline and a more assimilated middle class on the rise, the old radical and nationalistic responses to racism and discrimination did not strike a positive chord among the new Mexican American leaders.

Since World War I, the new reformer in the barrio was usually a veteran, a lawyer, an elected official, or a small-business owner who had learned to survive and often prosper in postwar America. This meant that like other Americans, these reformers were non-ideological and usually quite pragmatic.[3] While many had traces of the New Deal in their personal philosophies, most were simply individuals hypersensitive to the disparity between their community and the society at large. These individuals, unlike many of their African American counterparts, had a limited knowledge of their history. Though Carlos Castañeda had already written some of his better work on Mexican American history in Texas and George I. Sánchez had done the same for New Mexico, little of that information had reached most reformers.[4] Even those who were privy to the history of Mexican Americans saw their people as being victimized or saw them as misfits in American society. Their love of community seems now more emotional and sentimental than ideological or philosophical. This sentimentality did not diminish their tenacity for reform or necessarily temper their frustration with American society, but it did direct their efforts toward liberal reform rather than radical politics.

They thus looked toward politics as a solution, and they came to Los Angeles with expectations. One who had high expectations and a specific agenda was Hector P. García, founder of the American G.I. Forum. Unable to attend the convention, he sent a statement to the Democratic National Committee Nationalities Division on July 12, 1960. García, a medical doctor, had become involved in veterans' issues shortly after returning from the war to set up his medical practice in Corpus Christi, Texas. He first started helping veterans in their fight for adequate medical care at the veterans hospital, then ensuring that they knew their right to the G.I. Bill, and finally getting involved with the issue of discrimination in the hiring process for government jobs. Involvement with the veterans brought him in contact with other issues that affected the whole family. School segregation, poor housing, police brutality, blatant racism, and a host of other problems afflicted Mexican Americans in South Texas. To help Mexican Americans confront and resolve their problems, he helped found the American G.I. Forum.[5]

Since the late 1940s, the Forum had been fighting school segregation and advocating for the rights of migrant farm workers. Forum reformers were strong supporters of a minimum wage and better living conditions for farm workers. They also supported tougher border regulations to keep undocumented workers from entering the country and replacing Mexican American farm workers by offering their cheaper labor. They were particularly hostile to the *bracero* program—a bilateral agreement between the United States and Mexico that brought workers from Mexico and in theory provided them with better working conditions and the protection of the federal government. While not anti-Mexican, the American G.I. Forum did lay part of the blame for Mexican American unemployment and low wages on the Mexican workers. In practice, their advocacy for better conditions for farm and migrant workers did not distinguish between legal and illegal, but in theory and articulation, the Forum leaders projected a prejudicial attitude toward Mexican workers.

When García wrote to the national Democrats, he and other Forum officials were expanding their social and political agenda. While they sought to continue to protect the working class in employment and schooling, they also sought a larger role for the Mexican American middle class in American society. Unlike reformers of the past, these individuals wanted more than integration and opportunity. In the pre-war and early postwar years, reformers had simply wanted the benefits of an abundant society. By the late 1950s, they wanted to be the focus of government action, and they wanted opportunities to serve the nation.

García began his statement by underscoring the limited participation of minorities in the Democratic Party, citing the small number of delegates to the national convention and the even smaller number in the national committee.[6] He told the committee that the lack of influence at the national party level was reflected in state and county party positions and appointments. García accused the Democrats, as well as the Republicans, of carrying out a "selective exclusion" that kept Mexican Americans from gaining any influence in the political arena. Their "omission," wrote García, undermined any efforts to get Mexican Americans appointed to positions of leadership, particularly foreign-policy posts in Latin America.

He argued that the United States was "unable . . . to sell democracy because we are not making use of our greatest salesman [sic] of Democracy." That "salesman" was the Latin American.[7] This line of reasoning sought to place the resolution of the Mexican American's problems within the context of fighting communism and saving democracy. It is difficult to know if this was a ploy to garner sympathy or whether García and the Forum leadership did believe that they could save America from communism. The American G.I. Forum never developed a track record of anti-communist baiting. They were, however, veterans who tended to toe the foreign-policy line, never once engaging in a questioning of American "police" actions.

The American G.I. Forum fought hard for the rights of the Mexican American, but it did so within a limited political sphere. Radicalism or challenges to the fundamental principles of the nation were simply not options. The Forum leaders were not seeking to change American society, only to enlarge its parameters to include Mexican Americans. Their experiences in the military and their experiences at home were so contradictory that they had dichotomized their view of American society to make sense of it. They believed that the federal government and its institutions were good, but that local, county, and state political and social institutions were discriminatory.[8] They failed to realize that, in large part, their positive feelings toward the federal government were based on conjecture rather than reality. As veterans, they wanted so much to believe in their nation. Because the federal courts had helped dismantle de jure segregation against Mexican Americans, Forum leaders believed the federal government to be an ally. They believed this to be so in spite of the fact that Mexican Americans were invisible to government policy-makers and politicians. The evidence of neglect was obvious. Mexican American concerns failed to rate a mention in most government-sponsored studies, and domestic policies simply did not take Mexican Americans into consideration. With a friendly and, at times, romanticized view of the federal government, the Forum leaders found it reasonable to seek inclusion in the politics and bureaucracy of the federal government.

García called on the new president-to-be to "use [the] vast number of loyal citizens. We definitely want judges of Latin American origin, American ambassadors, and consuls of our own origin," García wrote.[9] This request—not yet a demand—signaled an expansion of the G. I. Forum's agenda. In the past, the organization had concerned itself with access to federal jobs, integration of schools, and with the elimination of all forms of discrimination and brutality against Mexican Americans. Many of the Forum reformers' concerns had focused on those who were voiceless and poor. But since the mid-1950s, a growing number of Mexican American veterans and others had attained the necessary education, employment experience, and economic stability to aspire to more than civil service jobs at the local and state level. These new aspirants revealed the diverse nature of the community and the challenge to the Forum to remain sensitive to the needs of its changing constituency. It also signaled that some members of the community were assimilating into the whole of American society. These individuals saw no need to remain in the barrio but in fact saw the need to spread out to the rest of the country. This new aspiration was not a one-way street. It revealed a belief in a fluid pluralism that many veterans believed they had experienced during the war.[10]

The emphasis on foreign-policy appointments reflected the nation's preoccupation with the Cold War and fears of communism in Latin America. It also revealed the reformers' belief that they must tie their reform activities to the anti-communist movement in order to be taken seriously. The foreign-policy focus also showed how cut off Mexican American reformers were from domestic policy-making. They were sensitive to the legal system—thus their request for judges—since many Mexican Americans were constantly dealing with legal matters in which they were almost always at a disadvantage. Also, the courts had been an ally during the litigious 1940s. Beyond the courts or politics, Mexican American reformers had little knowledge of the workings of government and so they had little to contribute. As veterans, they believed themselves to be more aware of foreign affairs. Since Kennedy had run a rhetorically tough campaign that emphasized foreign-policy issues, political novices like García sought to take advantage by jumping on the foreign-policy bandwagon to get Mexican Americans on the Kennedy agenda.

From foreign policy and political appointments, García shifted toward the exploitation of migrant workers, calling it the "greatest shame" of our country. He found it "hard to understand" the willingness of the federal government to protect foreign workers' rights while ignoring those native workers who earned as little as fifteen or twenty cents an hour. The Forum was particularly angered by the *bracero* program, which had the effect of forcing native farm workers into seasonal migrations to the fields of the Midwest and Northwest.[11]

Migrant workers' rights were thus one of the core concerns of the American G.I. Forum. Many of the Forum chapters in South Texas were founded in rural agricultural communities where thousands of migrant workers lived and labored. For at least a decade the Forum had been exposing their exploitation. Many first- and second-generation Tejanos could trace their family roots to the migrant fields. It is also possible that Mexican American reformers shared their Mexican counterparts' concern with the *campesino* or farm worker. Mexican symbolism relied substantially on the *peon* image. Many of the Tejano reformers had grown up in households where the Mexican Revolution and its war between the haves and the have-nots was a constant topic of conversation and romanticization.[12] This statement should not imply that the reformers' regard for farm workers was simply an exercise in romantic nostalgia. Rather, it is an indication that the reformers had a profound cultural and social concern for the downtrodden, *los de abajo*.

García, particularly, had undertaken to document with first-hand reports and photographs the plight of those people. To him, the treatment of migrant workers was a devastating indictment of America's inability to live up to its ideals. It is also possible that García and other reformers were aware of how federal government attitudes had changed toward migrant workers when the crop-following masses had become mostly Mexican or other peoples of color. Conservative legislators had dismantled the New Deal rural policy, and liberals had stopped advocating for migrant workers when they stopped being white. This change in the liberals' strategy may have been because Mexican and Mexican American workers were seen as temporary, but to reformers it may have seemed another example of government insensitivity.

From migrant workers, García shifted toward support for a civil-rights plank in the Democratic Party platform. Particularly urgent for García was finding an end to police brutality. He argued that most juries and investigative agencies did not seek justice but rather an exoneration of the police officer. Police brutality represented the most insidious and ruthless oppression that Mexican Americans faced. Violence against Mexican Americans had a long legacy in Texas and most other parts of the Southwest.[13] Border ballads were replete with tales of violence and resistance. In every period of Mexican and Mexican American activism, police brutality had been an important concern. García called for an oath to be taken by all law enforcement agents indicating they had no prejudices toward Mexican Americans. Members of juries should also be questioned about their feelings toward minorities, García wrote. "Today, more than ever we must prove to the world that we believe in the equality of man and today we must convince our minority groups . . . and their brothers in other countries that their abuse and exploitation is a thing of the past." García ended his statement with a reiteration of the need to save the country from communism.[14]

The statement reflected no particular ideology and only superficially touched on a number of concerns. Its two major requests—not demands—were appointments to government posts and a civil-rights plank in the platform. Except for the very minute discussion on the migrant workers' plight—all one paragraph of it—the statement dealt little with bread-and-butter issues. It reflected a middle-class agenda and a shift away from more traditional working-class issues. Issues such as dual wages, promotion discrimination, unsanitary working conditions, lack of collective bargaining, bad housing, and others which often highlighted class disparities were absent from the statement. Mexican American reformers, like many African American civil-rights advocates, revealed a developing class focus by concentrating on issues relevant to their middle-class status.

Even the discussion of police brutality revealed a middle-class perception that racism and discrimination could be eliminated by the use of an oath. This last perception reflected the belief of many reformers that if Anglo Americans would only take time to know Mexican Americans, they would abandon their prejudices. This was one perception that many working-class Mexican Americans had given up years before. The civil-rights plank, which would "legitimize" the rights of Mexican Americans, would be one major step forward for reformers like García. Once legally on a par with Anglo Americans and protected by the federal government, Mexican Americans would have few limits to their "pursuit of happiness."

They would be free to enter any arena, engage in any enterprise, and receive any benefit that their citizenship afforded them. At least that is how it seems Forum leaders saw the situation.

Unable to send people to lobby the convention politicians and with no other means of persuading the delegates, García sought to touch their hearts and gain their sympathy. He expected and hoped that the plight of the Mexican American would be part of the discussion over the Democratic Party civil-rights plank. But the letter seems not to have circulated much, if at all, among the delegates. Mexican Americans were simply not an important part of the discussions at the convention, and up to that time no one apparently saw reason to include them. The conflict over civil rights was being waged in the southern and southeastern parts of the country. The most articulate proponents and opponents also came from those regions. While places like Texas were also emerging civil-rights battle grounds, liberals and moderates there were still using a white/black dichotomy when they thought of civil rights. Simply put, Mexican Americans were considered a disadvantaged group but not one discriminated against in any collective fashion. What discrimination they suffered was the result of individual acts by unenlightened people.

Another reformer who saw the civil-rights plank as a crucial part of the 1960 presidential election was a county commissioner from San Antonio. Albert Peña, Jr., came to Los Angeles as the only Mexican American voting delegate from Texas. He also came with a commitment from presidential candidate Lyndon B. Johnson that the conservative Texas delegation would support the civil-rights plank.[15] Peña's political importance resulted from his leadership of the Bexar County delegation to the Texas Democratic Party convention. As the most liberal delegation, the group from San Antonio represented the only glitch in the pro-Johnson movement in Texas.

Peña's endorsement had been sought by the Johnson forces as early as 1959, but he had remained uncommitted to the Texas favorite son.[16] "I believe [the] debate on favorite sons is premature," he told the state convention of Democrats in 1959. "I believe first we must decide what we stand for; and then we must fit our selection of favorite son to a strong liberal platform," he continued. Peña had been involved in liberal Democratic issues since the Harry Truman race in 1948 and had become a well-known maverick who, in his words, refused to "take a moderate view, a middle of the road view" on issues of civil rights and justice. "You are either liberal or conservative," he told the Harris County Democrats in their quarterly meeting on July 4, 1959.[17] This unequivocal position represented a thorn in the side for Texas conservatives and for Texas liberals who had found a way to coexist with the conservatives.

When the Texas Democrats met in their state convention to select delegates to the national meeting in 1960, a rumor circulated among the delegates that the liberals, led by Peña, were going to walk out rather than support Johnson. The latter immediately and personally contacted Peña to find out what he wanted in return for his support. Peña had two demands. He wanted to have a Mexican American selected as a voting delegate to the national convention, and he wanted the Texas delegation to support the civil-rights plank at the convention. Johnson said yes to both demands and delivered despite the opposition of most of the conservative delegation.[18]

Peña represented a more political orientation among Mexican American reformers. Though a lawyer with nearly ten years' experience in civil-rights litigation, Peña believed that Mexican American civil rights were more likely to be protected through the political process than through the courts. In the early 1950s, he set out to take over the Bexar County Democratic Party by forming a coalition of Mexican Americans, blacks, labor people, and white liberals. In the westside of San Antonio he established the Loyal American Democrats to wrestle the Mexican American vote from the barrio politicos who were controlled by Anglo American politicians. "We demanded independence," said Peña years later. "You could not work for a politician or be a politician—you were strictly independent." This restriction did not apply to Peña, who was the consummate politician, dealing and wheeling throughout the county and the state. Yet he always remained independent. The Loyal American Democrats became the nucleus of *mexicano* politics in San Antonio.[19]

The group also became a vehicle for Mexican Americans to become involved in major political races while retaining independence for the barrio. The group supported Adlai Stevenson for president in 1956 and showed its strength by attracting ten thousand Mexican Americans to a Stevenson rally in San Antonio. Peña had sent a strong message to the Democratic Party of Texas that Mexican Americans were a force to be reckoned with. He had literally saved the day for the Stevenson Democrats; their rally was anemic until Peña and his supporters arrived, leading a procession of Mexican Americans from the west side of San Antonio. Peña had promised a big crowd to skeptical leaders, and he delivered. In 1958, the group supported the Henry B. González campaign for governor, which gave state Democrats a real scare by almost forcing the incumbent into a run-off.[20]

Peña came to the early committee meetings of the Democratic convention and tried to assess the impact that Mexican Americans would have on the convention. He quickly realized that it would be almost nonexistent. Nevertheless, he knew that as the lone Mexican American delegate from Texas, he did come with leverage, based on the Johnson promise on the civil-rights plank. While at the convention, Peña had little contact with the other Mexican Americans there.[21] He did, however, have discussions with Democratic officials who wanted him to head some type of get-out-the-vote campaign among Mexican Americans for the eventual nominee.

Interestingly, neither García nor Peña were initially supportive of John F. Kennedy. Peña remembers, "I was so hung up on Stevenson that I didn't care for anyone else."[22] For fervent liberals like Peña, Stevenson was the liberal in the race. García had committed to Johnson quite early in the campaign and had tried almost singlehandedly to turn Mexican Americans nationally toward Johnson. In fact, García had traveled through the Southwest polling Mexican American leaders on their presidential preference. He found many committed to Kennedy, and he found others who believed Johnson was just another southern bigot. García defended Johnson and changed some minds but did not rally much support for the Texas senator. For García, Johnson would always remain a friend to Mexican Americans because of his support for Forum activities.[23] One characteristic of García was his wholehearted, unequivocal commitment to those he endorsed. This commitment did not always mean long-range fidelity, but it did mean that the person of the hour was the most important person at that time.

There were, however, several prominent Mexican American elected officials who did support Kennedy. These individuals were Edward R. Roybal and Henry B. González. These two, as mentioned before, represented two of the three most recognized Mexican American politicians in the country. The third one, U.S. Senator Dennis Chávez, initially a Johnson supporter, would also become a Kennedy supporter when it became apparent that the Johnson effort would fail.[24] The three were avowed liberals, though they were more moderate than those Anglo American liberals who were wary of John F. Kennedy. Chávez knew Senator Kennedy through his duties in the Senate. González had met him while working on housing legislation, and they had been mutually impressed. Roybal had come to Kennedy's side the year before during a tough question-and-answer session that Kennedy had conducted in California.[25] While initially skeptical, Roybal came to view Kennedy as a Roosevelt-type politician with the right answers to the pertinent questions. The three, being loyal Democrats, were likely to have come to the side of the eventual nominee, whoever it was. While all three were feisty politicians at the local and regional levels, none of them ever showed themselves to be players in the battles over leadership at the national level. Their personal influence remained limited to that level, and before the Viva Kennedy Club movement, they had minimal collective strength to offer.

Roybal and González met during the convention to discuss Mexican American involvement in the national presidential campaign. Efforts to meet with other Mexican American delegates before the start of the convention had failed; thus, the two had set out to salvage an influence in the national campaign. The duo then contacted Chávez, whom they considered a mentor. The three agreed that a Latin American effort would be a way to shed light on the needs of the Mexican American. They then approached the Kennedy campaign and spoke to Robert Kennedy.[26] No specific strategies were suggested by either side, and none of the three volunteered to head the project, though they expressed their desire to be involved. Roybal remembers that the three did not bargain or negotiate for any specific compensation for the Mexican American community but did underscore the need to do something for Mexican Americans in the arena of employment and education. The three shared the concerns of other reformers that Mexican Americans were not getting government jobs and that schools remained segregated.

It is likely that John F. Kennedy's campaign staff saw this "Latin American" effort as one that would be integrated within the national campaign. There is no documentation or much recollection of what happened during this discussion, except that Robert Kennedy agreed with the idea of a strong effort among Mexican Americans. Interestingly, none of the three was placed in charge of setting up the national effort. That responsibility fell to Carlos McCormick, a native of Santa Barbara and resident of Tucson, Arizona, who served in the Kennedy campaign staff. McCormick, a senior law student at George Washington University, had taken a leave to join the Kennedy campaign in the West Virginia primary and had been put to work specializing in Spanish-language public relations and Latin American affairs.[27]

McCormick would prove to be the real catalyst for the Kennedy effort among Mexican Americans. Shortly after the Democratic convention, he contacted Peña in San Antonio and asked him for his support. McCormick presented himself as the chairman of the yet-to-be-organized and yet-to-be-named Kennedy movement. McCormick offered Peña the chairmanship of the effort in Texas. He had spoken to Mexican American leaders in Texas, and a number of them suggested that Peña be appointed to head the effort in the state. He was an elected official, headed an organization, had impeccable liberal credentials, and seemed the most likely to rally Mexican Americans behind the Democratic nominee.[28]

Peña responded positively but on "several conditions." The first condition was that those who supported Kennedy would be seen as a distinct political group, and this group would bypass the state organizations and work directly with the Kennedy staff. "They always sell us down the river," said Peña of the state party structure. The second condition required that Mexican Americans be considered for some high-level appointments in the new administration. A third condition required an effort by the new president to eliminate the poll tax. McCormick called Robert Kennedy from Peña's office. Recalled Peña, "McCormick handed me the phone and Robert Kennedy accepted the conditions and thanked me for my support."[29]

After securing Peña's support, McCormick went after the American G.I. Forum. As a member of the Washington, D.C., chapter of the Forum, he attended the national convention held in Wichita in August. The summer before, he attended the convention as John F. Kennedy's representative. That summer Kennedy had joined the Forum, though he never attended a Forum activity or had any contact with the leadership. At the time, Kennedy declared that he was honored to be associated with "this splendid veterans organization of Spanish-speaking ex-servicemen" whom he admired.[30] The membership seems to have been an election ploy in preparation for the presidential campaign. For Forumeers, however, the recognition by a national figure provided them evidence of the effectiveness of their work.

At the 1960 Forum convention, McCormick found the veterans expounding and expanding on García's statement to the Democratic Party.

Of the proposed resolutions submitted to the convention membership, three dealt directly with issues similar to those brought up at the Democratic convention. The first resolution put the Forum on record as supporting the sit-in demonstrations by black citizens throughout the South. The resolution recognized the sit-ins as having been conducted in "an orderly and mannerly fashion."[31] This resolution showed that Mexican American reformers were now willing to be more assertive in their actions against discrimination. In the past, most had gone as far as organizing rallies, boycotts, and protest marches but had normally refrained from being disruptive or challenging discriminating practices through direct action. This new aggressiveness sought to give civil-rights legislation a boost. It also signaled that Mexican American reformers now understood civil disobedience as an effective weapon. In a few years, one of their own—César Chávez—would make it his most important political strategy.[32]

The second resolution spoke to the emerging middle-class agenda. It noted the interest that the Forum had toward American foreign policy as it related to Latin America. It pointed out to those who would listen that communism as a political alternative continued to grow among the countries of the south, and it could be checked only by those who understood "the culture and heritage of the people in Latin America." It reminded Anglo Americans that the United States had citizens of "Spanish ancestry" who spoke, wrote, and understood the language of Latin America. Given that available resource to fight communism, the resolution called on the U.S. State Department to "seriously consider" appointing Mexican Americans and other Spanish-speaking individuals to diplomatic posts in Latin America.[33]

The third resolution went back to familiar ground: the migrant worker. It deplored the circumstances under which these workers labored. It condemned the living conditions, low wages, and the poor transportation provided them. It reiterated the Forum's commitment to work to change the conditions. The resolution called for "comprehensive and enforceable migratory farm labor legislation" to resolve the problems. It also called for the creation of a regulatory entity within state governments to administer the legislation. The resolution highlighted a growing demand for government involvement in migratory labor issues as well as other civil-rights concerns. In the past, union activity, litigation, and legislation had been the reformers' approach. The demand for government action signaled a realization by Mexican American leaders that institutionalized vigilance would be the only guarantee that the rights of Mexican Americans would be protected. This reluctance to depend on "good faith" revealed that the reformers' previous struggles had been both frustrating and educational. Despite the legal victories, most school districts throughout the country circumvented the law. Without efforts by state attorneys general to enforce the law, de facto segregation had replaced de jure segregation.[34]

Forum leaders considered it imperative that they attack prejudicial barriers as effectively as they had the legal ones. Though they continued to have faith in the "fairness" of American society, they were not dependent on that faith. Already within the Forum and among other reformers, there prevailed a coercive approach to Mexican American civil rights. More will be said about this later, but it is important to note that, within the Forum, the backers of different approaches to dealing with discrimination were battling for primacy. There were those who wanted the Forum to move more energetically in demanding the end of government indifference to the plight of the Mexican American. They were willing to "discuss" the possibility of civil disobedience. There were, however, others who believed that continual upward mobility, better education, and a steady growth of political clout were the best strategies for obtaining their goals. There were still others who believed that Mexican Americans already had all they needed to lift themselves out of their depressed conditions, and the Forum should serve as a motivator for them. These divergent views, however, came together in the belief that the Forum had to be a player in national politics.

The upcoming presidential campaign, the growing civil-rights movement, and the rising difficulty in social reform back home made for a spirited convention. It also created a good climate for a massive recruitment for the Kennedy campaign. Shortly after the end of the veterans' convention, McCormick invited a number of the Forum activists and leaders to a meeting to discuss presidential politics. Some twenty-plus people attended the Sunday meeting.[35] There, McCormick informed them that he was on the campaign staff and had been directed to coordinate the campaign among Mexican Americans. He then suggested that the attendees unite to form "Viva Kennedy" Clubs in their communities. The name, said McCormick, had actually come from the Nixon camp, where Latino supporters had urged the Republican to make a strong appeal to the Spanish-speaking community. Nixon had rejected the ethnic appeal, and the Kennedy campaign had quickly adopted the idea.[36]

The fact that Republican Mexican American supporters had been the first to suggest an ethnic angle to the campaign might have been a surprise to Forum leaders, but it was consistent with past experience. Mexican American Republicans had been involved in such efforts before. Rather than just trying a mass appeal, Republicans had targeted middle-class Mexican Americans (who voted regularly), veterans who were usually loyal to the commander-in-chief at the time, and those who could be motivated to vote if there were particular incentives; to reach this last group they worked through the barrio *politico*. The fact that the Kennedy campaigns had jumped at the idea of a Viva Kennedy effort underscored the Democrats' recognition that they had some catching up to do to beat the Republicans at targeting Mexican American voters.[37]

Ed Idar, Jr., editor of the Forum *Bulletin*, remembers that the group of reformers "immediately appreciated" the appeal of the name. "We [quickly] realized that campaigning for Kennedy under a slogan like that was going to be easy," he said. According to Idar, most of those in attendance were already for Kennedy. They found him *simpatico*, a candidate with tremendous appeal who could be sold to the Mexican American community.[38] This appeal meant that the Kennedy campaign would attract the attention of the media and the country and allow Mexican Americans to present their case to the American people. To have a role as a separate and distinct entity in a presidential campaign meant achieving the national recognition that Forum leaders so urgently sought. Another reason for supporting Kennedy was based on the possibility that the new administration might appoint Mexican Americans to the federal bench and federal bureaucracy as a payback for the support. This idea drew some discussion but received no confirmation by McCormick. Idar remembers that "we were rather naive. We were not professional politicians in the sense that we could work out deals."[39] As in the case of Peña, the Kennedy campaign had not been forced to commit to anything specific except to consider the "possibilities" of such appointments. This lack of details would later haunt the Viva Kennedy leaders.

There were probably two reasons why neither Peña nor the Forum leaders pressed hard for specific promises. Idar described the Forum leaders, himself included, as naive. This naivete came from their complete lack of experience as a lobby or pressure group. Their own activist experience had been one in which they identified a problem, brought it to the attention of the appropriate authorities, and demanded its resolution. Whatever negotiations occurred were those necessary to force compliance with the spirit of the law. Few times did Forum leaders have a hidden or political agenda that sought benefits for the organization or the leaders themselves. As patriotic Americans, these reformers continually stressed the need to do things right and for the right reasons. Whether their private motives always lived up to this high standard is uncertain, but their rhetoric and public stance always did.

The naivete also extended to their understanding of power relations. They did not understand the role of the power broker, and most did not even like that role. Their experience with the barrio *politico* had been a rather negative one. Most of those Anglo-appointed middle men had always "sold Mexicans down the river," according to Peña.[40] The reformers, so far removed from the centers of national power, did not always realize the number of lobby and pressure groups working full time for their political and organizational interests. Most were naive enough to believe that an "unspoken" commitment from the president would be enough to make up for the lack of lobbying and their nonexistent track record in political negotiating.

The second reason for their failure to negotiate assertively grew out of their uncertainty about how successful they could or would be. They did not lack confidence in their ability to organize people against segregation or for registering to vote or a myriad of other causes, but they had never engaged in a national effort.[41] Organizers had worked their own individual areas, but rarely had there ever been a tightly regulated link between organizers. The fact is, Mexican American organizational history lay littered with national and regional efforts that failed to maintain a working cooperation. The Forum's success had been based on the flexibility and autonomy of each chapter. The fact that most of its members were veterans and that the issues they debated were rarely divisive kept the Forum as a united national organization. But politics and ideology had always been divisive for Mexican Americans.

Some of these leaders reveled in their ability to persuade the mass of Mexican Americans to vote for Kennedy. Others remained uncertain of how many would register—where they still could—and then actually vote. They also knew that most state and county Democratic Party structures would be a hindrance rather than a help. This uncertainty kept them ambivalent about what they could or could not negotiate. This uncertainty probably also kept them from asking for any funds. Peña remembers that they never got any financial assistance from the Kennedy campaign, and that they never asked for any. "We wanted to do it on our own," said Peña.[42] Idar also did not remember any offers of money. In fact, the one-hour meeting produced no structure, no strategy, and no particular links to the national campaign. Instead, the attendees agreed that they would all simply go home to their communities to establish Viva Kennedy Clubs and participate in the campaign in their localities.[43] Fund raising would be conducted at the local level in the tradition of the barrio: dances, raffles, bingos, and food selling. To that would be added the sale of one-dollar "membership" cards.

Idar became one of the first of the Forum members to establish a Viva Kennedy Club when he called an organizational meeting for August 25, 1960, in the Hidalgo County courthouse in South Texas. Fifty-nine mimeographed letters of invitation were sent out to individuals who had experience working on issues pertinent to the Mexican American community.[44] While a large number were members of the Forum, others belonged to different organizations or were simply not affiliated. Both men and women were invited, though most who came were professionals and businessmen, or wives of those men. The county chairmen of the Democratic Party also attended. It was important that party officials attend, as Idar found little support among local Anglo American Democrats for developing a grassroots effort among Mexican Americans. He believed that some Democratic leaders in the Rio Grande Valley feared the rising number of Mexican American registered voters and were uncomfortable with their new assertiveness.[45] Idar, a feisty veteran of Forum activities, did not press hard to get official endorsements; instead he decided to form the Viva Kennedy Club through his own efforts.

At the state level, Viva Kennedy leaders had also found lukewarm support for the formation of a Mexican American political group. In a letter to Idar, Peña expressed his disappointment with state Democratic chairman Gerald Mann, who had set up a campaign committee with no minority or labor representatives. Mann assured Peña there would be a Latin American division, but Peña wanted representation at the coordinating level.[46] The state Democratic Party Committee would take almost another month and a half to fulfill its promise to Peña.[47] The Kennedy campaign had formulated a strategy to create numerous clubs and groups to attract not only loyal Democrats but also many others who were not particularly partisan. There were businessmen for Kennedy, Negroes for Kennedy, Citizens for Kennedy-Johnson, and a host of other clubs.[48]

The largest of these groups was the Citizens for Kennedy-Johnson Clubs. Warner F. Brock, one of the campaign executives, wrote to local organizers about these electioneering options: "Many voters are anxious to vote for Kennedy-Johnson, but they do not want to work for one reason or another in the county Democratic organization. Many [other] voters are undecided. We want to appeal to these voters." Brock, however, emphasized that the clubs would work along with the official organization.[49] As the Viva Kennedy Clubs took shape, they may well have seemed more permanent organizations than the national campaign staff had in mind. For party leaders, particularly those in communities with large numbers of Mexican Americans, the formation of groups with specific goals and agendas represented a challenge to the status quo. The fact that the groups were only loosely tied to the state organization revealed an independent attitude.

Idar succeeded in attracting a number of prominent members of the Hidalgo County community to his Viva Kennedy Club. In the group were several lawyers, business leaders, a pharmacist, and even a young district attorney. Also present were a number of women who had been active with the Forum's women's auxiliary or involved in civic functions together with their husbands. The group quickly elected Ramiro Casso, a physician in McAllen, Texas, as the chairman and Adolfo de la Garza of Mission as vice-chairman. Estela Lone Treviño of Edinburg was elected vice-chairwoman. Several campaign committees, including strategy, public affairs, finance, and women's activities, were established to carry out the functions of the club.[50] The designation of a women's vice-chair and women's activities committee indicated that the women were expected to be part of the overall effort. The G.I. Forum had proven quite successful at integrating women into their reform activities, and women would also perform ably in the Viva Kennedy Club movement. Since they had their own auxiliaries, the women never assumed leadership in the Forum, but as in the Viva Kennedy effort they often did important work.

The club officers decided not to set up by-laws or a constitution for the organization, since the campaign would last only three months. They also did not articulate among themselves any particular strategy. Since most were veterans of poll tax drives, get-out-the-vote campaigns, and numerous other civic functions, they simply decided to do what they normally did. The club had no budget. The expenses would be paid as the campaign went along, out of their own pockets or through small fund-raisers. The main campaign propaganda would be transmitted via Spanish-language radio announcements, neighborhood rallies, word of mouth, and visits by national and state Kennedy supporters.[51]

Less than a week after organizing the Viva Kennedy Club in Hidalgo County, Idar sent Senator Kennedy a five-page letter providing some information on the infant effort and asking for more information on the function of the clubs.[52] The letter began by reminding Kennedy that Mexican Americans in the Rio Grande Valley had supported the Democratic Party in 1952 and 1956. It was a proud achievement for Idar, given that Dwight D. Eisenhower had carried Texas by significant majorities in those elections. Idar then informed the senator that establishing the clubs would "secure the recognition" that he believed Mexican Americans deserved as a payback for the previously mentioned support. Idar then painted a picture of a region with a growing conflict between Anglo Americans and Mexican Americans. He accused the minority white population of paranoia as they saw the "Spanish-speaking" voters become the majority in the county.[53]

There was now, wrote Idar, "younger leadership . . . awakening" Spanish-speaking voters to their voter responsibilities. This awakening had reversed voter registration numbers in Hidalgo County to the extent that Mexican Americans now had a 60-40 majority. "Due to these underlying factors," wrote Idar, "there is much lack of trust and confidence between the factions and the leaders . . . that compose the Democratic Party." Idar stated that his group had agreed to work with the county Democrats only on the condition that they be recognized for their efforts.

Idar told Kennedy that his local club wanted to set up a direct liaison with the national campaign headquarters. Assuming a closer relationship, Idar continued his letter with a request for assistance from the candidate himself. He asked Kennedy's help in bringing Rep. Franklin Roosevelt, Jr. to speak to a county rally. He also requested appearances by Sen. Ralph Yarborough and by Henry B. González but cautioned that conservative Democrats such as the vice-presidential nominee and the speaker of the House of Representatives might try to block these "outside" Democrats from coming. The letter ended by requesting more literature on Kennedy and more information on the purpose of the clubs.[54]

Audacity is one way to describe the letter from Idar to Kennedy. The tone was that of one whom Mexicans would call an *igualado*, someone who places himself on par with someone else of much higher status. That attitude reflected two perceptions that would come to dominate the Viva Kennedy Clubs. The first was that John F. Kennedy was somehow different from the rest of the Democrats, particularly the southern ones. The second affirmed that the Viva Kennedy Clubs were going to be extremely important in helping change the political landscape in which Mexican Americans lived. The first perception hinged on the belief that Kennedy was a friend, someone who offered a partnership that transcended an unfriendly state Democratic structure. They believed that Kennedy, as a liberal northerner and a national figure, was beyond the reach of state party officials and political bosses who would be directly threatened by active Mexican American voters. Kennedy, as a friend, would be sensitive to their consensus. The second perception grew out of McCormick's pitch for support, and also from García's letters to Viva Kennedy Club members in which he painted a picture of a presidential candidate deeply and personally committed to Mexican Americans. In an undated letter to Club members, he stated that "John Kennedy and . . . Johnson beg us for our help."[55] Both McCormick and García had defined Mexican American participation in the election as crucial. Leaders like Idar came to believe that the candidate himself issued this campaign rhetoric. Thus, they set out to elect a friend who depended very much on their support.

The spread of Viva Kennedy Clubs throughout the country revealed a similar approach to the one in Hidalgo County. Civic-minded individuals, old reformers, hardcore Democrats, and novice individuals motivated by an impressive Democratic nominee came together to form Viva Kennedy Clubs. The initial wave of clubs sprouted in soil prepared well by the activities of the American G.I. Forum. In fact, the Forum became the backbone of the Viva Kennedy movement, as chapter after chapter temporarily shifted from their civil-rights agenda to work on the campaign. Forum leaders made sure to tell people that "the Viva Kennedy Clubs [do] not have anything to do with the American G.I. Forum." Still, Forum leaders acknowledged that chapter officers were transforming themselves into club officers almost en masse. Reported the *News Bulletin*, the

Forum newspaper, "Leadership in these Viva Kennedy Clubs is, for the most part, supplied by politically conscious persons who also happen to be members of the American G.I. Forum."[56]

This link made it possible for the Viva Kennedy Club movement to spread "like wildfire," even before the national organization could get staffed. The Forum's newspaper became an unofficial organ for disseminating the information. The initial thrust of the Forum leaders sought to organize clubs in thirty-two states, and these clubs began forming before the national organization could outline any structure or philosophy. In Corpus Christi, Texas, thirty South Texas political leaders were invited to meet with Hector P. García and Albert Peña, Jr. to set up a state structure. By this time, the local newspaper referred to García, Peña, and state senator Henry B. González as co-chairmen of the national clubs.[57] To those who would listen, García began expounding on a vision that went beyond the opportunity to participate in electing a president. He told a gathering of Viva Kennedy workers that it was "very necessary that we have a judge of Spanish-speaking descent to convince our brothers in Mexico that we have a Democratic government." He went on to tell them of the need to have Mexican American educational counselors, teachers, superintendents, college board members, and a host of other positions to "recognize" the Mexican American people. And he promised them that "if we win this election . . . we will have the recognition."[58]

For his part, Carlos McCormick busied himself appointing state directors and national chairpersons and getting as much media exposure as possible. Shortly after the Democratic convention, through McCormick's mediation, Dennis Chávez and Joseph Montoya were appointed to serve as honorary chairmen.[59] McCormick then set out to appoint co-chairs where he felt a sustained campaign could be waged. Appointed to these positions were Henry "Hank" López and Edward R. Roybal of California; José Alvarado of Illinois; John Mendoza of Nevada; Filo Sedillo of New Mexico; Stanley Valadéz of Pennsylvania; and Henry B. González, Albert Peña, Jr., and Hector P. García of Texas. Also named were Richard Rucoba and Joe Maravilla in Indiana; Frank Rubi in Arizona; Vicente Ximenes in New Mexico; Jesse Alvarado and David Vega in Kansas; Mrs. Agustine Olvera in Iowa; and a Mr. Coronado in Minnesota. Still others were recognized as leaders in the club movement in Nebraska, Colorado, Michigan, Florida, Ohio, and New York.[60]

To enhance the sense of organizational solidarity, the Viva Kennedy people came up with a symbol and a banner. The symbol was a drawing of Senator Kennedy riding on a burro wearing a large *sombrero* that had imprinted on it "Viva Kennedy."[61] The design was a bold "Viva Kennedy" in blue. This was created by Ben Alvarado, an artist from Kansas City who was a member of the American G.I. Forum.[62] The Viva Kennedy Clubs also provided a Viva Kennedy pin and a one-dollar membership card to each new member.

"The national Viva Kennedy Clubs will give the millions of Spanish-speaking Americans a direct line of participation in the presidential election," declared McCormick in early August. He added that the clubs had been promoted by those who appreciated "the deep interest Senator Kennedy has always shown in the welfare of American citizens of Latin American origin."[63] This was an attempt to create an image that a few Mexican American leaders had of Kennedy but which was largely unknown among the populace. Kennedy was, in fact, not that well known to many Mexican Americans. The strategy for McCormick and others revolved around connecting Kennedy with progressive politics, Franklin D. Roosevelt, aid to migrant workers, political appointments for Latinos, and a myriad of other issues that would provide him instant credibility.

The three most important selling points were that he was a Democrat, that he was sympathetic to Latin America, and that he was a liberal, and as such, sympathetic to the poor.[64] Two other lesser points were that he was a friend to various Latino leaders and that, as an Irishman, he understood the problems of being a minority in American society. A sixth selling point that Viva Kennedy Club leaders denied as a factor but did not discourage was that the Democratic nominee was Catholic and his wife spoke Spanish.[65] All of these points except the last surfaced in the campaign speeches, flyers, personal letters, and press releases. More will be said in the next chapter on the creation of Kennedy's image, but a discussion of these points will serve as a foundation for the view of Kennedy that developed among Mexican American leaders and their followers.

The party affiliation served as the first foundation of a campaign among Mexican Americans. Those individuals in the barrio who had been active in the electoral process had tended to be Democrats, at least when they voted in the national elections. Even among New Mexicans and Arizonans, who had been Republicans before the Depression, political affiliations had shifted toward the Democrats. For many Mexican American elites, the New Deal had awakened in them an interest in national politics. While there is little indication that Roosevelt's policies were any more sensitive to Mexican Americans than to African Americans, government programs did help some Mexican Americans find jobs and receive assistance. Mexican American writers and academicians also received jobs through the Writers Project, which paid them to collect folktales throughout the Southwest.[66]

Sen. Dennis Chávez, a strong supporter of the New Deal, had also pushed through Congress a bill creating the Fair Employment Commission. While far from effective, it had been one more indication of the government's concern. Finally, during World War II, Roosevelt had promoted better and more equal relations with Latin American countries. The education of Mexican American children had received federal attention as never before or since. If there was one politician most Mexican Americans liked, it was Roosevelt. Mexican Americans had also shown some interest in the Henry Wallace campaign for president and had been enthusiastic about Adlai Stevenson, though neither had promised much.

While most Democrats at the state and local levels had usually been callous toward Mexican Americans, national Democrats reflected a more liberal attitude. This liberalism became another selling point in the organization of Viva Kennedy Clubs. With the demise of organizations such as the Congress of Spanish Speaking Organizations and the Mexican American National Association, as well as numerous militant unions, ideological militancy had been replaced by liberal politics. Liberalism offered responsible political means of combating conservative politics, segregated schools, unlivable housing, and blatant stereotypes. Liberals had not really developed a minority agenda by 1960, but their rhetoric of a more sophisticated and open society—notwithstanding Cold War rhetoric—promised a more benign attitude. Also, the liberal support of civil-rights activities seemed to promise that they would be supportive of the reform agenda of the various Mexican American reformers. This vision of liberal support assumed a collective and concerted effort by liberal groups and politicians that had little precedence in history. Nonetheless, the flyers and other propaganda published by Viva Kennedy leaders depicted Democrats and liberals as those most interested in providing good jobs, fair housing, assistance to the elderly, and an end to discrimination. Kennedy strengthened his liberal credentials and his "civil-rights persona" among Mexican Americans by inviting them to a campaign-sponsored National Conference on Constitutional Rights in Boston during the month of October. There, among four hundred other civil-rights activists, Hector P. García; Ralph Estrada, Supreme President of the Alianza Hispano-Americana; and New York assemblymen Felipe Torres and José Ramos López heard Kennedy pledge to bring "an end to second-class citizenship in America." Never before had Mexican American reformers been part of a national gathering on civil rights or participated so extensively in panels and sessions. While none of the speeches or resolutions specifically noted their concerns, the Mexican American reformers could still claim that they were part of the larger effort to fight discrimination in America.[67] While progressive rhetoric had been used before by other Democratic candidates, never before had there been such enthusiasm or such promises of implementation.

Kennedy, during the primaries and early part of the election, had made fighting communism an important issue. While re-stating much of the usual Cold War rhetoric, he had deviated slightly by arguing that poverty pushed people in developing countries toward communism. Americans had to export not only ideology but also economic assistance and know-how. Kennedy had referred to Latin America as a place where poverty provided the potential for subversion. Viva Kennedy Club leaders were in agreement, and they saw his rhetoric as progressive and non-interventionist. His efforts to establish a good relationship with Latin American countries reminded them of Roosevelt's Good Neighbor Policy.[68] Also, Latin America was one place where they could be of service to the new administration. They saw themselves serving in diplomatic posts and having policy-making responsibilities. It is probable that they saw the new interest in Latin America as a way of enhancing the status of Latin Americans in the United States.

The fourth selling point, that of personal relationship to Kennedy, was only partially true. Given Kennedy's propensity for making political contacts during the years of preparation for the campaign, it is likely that he met some of the major Viva Kennedy Club leaders. With the exception of Chávez, however, he had very few dealings with any of them. He had joined the American G.I. Forum the year before but had not attended any of the conventions, even though he had been invited. He had never met Albert Peña, Jr., barely knew Hector P. García, and had only interacted with Henry B. González a few times.[69] Even Chávez had initially been a supporter of Johnson. The rest of the Viva Kennedy Club leaders had little contact with Kennedy. Even during the campaign, his contact with them would be limited. But a few letters from Robert F. Kennedy, the campaign manager, created in the minds of these leaders an image of friendship.[70] When they spoke of what Kennedy promised, they did so as if they were relaying a personal commitment from a dear friend who would not betray them. In presenting the message this way, the Viva Kennedy Club leaders also put their own reputations on the line and transformed a campaign promise doled out in the political arena into an agreement between intimate friends. It was a bold and dangerous move, but it was a calculated one. Delivering a high vote meant the difference between influence in the future administration or simply a "thank you" from a victorious campaign. While ethnic political campaigns usually have a personal tone, this one took that tone publicly with open letters and advertisements. Also, those promoting this type of campaign were not traditional ghetto politicians but reformers who always sought to be legitimate and sophisticated.

Kennedy's ethnicity also played a role in the campaign strategy, though probably a lesser one. Since Kennedy's forebears were Irish, a much more recognized immigrant group than others from Europe, he was somewhat different though still a mainstream Anglo politician. More important for the election, though, was that his ethnicity also opened the discussion of Catholicism and politics.[71] Being a Catholic Irish American placed Kennedy in a situation where Viva Kennedy leaders could argue his similarities to the mainstream of Mexican American voters. This tactic was dangerous since it accentuated the Mexican Americans' own divergence from American society, but at the same time it expanded the American mainstream to include the barrio residents. Kennedy's Catholicism would be downplayed at the public level, with no reference to his religion in pamphlets, letters, or other campaign paraphernalia. The debate over Kennedy's religious affiliation had ignited a storm in many communities, especially among conservative Protestants who questioned his ability to govern without interference from the Vatican. This caustic debate must have angered Mexican Americans, since most of the heated debates occurred in areas with large Mexican American populations. Having been discriminated against in most things, Mexican Americans must have felt that this debate over their religion only added salt to their wounds. Still, Viva Kennedy Club leaders sought to avoid the debate, and most would claim it to be a non-issue. But at the grassroots level people recognized it as a powerful selling point. Mexican Americans spoke about it, but they tended to do so in Spanish—the barrio's private language—and thus only among themselves.[72]

Kennedy's Catholicism may not have been a religious issue to most Viva Kennedy Club leaders, but it was to many of their followers. For Club leaders, Kennedy's religious affiliation represented a cultural bridge to the Mexican American community. His Catholicism meant that he understood religious and cultural prejudices. It meant that he understood the dilemma of the Catholic schools—an issue prominent in the minds of G.I. Forum leaders.[73] And it meant that he valued family and tradition. The fact that his wife Jacqueline understood and spoke Spanish meant that Kennedy could communicate with Mexican Americans and understand their needs. With these points to sell, Mexican American reformers felt confident that they could get barrio residents to vote for him. The fact that he was *simpatico* made it an easier sell.[74]

At this point, it is important to emphasize that the organization of the Viva Kennedy Clubs proceeded in an unregulated and uncoordinated manner. They appeared first in localities where the Forum had a presence, and group leaders in other areas simply copied the process, though not necessarily the strategy or structures.[75] They grew faster than the ability of the national office—comprising McCormick and one assistant—to keep up. And they grew disconnected, knowing little about each other's work. Ed Idar would admit years later that he had known almost nothing of the national organization and just as little about the Texas statewide coordinating body.[76] No major meetings would bring the state groups together, and few, if any, strategies were ever shared among state organizations, and only a little more within the states themselves. The thing that kept them bound as a "national" organization was the desire to elect John F. Kennedy president and the prospect of receiving a payback from a grateful winner.

3. Camelot, Mexican American Style

The effort to provide some structuring for the Viva Kennedy Clubs organization occurred in the heat of the campaign. Unlike the larger Kennedy organization, which had been years in the making, the Viva Kennedy Clubs came together without any prescribed strategy. They also lacked an ideological foundation, instead relying on the particular experiences of their founders. Unlike the later Chicano Movement groups, which sought ideological and organizational hegemony, the Viva Kennedy Clubs were meant to be adaptable to the particular community in which they were established. This policy reflected the independent nature of most of the reformers. The use of the term "policy" should not imply a conceptual approach but rather a consensual one. That is, most Viva Kennedy leaders accepted each other's autonomy.

These politicians and social reformers who came to lead the Viva Kennedy movement were individuals who best represented the integration of first- and second-generation descendants of immigrants. They were individualistic, often exhibiting an aggressive independence, but were collectively united in their efforts to be good Americans and to entice their community toward the same goal. They were, however, conscious that discrimination against their fellow Mexicans served to undermine the social and economic advancement of all Mexicans, whether foreign or native-born. These reformers, as a group, were a success story. They had good jobs, good educations, and usually a respectable standing in both their own and the Anglo American community. They exhibited a middle-class orientation toward higher education, personal discipline, and integration, though not assimilation into mainstream society. While some came from homes with activist or politically involved parents in Mexico or the early Southwest, most were not concerned with ethnic issues or civil rights in their early years, at least not in the context of a broader ethnic movement. Most, though not all, became interested in civil rights as they became more secure in their own brand of Americanism. These individuals perceived their childhood as a happy one that was not marred in any profound personal way by discrimination and racism.[1] While the later generation of Chicano activists was motivated by ugly encounters with prejudices, the major leaders of this reform movement seemed compelled—publicly at least—by an obligation to make the United States live up to its ideals.

These reformers were practical individuals. Henry B. González would declare, while running for governor in 1958, "I don't think of myself as a do-gooder or a big crusader. I think I have always tried to keep my feet on the ground and do the practical thing."[2] This practicality reflected the reformers' belief in the fundamental goodness of American society. They believed that most problems could be "harmoniously worked out between Anglos and Latins."[3] To them, there were no real divisions except those caused by ignorance and personal prejudices. They believed, at least initially, that most Anglo Americans were prejudiced only because they did not know Mexican Americans well; thus, the "practical" thing to do was to educate the American public and prove the Mexican American worthy of respect.

Mexican American reformers became interested in the political arena because it was the one avenue that provided an opportunity for the greatest interaction with mainstream society. Electioneering meant participating in one of the fundamental aspects of American citizenship. Those who chose to support particular candidates were going to be interested in platforms and political rhetoric and in discussion of major issues. The mere process of deciding for whom to vote meant that the Mexican American voter was making an emotional commitment to the American political system. The move toward electoral politics came about as a result of changes in demography. Mexican Americans were simply growing in numbers, particularly the native-born population. This growth, as discussed before, provided them a sense that political empowerment was possible in a number of places. Political control became important as Mexican American elites concluded that, in spite of some Anglo American sympathy, resolution of problems in the community would have to be resolved by Mexican Americans themselves. They perceived that Anglo Americans had a lack of faith in the Mexican Americans' ability to govern.

The Anglo American stereotypes of their "abilities" bothered them. The fact that they were seen as a supportive constituency and not a governing one made Mexican American elites anxious to prove otherwise. Mexican American middle-class reformers were also troubled by what they perceived to be a historical failure in their struggle for civil rights. Lacking historical perspective, they did not recognize the reform efforts of the past. They believed, in some respect, that they were the first to truly agitate for reform.[4] This view was partly based on the fact that they rejected radical and nationalist efforts because they moved away rather than toward integration into American society. Conscious of their factionalism, they continually criticized their people for not becoming "united."[5] Yet this factionalism was a middle-class dilemma that had rarely affected working-class struggles of the past. Nationalist-oriented groups had normally seen themselves as defending the community against an Anglo American cultural, economic, and social onslaught. Their "us versus them" mentality had forged a Mexican identity that Mexican American integrationists usually lacked. By seeking to find a niche in American society, these reformers navigated a much more complex road than their nationalist counterparts. They continually had to juggle their competing identities. Their Mexicanness created obstacles for them, but it also provided them a distinction from the society around them.

Their political style reflected their experience with the American political system and its social institutions. It also reflected the attitudes these reformers had about their own people. For the majority of Viva Kennedy leaders, the opportunities that American society promised were real.

There were social, economic, and professional opportunities for those who worked hard and knew how to take advantage of them. The lives of each reformer served as an example. Dennis Chávez, Henry B. González, Edward R. Roybal, Ed Idar, Jr., and Albert Peña, Jr. were lawyers or professionals. Hector P. García was a medical doctor, and George Sánchez had a doctorate in education. Heading most every Viva Kennedy Club were Mexican Americans who had professional degrees or were in the process of getting them. There were also business people, and below them in the hierarchy were skilled workers. These were men and women who had begun to see the fruits of their education and their skills. While some came from professional families, most were the first generation in their family to become educated and acquire professional jobs. They were exceptional individuals who had cracked through the barriers of the barrio to live their version of the American dream.[6]

Given the condition of the barrio in their childhood years, it is incredible that few, if any of them, had emotional scars from prejudices or discrimination. Little has been written of them, but what has been written reveals that most were not apt to believe—at least not at this stage of their lives—that they had encountered any significant obstacles to overcome. The chief obstacle was lack of financial resources, but that problem seemed to have been solved by hard work. Hector P. García's reminiscence is a Horatio Alger story of hard work, incredible patience and tolerance, and tenacity that enabled him to achieve the American dream. He grew up in Mercedes, Texas, in a middle-class family with working-class resources. He attended a segregated Mexican school, then an integrated high school. Later, he walked or hitched a ride daily to attend college thirty miles from home. Periodically assisted by a compassionate teacher or other individuals, García seems to have seen life as a challenge to be overcome. In retelling his life story, he mentions no particular incident of prejudice, though he admits there being many who did suffer discrimination. At the University of Texas, García had few of the comforts that many of his Anglo American classmates enjoyed, but he never felt discriminated against, despite the school's reputation for harsh attitudes toward Mexican American students. "We were too few," he would later tell an interviewer.[7] While there, he mostly kept to himself, rarely participating in the Alba Club, which brought together the most prominent Mexican American students on campus. From that club, most of whose members were from Laredo, would come some important reformers.[8]

But it would be years before García showed any inclination toward reform. Like most overachievers in the barrio, he concentrated on making good grades and taking advantage of opportunities that American society presented to well-mannered, highly motivated Mexican Americans. As a teenager he became involved in military training, which he loved to the point of considering the military as a career. That consideration became even more serious when he served during World War II and rose to the rank of major. Also during this time García met the Italian woman who later became his wife. Though García participated in numerous activities that might have exposed him to American racial and cultural prejudices—in high school, at the University of Texas, in the cadet corps, the army—he would still remember his early years as happy ones.[9]

Henry B. González also described a childhood without major incidents. González's parents had fled the Mexican Revolution like many other middle-class Mexicans and had settled in San Antonio. His father, a prominent but low-level politician in Porfirio Diaz's dictatorship, became the editor of the city's Spanish-language newspaper. The father's position made his home a place for important exiles to meet and discuss politics and philosophy. González would later remember lively discussions in his family's kitchen as expatriates debated the effects of the Mexican Revolution. Though raised in a stimulating home environment, he grew up a shy young man who initially struggled in school. An incident in which a teacher humiliated him for his language deficiencies would change his life dramatically. Motivated to prove her wrong, he became the most avid of readers and quickly rose to the top of his class.[10]

This reaction to a humiliating incident was another characteristic of this generation of leaders. Rather than become deeply offended or alienated, these individuals simply became more tenacious in their acquisition of skills and knowledge. They were not blind to discrimination's effect on their people, but they dealt with it on a personal level. One reason may be that for those persons who were first-generation Americans or immigrants raised in the United States, their parents had made a conscious decision to come to this country. They did not lament their being in the United States and not in Mexico. Since many of these parents saw themselves as immigrants, they tried hard to play by the rules of their new land. With time, and because of Anglo American retrenchment, many would develop a harsher remembrance, but at this juncture they were still optimistic and less bitter.

González attended the University of Texas for one year, but his lack of money meant days without eating, a hardship which caused him to drop out. He would finish college in his hometown of San Antonio. He completed law school by attending evening sessions, but he would never pass the bar. González never did enter a profession or even have a job that lasted long or provided him an adequate income. He was fiercely independent, and he had a quick temper. Politics would become his profession, beginning with his election to the city council, the state senate, and eventually the U.S. Congress. González simply survived as best he could economically while dedicating his time fully to his political responsibilities. The fact that he devoted more hours to working for his constituencies and was willing to sacrifice more of himself than most of his opponents or friends allowed him to achieve success in politics. For González, a refugee from the Mexican Revolution, political mobility remained the best option for someone without a profession or family money.[11]

For those like Dennis Chávez and Joseph Montoya, whose families had been in the United States for a longer period, making American society work seemed the only option. Born at a time when Mexican Americans were the majority in New Mexico, Chávez and Montoya had grown up with less of the insecurity that other Mexican Americans had. After all, New Mexico provided role models and somewhat more opportunities than other Southwestern states did. They both had followed the pattern of former New Mexican leaders who worked hard in local and regional politics, waited for the right opportunity while building strong political and financial support, and then jumped at the opportunity to be elected.[12] As congressmen, they had learned to wield tremendous power in their committee assignments and powerful influence in statewide politics. New Mexico's political arena, very unlike that of other Southwestern states, provided vast opportunities for Mexican Americans to make political careers. Because they had forged careers in the political arena, Chávez and Montoya were committed to the electoral process, though by 1960 they were both concerned with the changing social climate in New Mexico. Both had seen the decline of the Hispanos' power and prestige with the large influx of Anglo Americans into the state. Chávez, in particular, who was an avowed and outspoken liberal, had been involved in divisive and hard fought re-election campaigns because of the growing conservatism in the state. As early as the late 1940s, Chávez had warned Hispanos that if they did not actively participate in the electoral process, they would soon lose their political power to a newcomer less concerned about maintaining the fragile calm of ethnic relations in the state. The Hispanos' decline in status was compounded by the state's lack of wealth and its economic dependence on military bases and defense technology industries. Yet New Mexicans were a proud people and instilled in their children a will to succeed. It seems rather certain that, unlike those of the later Chicano generation, their families spent little time bemoaning the unfairness of American society. This, despite the fact that a number of these reformers' parents were involved in some form of social action.[13]

Others shared some of the core values of the aforementioned reformers. María Urquides of Tucson, Arizona, the only woman to serve on the national Viva Kennedy Clubs board, was one of those. Her biographer tells of a happy childhood in which sensitive Anglo American teachers helped her to adapt socially and academically in school. She tells of a time when her second-grade teacher made all the students take off their shoes to make a shoeless María feel at home.[14] She also tells of teachers who took time to help her become an overachiever in her early grades. In fact, Urquides blended so well with her Anglo American teachers and friends that she felt "alienated" from her Mexican American friends. Yet Urquides remembers not being able to visit her Anglo American friends' homes because it was socially unacceptable. This social irony would plague other Mexican American reformers, but it was such a part of the social circumstances that few made much of an issue over it. It is also quite possible that they did not connect their friends with the action of their parents or the attitudes of the society at large.[15]

Urquides, who came to be known as the mother of bilingual education, became a teacher in the elementary grades and then at the high-school level. When she and an English-surnamed friend applied for a teaching position, she got the job, and it dispelled, according to her biographer, the "feelings of discrimination that she thought might have prevailed at college."[16] For the rest of her life, Urquides would see—as would many other Viva Kennedy reformers—success as a re-affirmation that discrimination was not a problem for them even if it was for others of their kind. As a schoolteacher she was known as a disciplinarian and as a strong promoter of patriotism. Her class always won the city championship marching award during the Armistice Day parade.

In spite of her commitment to Americanism and to the teaching of English, she sought to promote the students' Mexican culture and a greater fluency in their native language. She promoted bilingualism in the public school years—but not in college—and a bicultural lifestyle but not a Mexican one. She never visited her relatives in Mexico, and she clashed with Chicano activists years later over their cultural nationalism.[17] In doing so, she reflected her cohorts' cultural and philosophical duality. Her whole career involved working with mostly Mexican American students and parents, but her major goal remained making them better Americans. Her commitment to American middle-class values meshed with her exprience as an overachieving Mexican girl from the barrio to produce a Mexican American educator and reformer with a profound belief in the goodness of American society. But this philosophy rested on a profound belief in the need for personal and collective respect for American institutions.

The Viva Kennedy Clubs brought together two generations of Mexican Americans. George Sánchez and Dennis Chávez represented the older, more established generation, and González, García, and Albert Peña, Jr. represented the emerging one. Edward R. Roybal represented a period in between those two. Sánchez and Chávez, having grown up before the Depression, participated in World War II home-front politics, and matured during the desegregation battles of the 1940s, were the more militant of the group. Their perspective represented a hybrid of southwestern nationalism, New Deal politics, and middle-class accommodationism. The fact that both were from New Mexico provided them a better sense of the history of the Mexican American experience. They had seen their fellow New Mexicans live the dichotomy of assimilation and cultural resistance. While New Mexicans clung fiercely to their cultural traditions, they also participated more fully in the American social and political system than their counterparts in other southwestern states. New Mexicans tended to be primarily native-born and for the most part were less inclined to look toward Mexico as a cultural center. Yet their rural predominance made them much more culturally Mexican than they admitted. Their own native-son folklorist, Arthur L. Campa, would deflate their claims of being "Spanish" and not Mexican.[18]

Both Sánchez and Chávez believed that an active federal government could resolve many of the problems that Mexican Americans faced. Without federal assistance, the state could not provide adequate health maintenance systems, public schools, or housing. The fact that mining, agricultural, and other industrial interest groups dominated New Mexican politics made it unlikely that state government would be sensitive to the needs of the rural and urban poor of the state. Both men, but particularly Sánchez, also believed that Mexican Americans simply lacked the political, cultural, and economic sophistication needed to make the changes themselves. Thus, the government had an obligation to resolve the most critical problems and bring the Mexican American into the "American fold."[19]

The Roosevelt programs during the Depression and World War II contributed another factor to their philosophy. Chávez had been in the House of Representatives when Roosevelt assumed the presidency. As a loyal liberal Democrat, Chávez had supported Roosevelt's numerous proposals to save the nation from the grips of unemployment and poverty. He had even written a crucial bill creating the Office of Fair Employment to give minorities an equal chance to benefit from federal labor legislation. His own state of New Mexico had been a prime recipient of federal funding. New Mexican writers and scholars would be major beneficiaries as they were hired to record the folklore of the region. For Chávez, as with other Mexican Americans, the New Deal represented a significant effort to provide the benefits of American society. As a senior-ranking senator, he had faith in the ability of the federal government to make significant changes in the lives of ordinary people. He also recognized that federal action could circumvent the prejudices and narrow-minded views of local and state governments. Ironically, the New Deal may have reminded Chávez and many others of the Mexican Revolution, another major social and political event undertaken on behalf of the poor. For Mexicans, it seemed that these major social or political contortions were necessary for change to come to their lives.

For Sánchez, World War II provided the context for an active federal government. As an educator at the University of Texas, he became involved in federal efforts to provide a better education for Mexican American children. This new benevolence toward the Spanish-speaking came out of the attempt by Roosevelt to develop a "good neighbor" policy toward Mexico.[20] This policy had a two-fold purpose: to gain moral and eventually military support for the war effort and to alleviate Mexico's concerns about sending hundreds of thousands of its citizens to work in American agricultural fields. Sánchez served on a number of committees at the state level and even one at the federal level. During this period of time, he and other Mexican American and Anglo American educators promoted numerous ways to resolve the educational problems of the

Southwest. At no other time in the history of the Mexican presence in American society had government seemed so interested.[21] Numerous Mexican Americans received appointments to war-time committees, positions which these reformers used to extend their fight for rights and benefits in education and housing. They also worked to promote a better relationship between cultures. The war seemed to provide a new basis for friendship, cooperation, and understanding.

With Sánchez in the lead, Mexican American reformers challenged the interpretation of their "problem." They rejected the stereotypic view that Mexican Americans were a non-achieving homogenous group whose cultural inadequacies compounded the problems they faced because of poverty and a lack of English proficiency. Replacing that typology was the view that Mexican Americans were a heterogenous group of people with very defined cultural, linguistic, racial, and economic differences. While this "new definition" sought to combat prejudice, it did not, however, go far enough in defining the unique challenges that Mexican American children faced. Guadalupe San Miguel argues that this definition made Mexican American children like any other American children except with the need for more English instruction.[22]

Interestingly, although Sánchez believed that Mexican Americans were victims of the U.S. conquest of the Southwest, he did not, unlike Chicano scholars of the 1960s, develop a critique of the American educational system that rejected its values and principles. Sánchez wanted to end segregation, provide bilingual education, and improve instruction. He also shared his Chicano counterparts' desire for the introduction of Mexican American history into the curriculum. But all of these steps were to make Mexican American children more American and not less. His preoccupation with the cultural and educational deficiencies of Mexican Americans made him an aggressive exponent of an integration that respected cultural and linguistic differences. His dream would be shared by Hispanic educators of the post–Chicano Movement era.

In California, Roybal led a slightly younger and more politically aggressive group. The heterogenous and seemingly more politically open California society presented opportunities for young reform-minded Mexican American *politicos* who could put together effective voter-registration and get-out-the-vote drives. Roybal did just that in 1949 to win the ninth-district city council seat in Los Angeles.[23] The victory came after a successful voter registration that added 15,000 more Mexican Americans to the voter rolls. With these new votes, Roybal increased his earlier vote total nearly six-fold. An earlier defeat had taught Roybal that organization, registration, and an appeal to ethnic solidarity in the barrio would be necessary for victory. The first two strategies were typically American, and the last was a time-tested barrio strategy. Yet within the strategy was always an effort to persuade Anglo Americans that Roybal was not an ethnic candidate but simply the "best man" for the job. Thus, Roybal played the ethnic card in the barrios while running a traditional liberal campaign in the rest of the city council district.

Roybal's victory provided a pattern for future California races involving Mexican American candidates. These candidates waged voter-registration drives for specific elections, and their efforts at stimulating civic duty were centered on their personal campaigns. With the founding of the Community Service Organization by Roybal and others, politics in East Los Angeles became ethnic-specific even while Mexican Americans sought entrance into the mainstream.[24] While ethnic solidarity had always been part of electoral rhetoric in the barrios of Southern California, the CSO, under Roybal's leadership, created an ethnic agenda that identified most of the issues as "Mexican" issues. This meant that Mexican American candidates could not simply request support because of their personal ethnicity; they now had to promote a Mexican American agenda. This strategy sought to eliminate barrio opportunists and those who were political lackeys of Anglo American power brokers. The CSO would eventually have hundreds of Mexican Americans involved in defining, articulating, and attacking the problems of the barrio. Committees to tackle almost every problem became a permanent part of the CSO.[25] The organization sought to teach Mexican Americans to resolve their problems the "American" way—through politics and the ballot box. By placing the electoral campaign within the cultural and social confines of the barrio, American democracy became the philosophy of reform, replacing militant unionism and Mexican nationalism as the dominant ideologies for reform. This Americanization, ironically, depended on the playing of the ethnic card. Like Chávez and Sánchez's governmentalist view, this Mexicanization of American politics contributed to a changing perception of reform.

Texas reformers and politicians would provide other elements to the reformers' perception of how American democracy worked and how Mexican Americans could use it to their advantage. By consensus of most reformers, Texas represented the most repressive political climate of any state in the Southwest. Yet Texas also proved to be the most fertile ground for reform activities. Texas had sprouted LULAC, the American G.I. Forum, and a host of other integrationist organizations that fought for the rights of Mexican Americans. By the late 1950s, the truly militant and nationalist organizations had given way to the new associations of professionals, veterans, and skilled workers. These new organizations were led by individuals whose sense of Mexicanness had been reconstructed to fit within American pluralism. Rather than see themselves as a distinct group with a variant history and a distinct future, they saw themselves as having always been American. Their immigrant or first-generation status served as a starting point for their Americanism and not a juncture in their Mexicanness. For the most part, they were proud of their ancestry and usually retained their connection to the barrio and its residents. But this social and genealogical foundation merely pointed out that they were part of a diverse American society, not that they were alienated from it. The Texan-Mexican, the most oppressed of the border Mexican Americans, also became the most tenacious in clinging to his or her Americanism.[26]

Three particular individuals stood out in the Texas political scene of the 1950s. They were Henry B. González, a state senator; Albert Peña, Jr., a county commissioner; and Dr. Hector P. García, American G.I. Forum founder. Each one of them brought a particular style to the politics of reform, but they all promoted a fierce loyalty to American ideals. González's activities reflected the lone wolf approach. He was an avowed liberal who spoke out against segregation and discrimination on behalf of all minorities without using the rhetoric of ethnicity or race. He cemented his support in the barrios by speaking out forcefully against abuses and by his exhaustive services to his constituents. He gained support from liberals, union members, blacks, and moderates by his fierce defense of the working class against the powerful economic interests in Texas.[27] An extremely articulate politician, González disavowed the ethnic politician label even as he developed into the most successful and popular Mexican American politician in Texas. In many ways, he represented the epitome of the Mexican American renaissance politician. He was well educated in the Anglo world, but spoke perfect Spanish; he was a loyal American but came from a prominent Mexican family; he was loved by his people but feared by his Anglo American adversaries; he was a strong advocate for the *mexicano* but he was an American leader. González took the Mexican

American's yearning for legitimacy and forged it into a solid support for his electoral efforts. And he did it at the same time that he encouraged liberals and others to see him as a product of America's tolerance and pluralism.[28] Even some conservatives would come to grudgingly admire him because he exuded American ideals and remained a Cold War warrior throughout the 1950s and 1960s. González's brand of politics kept Mexican Americans connected to traditional liberal politics even as their particular issues were addressed by a Mexican reformer. Few Mexican American politicians would ever live the American dream as well as González.

Albert Peña, Jr. represented another political style. While González remained throughout his career a loner, an individual against the forces of prejudice, Peña would best be known as a coalition builder and a consummate ethnic politician.[29] His early experience as a civil-rights lawyer convinced him that he had the ability to organize Mexican Americans to action and to attract open-minded Anglo Americans to his point of view. His experience integrating several public schools without the use of outside support or litigation led to his belief that political coalitions that could threaten and take political or physical action—such as walkouts or protest marches—were more effective than costly lawsuits or appeals to the goodness of those who governed. Peña developed the reputation of being a confronter whose bombastic oratory relied on the rhetoric of race and equality. Rather than just rights and privileges, Peña wanted empowerment for Mexican Americans. They should govern where they were the majority. While González attacked Texas conservatives through the rhetoric of inclusion and fairness, Peña assailed them with the rhetoric and actions of political empowerment. His coalition of liberals, blacks, union members, and Mexican Americans eventually took control of the Bexar County (San Antonio) Democratic Party and made it one of the largest and the most liberal Democratic Party organizations in Texas. His own westside group, the Loyal American Democrats, became a pseudo-political machine in the barrios of San Antonio, influencing much of the politics among Mexican Americans there.[30]

The third prominent reformer in Texas, García, proved to be the most traveled and tenacious proponent of Mexican American civil rights of all the Texas reformers. As founder of the American G.I. Forum, he dealt with bread-and-butter issues constantly. His efforts kept him in contact with working-class Mexican Americans, unlike González and Peña, who depended heavily on middle-class support for their electoral efforts. García traveled throughout Texas and the Southwest establishing Forum chapters and state organizations, thus becoming one of the few national leaders of the 1950s. His approach to organizing Forum chapters differed greatly from the efforts of the aforementioned politicians in that he allowed greater autonomy to his followers. García sought to develop reformers in every community, and once developed, they had more than adequate space to engage in the activities appropriate to their communities.[31] Forum leadership, at least at the local level, was not always professional or middle class, and its activities were often in behalf of poor Mexican Americans and Mexicans.

The Forum's initial agenda facilitated the rendering of government services to veterans and their families. Before the Forum's founding, Mexican American veterans encountered numerous obstacles in getting medical treatment, receiving the G.I. Bill, finding federal employment, and obtaining home and business loans. With the Forum's aggressive lobbying, those problems were usually resolved. But in becoming involved in those issues, Forum leaders became aware of a number of other problems that veterans faced because of their ethnicity. Segregation in schools and housing remained prevalent. Stereotypes and degrading depictions of Mexican Americans still circulated, and, more important, Mexican Americans remained politically powerless even in communities where they constituted the majority of the citizenry.

While Mexican Americans sought redress as American citizens for years, their citizenship seemed to offer little protection as witnessed by the deportations, the policy brutality, and the voting fraud committed against them continually. For García, Mexican Americans had to demand their rights not only as citizens but also as veterans who had offered their lives to defend their country. Their status as veterans provided them a platform that Mexican Americans had lacked before. They could speak as equals, and their demands were nothing more than a payback for their sacrifice. Having participated in this country's most significant event of the twentieth century, they could not be classified as foreigners and Johnny-come-latelies. Fortifying their position even more was the protection that veteran status gave them against being labeled communists or radicals. Veteran status allowed them to be forceful in their demands and confident in their action. Their patriotic service also provided the parameters to their activism. As defenders of the "American way," they were rarely tempted to radicalize or to become too nationalistic. They were

American soldiers continuing the war at home that they had begun over-seas. Eventually García would see all Mexican Americans and Mexicans as part of an enlarged veterans' community.[32]

Other reformers throughout the nation fit into one or more of the political styles reviewed. They, along with Chávez, Sánchez, Roybal, González, Peña, Urquides, and García, created a political ambience that provided the framework for the goals of the Viva Kennedy Clubs. The as-pirations of these reformers may be broken into five major goals: accep-tance into the American fold; cessation of all discriminatory and violent acts against Mexican Americans; access to political and economic power; recognition of Mexican American contributions to American society; and the pluralistic Americanization of the Mexican American community. All of these goals were believed to be possible in a Kennedy administration that would promote an active federal government, support strong civil-rights legislation, appoint Mexican Americans to important government posts, and recognize its political debt to Viva Kennedy Club support. A friendlier federal government led by a charismatic Catholic with sympa-thies toward Latin America would surely attract more Mexican Ameri-cans toward the American mainstream. In doing so, many of these re-formers could move toward leadership in the larger American society and not just in the barrios of the United States.

Given these reformers' aspirations, the Viva Kennedy Clubs became more than just a vehicle to promote a Catholic candidate with a wife who spoke Spanish. The Kennedy campaign, rather, provided a much-sought forum for Mexican American reformers to present their case to the Ameri-can public. For years they had cried out for attention with little success. With the Kennedy campaign, they moved quickly to proclaim their exis-tence. In the process of becoming public, they created an image of their cause. Although they wrote very few political statements, the Viva Ken-nedy Clubs of Texas did, however, outline their goals in a statement they titled "The Americans of Mexican Descent, A Statement of Principles" and distributed to their supporters, the Kennedy campaign staff, and the media.

One of the things that is apparent from reading the statement is that these reformers did not base their philosophy on interpretations of Ameri-can history that conflicted with the traditional American historical nar-rative. Much of their historical perspective is based on references to soci-ological and statistical reports that American academics prepared in the late 1940s and 1950s. These reports tended to blame Mexican Americans for their problems, though they did provide substantial evidence of Anglo American prejudices. This dichotomy reflected, in part, the view of many reformers who saw Anglo American prejudices compounding the problems inherent in the barrio. The dichotomous dilemma made it difficult to resolve the problems confronting Mexican Americans, because two problems had to be corrected simultaneously. Mexican Americans had to abandon those cultural and social traits that disadvantaged them, and Anglo Americans had to abandon those prejudices which also disadvantaged Mexican Americans.[33]

The Viva Kennedy statement of principles begins with a cursory history to remind the reader that the four million "Spanish-Mexicans" were descended from the peoples of Spain and New Spain and had been in the country in one capacity or another since "time immemorial." "In other words," the document stated, "historically and culturally he [the *mexicano*] belongs here." This line of thinking follows that of both George Sánchez, the primary author of the statement, and historian Carlos Castañeda. Both had argued in their writings that American history could not be seen as linear, that is, beginning in Europe and moving west. Castañeda emphasized Spanish exploration, and Sánchez emphasized the development of autonomous communities in the Southwest, both of which predated English colonization.[34] The introduction points out that the "Spanish-Mexicans" were not an immigrant group but actually a people living in their "traditional home." The Mexican American's right to be here, continued the statement, "has been dramatically attested to by his spectacular loyalty to this country in time of war."[35] The introduction categorically rejected any notion that Mexican Americans could leave if they did not like their treatment. For these Mexican Americans, most of them veterans, World War II had been the time of the community's greatest integration into American society. A reference to the great conflict where Mexican Americans had participated fully provided legitimacy to their demands. Unlike Mexican nationalists of the past who extolled Mexican historical events, these veterans saw World War II as the most significant event in Mexican American history. The fact that the war had occurred during their maturing years partly explains this presentist viewpoint. The other part of the explanation may be that, of those bits and pieces of Mexican American history that were familiar, only a few did not describe a tragic story, a failure, a short-lived victory, or a re-affirmation of Mexican

American second-class status. This defeatist view of their history would naturally lead them to think of World War II as a triumph, a new departure for the Mexican American narrative.

The statement then shifts to a discussion of the "forgotten" status of Mexican Americans. For the Kennedy Democrats, nothing grated on them more than the fact that American society had little consciousness of them. Books and reports with titles such as *Strangers in Our Fields, Forgotten People, Frustration, The Uneducated, Roots without Rights, These Are Braceros,* and *This Is the Migrant* seemed to always be introducing Mexican Americans to the larger society but never integrating them. For them, having been first in the land gave them historical precedence over other groups. At this stage, the writers of the Viva Kennedy document provided one of the few truly nationalist concepts. "In moments of bitterness over the sad state affairs among our people," they declared, "we might well point out that we did not ask the United States to come here—that we are, in effect, subject-peoples."[36] Sánchez, in his book *Forgotten People,* had referred to New Mexicans as children of the conquest, people cast into a new world by no choice of their own. The people had lost their lands and their political power, had been economically dislocated, and for all practical purposes had lost their history. They continued to suffer the consequences of not being able to compete in American society. In essence, their whole history seemed to be one adjustment after another to American prejudices. This status as "subject-peoples" kept them from controlling their own destiny, and, consequently, they remained invisible as long as American society chose to ignore them.[37]

At this juncture in the statement, the authors had an opportunity to provide a truly nationalist critique of the Mexican American experience in the United States. Tying together the military conquest, the forced subordination, the indifference of American society, and the continuing racism, the authors could have written a defining document that reinterpreted history and took Mexican Americans out of the pool of minority mini-narratives that dominated American thought even in geographic locations with high concentrations of Mexican Americans. But the authors seemed not to have had any grasp of a historical vision that would differentiate them from the identity imposed by American history.[38]

The nationalist critique, thus, faded into these words: " . . . [subject-peoples] for whose well-being the United States has a special obligation, an obligation that has been most pointedly overlooked." The paragraph goes on to say that American society had recognized its moral responsibility to the Indian, Negro, Filipino, and Puerto Rican but had ignored the Mexican American. The philanthropic institutions, the mass media, and even the public officials who had been elected by Mexican Americans had "barely stirred over his plight." "It is wondrous . . . that he [the Mexican American] has not become permanently embittered and thoroughly disillusioned."[39] The writers then remind the American public that Mexican Americans had faith in the system. This faith was a testament to their devotion to the United States. Rather than define themselves as a people, they chose to see themselves as a neglected group within American society.

In the next several pages, the creators of the document go on to cite what they consider the most important effects of the neglect. They point out that Mexican Americans were at the bottom "of the scale on virtually every criterion measuring health, wealth, education and welfare."[40] These factors, they stated, had caused a high rejection rate for the draft among Mexican Americans, while also contributing to a high infant death rate and a high incidence of tuberculosis. While hundreds of thousands of Mexican Americans had served proudly, many South Texans had been rejected for military service. For veterans this was intolerable. As for infant mortality, Texas contributed one-fourth of all deaths nationally, and most of those came from the areas of high concentration of Mexican Americans. Tuberculosis claimed 160 deaths per 100,000, four times the rate among Anglo Americans. Those shameful statistics were duplicated in the areas of housing and income.

From health, the document moves to government jobs and political appointments, decrying the fact that even if one counted janitors, the paltry numbers of Mexican Americans in government work was a national scandal. Being cut off from federal jobs not only denied them government dollars but also denied them an influence in government. The Viva Kennedy Club leaders did not demand proportionate representation, but they did point out that qualifications or lack of them had little to do with the situation. This scandalous situation, they stated, cut across class lines as Mexican Americans, no matter their education or training, suffered discrimination. Here, the document emphasizes that not all Mexican Americans were poor or uneducated. There were significant numbers with college degrees, professional training, and business experience. By all measures, they were successful individuals with the potential to assume leadership in the larger society. Yet they continued to be passed over for less qualified individuals. While claiming to speak only for the Texas Viva Kennedy Clubs, the authors surmised that the situation reflected the Mexican American experience throughout the Southwest, where a "Spanish surname places the applicant 'behind the eight ball,' in public employment . . . and where, in business or the self-employed professions, his name militates against his getting a fair shake."[41] For Mexican American reformers, their lack of influence in business, government, and other sectors in public life made them worse than second-class citizens. In fact, many of them were conscious that while their oppression was not as intense as that of the black American, their neglect was more profound. There were simply few philanthropists, social advocates, or politicians who were as concerned about Mexicans as they were about African Americans. The American mentality seemed to be that all individuals of Mexican descent were immigrants, poor, uneducated, spoke only Spanish, and were largely uninterested in what happened in the larger society. And as other non-black immigrants had done, they were likely to quickly assimilate. This perception and the neglect it engendered, the reader is again reminded, is a betrayal by a government to whom Mexican Americans had been fiercely loyal.

The influence of the American G.I. Forum's campaign on behalf of the Mexican American farm worker and against the Mexican *bracero* becomes explicit in the next section of the Viva Kennedy statement. It makes reference to the flagrant exploitation of workers in the agricultural fields. Here the document writers show their ethnocentricity in making the Mexican workers the cause of the depressed wages in the border areas: "We have seen the hundreds of thousands of 'wetbacks' who are permitted to swarm across our southern borders to earn as little as 15 cents an hour, to live in the most profound misery and to create misery for the American citizens whom they displaced. Hundreds upon hundreds . . . commute . . . from Mexico . . . to take jobs that are sorely needed by American citizens who live in extreme poverty because wages are so depressed . . . by that commuter, by the bracero, by the wetback. These [Mexican Americans], indeed, are forgotten people. Millions of them, strangers in their own homes. In comparison to a recital of the woes of the Mexican American, Steinbeck's *Grapes of Wrath* is cheerful."[42]

One should not infer from the above that Mexican American reformers were not sensitive to the plight of the Mexican worker. They were.

Even the American G.I. Forum activists who had worked hard against the *bracero* program did not differentiate the citizen from the non-citizen when it came to demanding better conditions. But for the Viva Kennedy Democrats, there was no ideology that saw them as Mexicans without borders. Race and ethnicity held no ideological or political bonds beyond the border. Their personal philosophy made them Americans who happened to be of Mexican descent. While they were often proud of their heritage, their citizenship played a more important part in their political views than race, class, or national origin. This attitude was part of a historical alienation from past activism that had been occurring since the rise of what Mario T. García calls the Mexican American Generation.[43]

This generation, but particularly the Kennedy contingency, had accepted political borders that were not only geographically restrictive but which divided Mexicans from Mexican Americans. The fact that these reformers were moving toward greater political integration meant that the borders were becoming more defined and more rigid. While this did not necessarily translate into insensitivity toward non-citizens, it did mean that the Mexican immigrant played a lesser part in the ethnic ideological dichotomy. For old-time reformers like Sánchez, the immigrant, at times, represented a foreign entity rather than part of an extended family. The future Chicano cry of *"somos un pueblo sin fronteras"* (we are a people without borders) had no foundation in the Viva Kennedy Club politics. This should not be taken to mean that there were not some who felt a strong solidarity with Mexicans across the border. There were, and even some of the Club leaders may have been sympathetic to that ideology, but since they were writing for an Anglo American audience, they avoided any discussion of racial solidarity with a "foreign" people. This generation of leaders played their politics in the open; thus, they were always limited to what was publicly appropriate. In this, they were honest politicians. Unfortunately, what was appropriate for a Mexican American reformer to think was rather restricted, and this circumstance limited any profound discussion of what it meant to be Mexican in American society. It limited proposals to those acceptable to the American mainstream.

Calling for a "brighter tomorrow," the statement of principle put forth nine recommendations. Together these recommendations called for inclusion of Mexican Americans into all sectors of the American mainstream, for political appointments to government posts at all levels, federal involvement to tackle problems that local and state governments had ignored, and finally an affirmation that Mexican Americans should be the leaders of their own communities.

The first recommendation called for a comprehensive study of Mexican Americans nationally. Citing such works as Howard Odum's *Southern Regions of the United States,* Edwin Embree's *Brown Americans,* and Gunnar Myrdal's *An American Dilemma,* it bemoaned the lack of interest by government and philanthropic foundations in studying the Mexican American population.[44]

The importance of these kinds of studies can best be understood by the effect that they had on the government and the American people. The works brought recognition to particular regional and economic problems and treated them as part of the larger union. Whatever failings were highlighted were the responsibility of the government and society in general. A similar study of Mexican Americans would allow them to fit into the American union, calling attention to a forgotten people. No such study would be conducted until the 1970s. The only works that could claim to be an attempt at a broad study were Manuel Gamio's *The Mexican Immigrant: His Life Story,* and Paul S. Taylor's *An American-Mexican Frontier: Nueces County, Texas.*[45] Neither, however, had received the recognition of the earlier cited works. The lack of this type of comprehensive study meant that Mexican Americans continued to remain outside the mainstream, with no authoritative view on how they fit into the American whole. This lack of scholarly work simply re-affirmed that Mexican Americans were a forgotten people, an invisible minority.

Five of the other recommendations (2–5, 7) called for federal intervention in the areas of health, education, and the protection of the migrant worker. Repeating the special obligation that the nation had toward these "subject-peoples," the recommendation called for federal aid specific to the educational needs of Mexican Americans. This aid would assist in hiring Mexican Americans as teachers and in higher-level government posts, possibly those dealing with educational policy. "We are not at all frightened by the dire predictions of 'federal control,'" declared the document's authors. "We are much more frightened by the demonstrated irresponsibility of local control in the education of our children," they stated.[46] For decades Mexican American schoolchildren had been segregated, badly educated, and mistreated by public schools governed by boards composed of Anglo American citizens with deep prejudices or neglectful indifference toward Mexican Americans.

These recommendations reflected the New Deal idealism of George Sánchez and other liberal members of the Viva Kennedy leadership. They also reflected the distrust that they had of local, regional, and state governments; school boards; and social agencies. These recommendations revealed that many reformers were not certain that time and opportunity would resolve the major dilemmas of the barrio. In the past, LULAC members and other middle-class reformers had simply sought accessibility and opportunity. They had rejected special programs as an indication that they could not fulfill their obligations as Americans. The Viva Kennedy people were changing the approach by demanding that government assist in resolving problems that required the force of law or which demanded resources beyond those that the barrio had.

In the area of migrant work, the Viva Kennedy leaders called for a minimum wage, educational opportunities for migrant workers, and a reinstatement of the power of the United States Employment Service. Coupled with those changes, they called for a stringent patrolling of the border to stop what they called "the perennial free and easy dipping into the cheap labor reservoir of Mexico." The document writers, however, made sure to say that they had no problem with the United States helping "rehabilitate" Mexico or with growers making their profits. Capitalism was not one of their enemies. In the style of traditional liberals, they wanted an inclusive capitalism, not a redistribution of wealth. But they also did not want to "subsidize . . . Mexico or . . . our businessmen with the misery of the Americans of Mexican descent."[47]

Recommendations 2, 8, and 9 offered the Mexican American professional as a valuable resource for the federal government. "These well-educated and experienced persons," stated the document authors, "constitute a reservoir of talent for the immediate needs of the United States in foreign affairs that otherwise would take many years to develop. It would be," continued the statement, "short-sighted . . . to ignore this native cultural resource." The document then went on to refer to Mexican American professionals as "strategic," "best in their particular endeavors," "particularly significant," and as persons who would provide "an enhancement of national prestige." This offer to serve the nation in federal posts and foreign embassies became a recurring theme for these leaders who saw themselves—if not their people—as ready to serve at the highest levels of American society. Government service seemed to them the clearest sign of their integration into American society.

Recommendation 8 called for Mexican Americans to be the representatives of the Mexican American community. It criticized non-Latino officials who made poor but far-reaching judgments that adversely affected the Mexican American community. It also attacked those Latins who were "only incidentally concerned over the crisis faced by [their] fellows." This was a direct affront to the Mexican Americans who got themselves elected by participating in numerous Anglo American associations that governed many of the predominantly Chicano South and Central Texas communities. "It would be well to assess carefully the claims of any individual . . . who would speak for us," stated the document.[48] Declaring that local and state officials rarely filled the role of leaders for Mexican Americans, the Kennedy Democrats boldly stated, "It is our purpose . . . to underline that only the *mexicano* can speak for the *mexicanos.*"[49] This last statement foreshadowed the more separatist rhetoric of the Chicano Movement, but it also reflected nationalistic tendencies of past *mexicano* activism. When frustrated, these leaders were not beyond reverting to racial rhetoric. The Viva Kennedy leaders would stop short of developing a separatist ideology, but they began a process of identity-building that would eventually lead to nationalist notions of self during the Chicano Movement. This identity-building became necessary because they rejected the Mexican orientation of the working class and what they considered the too accommodating and too elitist middle-class orientation of the early postwar years. This identity-building process re-affirmed that strain in Mexican American intellectual thought which sought to promote the duality of the barrio's experience. Since the Texas Viva Kennedy Clubs lacked any real ideology, the process remained underdeveloped.

The quest for *mexicano* leadership had two purposes. First, it sought to eliminate the often insensitive Anglo leadership in the barrio. Second, it sought to get rid of the barrio politician who did not truly represent a constituency. The vacuum created by the removal of such leadership would be filled with a new, more liberal and well-educated Mexican American leadership. This leadership would be beholden to no one and would better be able to articulate the needs of the barrio residents. These leaders would also do a better job of Americanizing Mexican Americans, thus resolving many of the problems that came with the residents' inability to conform to the demands of American society.

In this statement of principles, which seemed put together rather quickly and which had no consistent ideological framework, the Viva

Kennedy Democrats did create a trichotomous view of themselves. They saw themselves as forgotten, despite their war contributions and their civil-rights activities during the postwar years. They saw their problems as solvable only through federal intervention and by national leadership. They also saw themselves as a reservoir to handle the professional jobs and political appointments required to make the changes in the barrios and to represent the United States in foreign affairs, especially in Latin America. The Kennedy Democrats saw hypocrisy in an American Cold War policy that promoted human rights and capitalism abroad but had no concern for the internal problems of the Mexican American. The document asked what "the uncounted millions of underprivileged peoples [of] the world think of the foreign policy protestations of the United States as they learn of the circumstances of these millions of Americans of Mexican descent."[50] The statement of principle in conjunction with the Kennedy rhetoric and the political orientation of the Viva Kennedy people provides a clue to the Mexican American version of Camelot.

This view was Camelotish because like that wondrous, chivalrous society of English mythology, it was based on utopian notions. This was not a utopia of collective welfare with a singular purpose. Rather, this was a utopia of affluence, of an active but unobtrusive government, of military power but with an admired democracy, and of a homogenous society which respected pluralism. It was 'a utopian America where fine-tuning was always necessary but fundamental change never a need. While these reformers constantly identified the lack of fairness in the larger society, they never rejected the 1950s vision of an America of plenty, of power and prestige, and yes, of fair play.

It required living a contradiction to mesh their two experiences— equality/affluence and poverty/discrimination—and most of the reformers lived the illusion. They did so because for many of them life remained comfortable and at times rewarding. The failure of reforms never brought to these middle-class citizens the personal tragedies that beset labor organizers and nationalist leaders of the past. Because they had accepted American capitalism and the American political system wholeheartedly at an early age, Camelot and not Aztlán became the goal.[51]

In this Camelot, Mexican Americans could find a home, a job or a government appointment, and a niche in the historical narrative. They would not have to lose their culture, but instead it would become part of the quaint, praised and promoted every time the United States sought to remind the world of its pluralistic democracy. The Mexican barrio would become like the suburbs, and every young Mexican American could dream of going to the best schools, yet remain ready to defend their country in time of war. All of this would be accomplished through affluence—Camelot was not poor—and dynamic leadership by the best and the brightest that America had, including Mexican Americans.

The fact that Camelot had European roots indicates the source of the Viva Kennedy reformers' inspiration. It would take several more years before Mexican American activists would look within the barrio and south to Mexico for inspiration. In 1960, they were in search of Camelot, not Aztlán.

4. La Campaña: Electing JFK

The campaign of the Viva Kennedy Clubs varied depending on location, each having different strategies and different purposes. The group's strength lay in the leadership of
each locality. These men and women understood the people
they were working with, and they also had experience working with the existing party officials and neighborhood and
organizational leaders of their communities. They depended on time-
tested strategies that got people involved. These strategies were based on
uniting former activists and reformers, voter registrants, educators, patriotic group leaders, LULACers, Forum members, and countless others
into a cohesive political force. These organizational and reform leaders
were apt to know who to contact, who the most likely voters were, and
who were the most likely to get involved in a new organization. The Viva
Kennedy people relied on seasoned individuals.[1] While they sought to

register new people and to try to get out a large mass of Mexican Americans voters, they understood that there existed a core group who always voted, and within the periphery of that group another group that voted whenever it was inspired to do so or when it found it could have an impact on the election. They depended on these groups to heighten the excitement and attract the peripheral voters.

The electoral efforts, in some ways, paralleled those of the past; even the enthusiasm may have been similar. The difference in this campaign lay in the overarching theme and in a candidate who could rally the troops. Because this major candidate was a candidate for the presidency of the United States, it gave Viva Kennedy people a sense of importance that they had never had before, either in running their candidates, many of whom ended up losing, or in supporting Anglo American candidates who, while they may have promised things, really seemed not in position to deliver. This presidential candidate provided them not only specific promises but also a sense of recognition. A feeling permeated the Mexican American community, particularly among those who participated frequently in politics, that government had a role to play and that when the federal government focused on the needs of the Mexican American, things could really happen. They had seen government as an active agent through Franklin Roosevelt's programs, as limited as they may have been in helping Mexican Americans. They saw government sensitivity in Truman's efforts to desegregate the armed forces and to provide certain national benefits. They also saw in the conservative presidency of Dwight D. Eisenhower an active government, constructing highways and providing funds for colleges and universities.

Mexican American reformers could look at the landscape and realize that not much was or could be done at the local or regional level. Neither the commitment nor the resources existed. Sánchez, in his book *Forgotten People,* argued that New Mexico had not the ability to make the kind of changes that Mexican Americans needed to fit into the American fold.[2] There simply were not the resources at the state level, so the federal government had to become involved. This view prevailed among Mexican American leaders and among Mexican American voters.

Mexican American leaders believed that a charismatic Anglo American had the potential to attract tremendous support in the barrio. By their own actions, they contributed to the idea that someone from the outside could come and resolve the problems and challenges that Mexican Americans faced. Having found support among Anglo Americans for their own reform activities, they were not adverse to coalitions with them, though at times they were ambivalent about accepting Anglo American leadership at the local level. Since they often had unrealistic expectations about the "obligations" of being an American, it is reasonable to believe that Anglo Americans were the model to emulate for achieving the status of first-class American citizens. The higher the role model's status, the more important that role model became. The fact that Mexican Americans had to depend on the benevolence of Anglo Americans added to the asymmetric relationship between the groups. Consequently, a charismatic Anglo American politician who spoke on their behalf became a prominent figure in the barrio. This status was bestowed on very few Anglo Americans, but once it was, the role took a life unto itself.[3]

The Kennedy campaign brought together many elements within the barrio. Since Republicans had rarely become involved in promoting Mexican Americans at the local level, it meant that anyone active, from the barrio politician to the reformer, based his or her alliances on connections to Democrats. This situation made it easier to rally the traditional Mexican American Democrats and, from that group, to get volunteers for a recruiting effort among the less politically inclined. Since these reformers were trying to attract the citizen rather than just the person of Mexican descent, they emphasized the Democratic Party's recent commitments to helping the underprivileged. Declared the *Latin Times* of East Chicago, "In John F. Kennedy we have a man who not only understands the problems of the working class, the elderly and the minorities but is committed and able to do something about it."[4] But the newspaper tempered that emphasis with the promotion of an active community that had more than poor and uneducated members, ready to save the U.S. and Latin America from communism. The message resembled the Democratic Party liberals' own efforts to come across as compassionate to the poor but belligerent to the Soviet Union.

Some aspects of the "pitch" of the Viva Kennedy leaders, however, revealed a class duality within the reformers' philosophy. While no doubt sensitive to the needs of the community, their political solution centered not on empowerment of the community but rather a magnification of their role as power brokers. This could be seen in their constant promotion of an almost non-existent "friendship" with the candidate and their frequent offer of a Mexican American elite that could serve in ambassadorships and other federal positions to save democracy in Latin American and the world.[5] They closely tied the support of Kennedy to the recognition of themselves as leaders. Many of them seemed to believe sincerely in a trickle-down theory of politics. The more Mexican American elites rose on the political and bureaucratic ladder, the more benefits would find their way down to the barrio. Consequently, the campaign for enthusiasm and fervor for Kennedy was also a search for their own confirmation as leaders. Because of this approach, the organizational effort took on a much more intense appeal for political activity among the less political sector in the barrio.

These organizational efforts occurred throughout the traditional Southwest, but they also occurred in other places. Some of the most active Viva Kennedy Club organizations turned out to be those in the Midwest. On September 30, Carlos McCormick called a meeting at the Sherman Hotel in Chicago to rally support for the campaign and to organize Viva Kennedy Clubs in the region. Representatives from the communities of East Chicago, Hammond, Highland, and Gary attended. Joseph Maravilla, Charles Cañamar, and Richard Rucoba were appointed co-chairmen of Viva Kennedy for Indiana. In Illinois, José Alvarado became the state chairman. Within a matter of days, Viva Kennedy headquarters opened in East Chicago, Calumet City, Indiana Harbor, and Chicago.[6]

These midwestern cities had Mexican American and Latino communities that dated back almost fifty years. Because these communities were relatively new and isolated compared to those in the Southwest, they responded well to a nationalistic pitch about Mexican Americans being an important bloc in the 1960 campaign. Most midwestern Latino middle-class individuals were one generation, at most, removed from the fields, the packing plants, and the slaughterhouses. The Mexican American and Latino communities had developed their internal structures in ways similar to those in the Southwest, but while often segregated, they were much more connected to the larger society because they were far from the border and close to major industries.[7]

In both Indiana and Illinois, the Viva Kennedy Club movement included a women's auxiliary. The women quickly integrated into the middle ranks of the club hierarchy or formed their own Viva Kennedy Clubs. Their importance quickly became apparent as they recruited other women, distributed campaign literature, and registered voters. Their legwork in going from one high-rise apartment house to another made up for the lack of resources that plagued the midwestern Clubs.[8] The women also formed the core of the fund-raising efforts. Housewives and working women came together to form a small but aggressive army of volunteers who shouted the loudest at the rallies, made the largest posters, and prodded the more reluctant men. These women were part of an emerging female sector in Mexican American politics that had gained its experience in local electoral activities and in the organizational efforts of such groups as the American G.I. Forum and LULAC, as well as the numerous patriotic clubs common in the Midwest. Lacking money and volunteers, most male-led organizations were happy to allow women to participate at the grassroots level.[9]

The groundswell of support for Kennedy among midwestern Mexican Americans and other Latinos created an opening for them to link up with the larger Democratic Party structures. Since Illinois and Indiana were Republican strongholds in presidential elections, the rise of a new Democratic Party constituency was welcomed by regional and national Democrats. Unlike areas in Southern California, South Texas, or southern Arizona, Mexican Americans in the Midwest posed little threat as an organized political entity. They were looked at more as a supplementary voting bloc that could prove handy in tight races. This meant that Democratic leaders in the Midwest were quite open to the organization of Viva Kennedy Clubs.[10]

Gary, Indiana, was one place where Mexican Americans came together. Their sense of isolation or the fact they had to come together to survive so far away from the traditional Mexican American homeland caused them to be highly enthusiastic. They organized through the efforts of the small middle- and skilled-class sectors, and got local Anglo American politicians involved, thus enhancing their efforts. They were able to bring in individuals like U.S. senator Dennis Chávez, Texas state senator Henry B. González, and Los Angeles city councilman Edward Roybal and create an event simply by having these Mexican American leaders from the Southwest travel to the Midwest.

Each visit became a boost for the local effort and a way to impress their southwestern friends with their organizational zeal and their ability to bring out the people. Roybal remembers being surprised by the large turnout in a Chicago rally in which he was the featured speaker. The event organizers proudly told him that those in attendance represented only a small portion of the Mexican American community.[11] In some way the visits of these leaders validated the midwestern communities as places where Mexican Americans also struggled for their own civil rights and for recognition. That these leaders personally visited the midwestern clubs was important to those far-flung Mexican American communities.

Senator González would be a bigger attraction in the Midwest than he was back home because he was an elected official coming to a place where Mexican Americans were not ready to elect their own people. When he spoke in East Chicago and other areas of Indiana and Illinois, he found himself promoted as the *honorable* Enrique González in a full-page ad in the *Latin Times*. The bilingual newspaper reminded its readers that González had filibustered for twenty hours to prevent a discriminatory bill from being passed into law by a Texas legislator. They were not, however, told that his effort failed.[12] Seven days later, the *Latin Times* assessed González's visit as a successful campaign stop. It also made much of the state senator's "friendship" with the presidential candidate. It quoted him as saying that the Kennedys were "men of vision; sensitive . . . and understanding of the problems confronting Hispanic peoples everywhere."[13] The *Tribuna,* another Latino newspaper in Indiana, described how the state senator had had breakfast with the mayor of Gary and how he had been given a tour of the U.S. Steel mills. González had received the courtesies usually reserved for much more prominent politicians. Accompanying González in Indiana was Alfredo Vidal, a Puerto Rican representative from New York.[14] The appearance of both at the rally represented an effort to bring together two communities which had rarely united on any issue. The *Latin Times* editorialized, "We are united as never before. Now let's see about this unity when the time comes for choosing our candidates." For the meantime, unity reigned supreme.[15]

East Chicago and Chicago were two other places where Viva Kennedy struck a friendly chord. They became hubs of tremendous Viva Kennedy activity, to the point that they challenged the traditional places like San Antonio and Los Angeles in terms of fervor and organizational zeal and in terms of how many people they could pull together for a rally. They engaged in activities that accentuated their Mexicanness. Some of them were stereotypic, such as getting two burros to represent the Democratic Party, putting sombreros on the animals, and parading them around as mascots.[16] It was, in a sense, the kind of political showmanship that did not offend the Anglo Americans and may have gone along with prevalent stereotypes. This generation of middle-class and labor people wanted very much to be accepted, and the Viva Kennedy campaign represented to these people a way to become legitimate. Their connection to a national political campaign allowed them a link to American society and to the rest of Mexican America. That they were extremely fervent and passionate might be an indication of how isolated they felt and how much they wanted to prove that Mexican Americans in places such as Gary, East Chicago, and Topeka were just as Mexican American and just as fervent as those in the Southwest. In fact, in these areas there were more flyers and announcements in Spanish, and the reformers were much more connected to the traditional Mexican patriotic organizations involved in the struggle for legitimacy and civil rights.

Ironically, the more they stressed their Mexicanness, the more they became committed to the American electoral process. What they really seemed to be promoting was their civic participation. Since many felt isolated from the American mainstream, they then played out their civic-mindedness in the Mexican festivals and Mexican American organizational functions. Elections were another time when they could express their civic responsibility. Thus, those who often seemed to be the "most" Mexican were in fact those more committed to assimilation once the opening became available.

Much of the campaigning bordered on the traditional. There were rallies, car caravans from the smaller communities to the larger communities, picnics, *tardeadas* (afternoon gatherings), fund-raising dances, tamale sales, and music at the park before the politicians spoke.[17] The traditional activities connected with the large presidential campaign and enhanced the significance of the barrio campaign without changing its style or structure. When Kennedy—or someone important to the campaign—visited a number of these areas, the stock of the local Mexican American elite rose. The campaign became a way to rub shoulders with local, county, and regional Democratic leaders who realized the tightness of the race and welcomed help from any quarter.[18] This proximity caused a coalescing of local, state, and national Democratic leaders with Mexican Americans. Conservative and moderate Democrats and Mexican American liberals, one-time opponents, came together with the intent of electing Senator Kennedy to the presidency. The Viva Kennedy campaign allowed Mexican Americans to be at the table, to be part of the whole. In the larger rallies and political meetings, the Viva Kennedy people were not prominent, but in the Viva Kennedy rallies they were. And they played their role to the fullest by basking in their organizational success and receiving legitimacy by the close association of local and national leaders.

The Viva Kennedy people attempted to be a presence in the larger rallies by wearing their sombreros and by placing their unusually large signs in the most visible locations. During Kennedy's visit to Chicago, the Viva Kennedy signs stood out among the rest.[19] More than in the Southwest, these reformers tied their campaign activity to their Mexicanness. They constantly mixed their *charro* queens, *mariachi,* and other symbols of Mexican culture. Their humor was at the expense of their ethnicity with their depiction of John F. Kennedy riding a burro and wearing a large sombrero. However, they never doubted that, despite their efforts and accommodation, they were only the "extras" who were going to help the Kennedy campaign go over the top. Kennedy took pictures with them and so did some of his campaign people. The pictures were then prominently displayed in the Spanish-language press (if not in the major newspapers). This sort of publicity reinforced among their people the idea that they were prominent in the election and among Anglo Americans, the idea that the Latinos were a necessary addition to the Democratic effort.

While still predominantly Mexican American, these Latino communities in the Midwest and upper Midwest had a great number of Mexican immigrants. Although unable to be directly involved, they could support the fund-raisers, dances, and tamale sales. These people gravitated to those activities that brought Mexicans together. The Spanish-language press, often more geared toward the immigrant community, generally supported the Viva Kennedy effort because it accentuated the presence of the community. Also, as mentioned in chapter 1, most of these newspapers promoted integration even as they promoted their community's ethnic distinctiveness. The Viva Kennedy Clubs brought Latino groups together that in the past had not worked with the Mexican Americans. The Puerto Ricans, Cubans, and others from South and Central America joined the Viva Kennedy effort, though in smaller numbers. The Puerto Rican leadership participated and even campaigned in predominantly Mexican American areas. The Viva Kennedy effort in the Midwest gave many reformist groups and patriotic associations an opportunity to come together and work for one cause. It brought the traditional Latino middle class together and recruited new members to its ranks. It also got labor people involved with a middle class it had once viewed with suspicion.

In California, the Viva Kennedy effort fell on the shoulders of the

Mexican American Political Association (MAPA) and the Community Service Organization (CSO) members. Members of these groups had participated in local politics since the first Roybal candidacy in the late 1940s. Like the G.I. Forum chapters in Texas, the MAPA chapters provided much of the support staff for the Viva Kennedy Clubs.[20] CSO members also assisted, although the organization itself continued to seek out citizens to register to vote. Ralph Guzmán headed this effort for CSO and the Viva Kennedy Clubs. A political science graduate student at UCLA, he created his own staff of five Anglo American students who helped him register hundreds of voters in East Los Angeles.[21] Carlos McCormick would claim, by the end of the campaign, that California Democrats had registered more than 130,000 Mexican American voters, with a large number of those coming through the efforts of the Viva Kennedy Clubs.[22]

Roybal, once selected as a leader of the Viva Kennedy organization, sought out his long-time supporters, as well as others he met during his time as director of the Tuberculosis Association of Los Angeles, and got them involved in the campaign. The Viva Kennedy groups became linked throughout Southern California, though they were much more loosely organized than those in other places. They did not meet regularly as clubs nor were they centralized.[23] This was the result of the MAPA and CSO chapters' unwillingness to lose their own identity. The clubs would meet, plan strategies, and then send those plans to Roybal for approval. Roybal remained the liaison between the California clubs and the national headquarters. He also coordinated the visits of Kennedy and other national leaders.[24] Roybal, as the most significant Mexican American leader in California, controlled the efforts in his state like no one else. Only Chávez came close to having the same kind of prominence in New Mexico that Roybal had in California.

The Viva Kennedy Clubs of California did establish a statewide headquarters that published a mimeographed news bulletin informing the state chapters and other clubs about the latest schedule of speakers, meetings, rallies, and fund-raisers. It also provided news about appointments within the campaign as well as campaign policies or activities. While geared toward the state clubs, the news bulletin also served to impress the national campaign headquarters with the work done. There was, in the tone of the news bulletin, a competitive spirit that seemed to pit California's effort against that of others.

The bulletin constantly reminded the local clubs that the campaign needed money and members.[25] The Viva Kennedy people were also reminded that numbers were important at the rallies. The bulletin of October 3, 1960, chided sixteen executive and field officers for having been absent at a rally in which Representative Montoya spoke. It also chastised club officers for not following through on assigned tasks. Revealing a fondness for military hierarchy, the bulletin spoke of "following orders," of the "high command," "field officers," and of being "victorious." The bulletins also emphasized training and trial runs as the last days of the campaign approached.

While the bulletin indicates an intense campaign and promotes the California structure as a model for other states, Roybal remembered a somewhat less coordinated and structured Viva Kennedy effort. He did not remember records being kept of how many members there were nor of there being a consistent flow of information between regions or clubs.[26] Though there were many reformers involved, no real strong connection existed between them. That would come later with the strengthening of MAPA. In the meantime, the Viva Kennedy people concentrated on promoting the campaign in their localities and adjacent areas. The main pitch for the California Kennedy Democrats dealt with education, health, and employment. These were issues that had been prominent in the Roybal campaigns and in the civil-rights crusades of the 1940s and 1950s. While no specific strategies had been designed, these three issues were capable of arousing the interest of Mexican American voters. Segregation, health problems, and unemployment were a constant concern.[27]

Roybal crisscrossed the state for the Kennedy candidacy and also traveled to Arizona, Texas, New Mexico, Illinois, and Kansas. In those stops he pointed out that discrimination had become more subtle but remained entrenched. He recounted the time that he, a sitting city councilman, had not been allowed to buy a house because he was Mexican. Roybal believed that most Mexican Americans harbored memories of the same type of experience. Once he had re-sensitized the people to their condition, Roybal would present Kennedy as the one candidate who could change the situation through government action and moral leadership. Roybal personalized his relationship with Kennedy and encouraged the crowds to befriend Kennedy by proxy. While Roybal had actually had little personal contact with the candidate, he believed that Kennedy had the capacity to befriend those with whom he spoke.

This proxy friendship had come through a pre-campaign forum that

Kennedy conducted in Los Angeles. In that public display, Kennedy persuaded Roybal that he was a friend of the Mexican American.[28] Kennedy's Catholicism undoubtedly assisted in this bonding. Roybal would be one of the few Mexican American leaders willing to acknowledge that Kennedy's religion made him a much more attractive candidate to the Mexican American community. In fact, he remembered a number of Viva Kennedy Club leaders in California stating that while they did not believe a Catholic candidate could win the presidency, they were going to try their darndest to elect one.[29]

In New Mexico, the campaign followed a more traditional approach. The Viva Kennedy Club movement there relied on the Hispano organizations and individuals who had been most active in the political process. These groups of individuals had elected U.S. senator Dennis Chávez, Rep. Joseph Montoya, and many other Mexican American candidates to local and statewide office. Electioneering by New Mexico's Hispanos had been nurtured by divisive statewide campaigns pitting Mexican American native sons against Anglo American newcomers. In the late 1940s, Chávez warned the state's Hispanos that they were losing ground to new arrivals who disdained the old balance of power that existed between the communities in the early years of the twentieth century. New Mexico's Hispanos needed little prompting to support Kennedy, but they did need a strong turnout to offset the large conservative Anglo American vote.

Once the campaign got into full swing, Senator Chávez launched his own one-man crusade to elect Kennedy. His travels took him throughout New Mexico and to Arizona, California, Texas, and the Midwest. Although seventy-two years old at the time, he maintained a hectic pace, speaking at rallies, breakfasts, luncheons, and dinners. Each stop at a major city came with short detours to smaller surrounding communities. At each stop, Chávez presented two speeches, one in English and the other in Spanish.[30] The political speech in English centered on general liberal themes about the rich getting richer and the poor getting poorer. "The Republicans haven't changed their thinking since the days of Alexander Hamilton," he told a Fresno, California, crowd. "They believe that if the rich get richer, something will trickle down to the poor."[31]

He criticized the Eisenhower administration and the Nixon candidacy as relics of the past and as anti–working people. He charged that the industrial and agricultural corporations were reaping excessive profits while the workers continued to work for low wages. A committed New Dealer,

Chávez never fully left behind his populist disdain for the larger corporations and agribusiness. He favored strong regulation of both. He also attacked American foreign policy which, he declared, had caused relations with Latin America to deteriorate. American military intervention and business intrusiveness had caused popular hostility toward the United States in Latin America. Only a few years before, the vice-president had been pelted with tomatoes and other objects on his visit to Venezuela. American foreign policy was perceived to be imperialistic and responsible for keeping dictators and military leaders in power across Latin America. Chávez continually linked the Kennedy-Johnson ticket with the idealism of the New Deal's Good Neighbor policy during World War II. In the minds of many liberals, that period had been a golden era in U.S.–Latin American relations.[32]

In his Spanish speech, Chávez expounded two themes: Kennedy's humanity and Mexican Americans' responsibility as American citizens. To the same Fresno crowd, he said, "Jack Kennedy has more humanity in his little finger than Nixon has in his whole body." In Corpus Christi, he called the Democratic nominee a man whose "decisiveness, firmness, know-how and heart" had prepared him to work for the people.[33] This personality-creation was Chávez's way of constructing Kennedy in the image of Roosevelt. Like many other Mexican American elites, Chávez came to see Kennedy the way he needed to see him. This new image had been constructed since the Los Angeles convention because initially Johnson had been his candidate.

For Chávez, presenting the candidate as a compassionate and caring friend was important in rallying Mexican Americans to come out and vote. Few Mexican Americans had experience with politicians who truly delivered on campaign promises. For this reason, most Mexican Americans learned to look beyond rhetoric and platforms in choosing among Anglo American candidates. Most of the time, the choice centered on which of the candidates would be the friendliest or most compassionate to the people in the barrio. Mexican Americans' lack of real political power made them constantly search for the "friend" or the "friendliest person" in the race. Voting for friends and actively seeking their election meant meeting the obligations of citizenship. Chávez, like most reformers of his time, wanted Mexican Americans to take responsibility for their lives. Unlike the Chicano activists of the future who sought to alleviate Mexican American concern over their inefficiencies, this generation of leaders wanted them to recognize their shortcomings and then correct them. Chávez told a group of Del Mar College students in Corpus Christi that they lived in a land of opportunity, "where the constitution says nothing of any particular origin." He continued, "When a boy named González goes off to war, he doesn't wear a Mexican uniform. He wears the uniform of the United States of America. There's nothing for him as a Mexican, but there is everything here for him as an American."[34] Often pointing his finger at the crowds of Mexican Americans, he would remind them that complaining about police brutality, discrimination, and other barrio woes would accomplish little if they did not go out to vote. "You'll deserve what you get," he repeated often.[35]

Chávez reflected his generation's ambivalence about the ability of Mexican Americans to correct their situation. Though they fiercely protested stereotypes of their people, they often accepted part of the stereotype. What they seemed to reject was not always the stereotype but the roots of the behavior. That is, Mexican Americans might act foolish or against their own interests, but they did so because they had been conditioned to do so. Reconditioning Mexican Americans meant reminding them of their shortcomings and instructing them on how to change them. Chávez's experience in New Mexico had taught him what Mexican Americans could do if they involved themselves in the electoral process. But the fact that Hispanos in New Mexico were losing power emphasized to him the precarious situation of most Mexican Americans nationwide.

The Viva Kennedy efforts in Arizona were led by members of the Alianza Hispano-Americana and by the leadership of the Mexican American copper miners' union. The copper state presented a rather unique political landscape. In places like Tucson, Nogales, and South Phoenix, Mexican Americans had an economically well-adjusted middle class.[36] They also had a history of civic participation and an active cultural and social life. But beneath the surface of middle-class integration lay a stratum of working-class Mexican Americans who suffered de facto segregation, poor employment opportunities, bad health, and who were subject to condescending stereotypes. Since this group was the largest in the community, it meant that Mexican Americans overall were second-class citizens in the political and social world of Arizona.[37]

The two major proponents of reform in Arizona were the Alianza Hispano-Americana and the Mexican American–dominated local unions and branches of the International Union of Mine, Mill, and Smelter

Workers. While one confronted stereotypes and made legal challenges to segregation, the other fought for bread-and-butter issues confronting Mexican Americans in the copper mines and smelters of Arizona.[38] These two organizations would support the Kennedy candidacy, though they would not really unite, except in small communities, to build a strong Viva Kennedy effort.

Arizona was Carlos McCormick's home state, and he established one of the first Viva Kennedy chapters. Here, as had MAPA in California and the G.I. Forum in Texas, the Alianza Hispano-Americana became an important base for the Viva Kennedy Clubs. But according to Ernesto Portillo, a radio personality for many years in Tucson, a new group of Mexican Americans was on the verge of assuming a more public role. These "new" Mexican Americans were anxious to become more politically active and were more demanding in their efforts to acquire a larger role for their own in Arizona. These new participants were more likely to join a Viva Kennedy organization than the old Alianza. While the Alianza would remain the organization most capable of being a foundation for the Viva Kennedy Clubs, these individuals would eventually emerge and coalesce after the 1960 election campaign to play a more important role in the state.[39]

One of those important individuals was Raul Castro. He would eventually be the first Mexican American governor in the state and the country. Roybal remembers him as the person who most symbolized the Kennedy effort in Arizona.[40] Yet, despite Tucson being McCormick's home and Arizona having such a significant Mexican American middle class, Arizona would be one place where the Kennedy campaign would not take off at the same level as in other places. Still, the fruits of Viva Kennedy would come to Arizona.

The Viva Kennedy campaign in Texas relied heavily on the efforts of local groups and individuals who had a history of political involvements. Unlike the California Viva Kennedy Clubs, no all-encompassing structure arose. There were simply too many individuals with their own independent styles to try to create an umbrella organization that could regulate their efforts. Peña, the first state director of the Texas Viva Kennedy Clubs, traveled throughout the state organizing clubs and promoting the Kennedy candidacy, but he made no effort to create a unified structure.[41] Hector P. García would be named a national co-chairman of the Viva Kennedy Clubs but would limit most of his efforts to Texas. He also traveled the state. More importantly, he wrote letters to G.I. Forum leaders urging them to support the campaign. His flyers became the standard literature on Kennedy for Texas. Other Tejano leaders would also become deeply involved in the effort, but most of their activities would be of an individual nature, relying on their former networks and on their ability to rally people to the Kennedy cause. While Tejano leaders had extensive experience in organizational activities, their success always hinged on allowing individuals autonomy in their membership. This meant that inspiration and motivation and not organizational discipline would be the mode of operation.

In a flyer credited to Hector P. García, Henry B. González, Roberto Ornelas, and Albert Peña, Jr., Mexican American voters were reminded of their significance to the campaign and the manner by which they could make a difference.[42] The open letter pointed out that in 1956 more than 100,000 Mexican Americans had failed to vote. "Because of that we lost," the letter stated, exaggerating the potential outcome since Eisenhower won the state by a huge margin. Either intentionally or unconsciously, Mexican American leaders continually described their electoral involvement as the key element of the campaign. They were not contributors to the victory but the actual determinants. They heard similar language from the Kennedy staff and repeated this so often that they came to believe it. This line of thinking would provide the excuse for Texas Viva Kennedy Democrats not to engage in a discussion of the issues that were pertinent to the community. The statement of principle discussed in the last chapter did not become an important issue for many of the campaigners even though it had the potential to create a dialogue within the community as to the nature of political empowerment. The emphasis in Texas was on the Mexican American being crucial to the election.

The letter also advised the Mexican American voter to pull the lever that provided a straight Democratic ticket vote. This practice was, according to the letter, a way to "avoid difficulties and errors."[43] While straight-ticket voting had been around for years, usually mandated by political machines or barrio politicians, this was the first time that Mexican American reformers were promoting it as a progressive idea. This campaign technique would become a permanent fixture in the barrio and prove to be a tremendous obstacle for Mexican American and Chicano activists in the future. The call for such action seemed to contradict the Viva Kennedy concept of distinguishing the Mexican American voter from others.

In this case, Mexican American "collective individuality" in politics depended on losing itself within the mass of Democratic voters. This, again, was an indication that the value of the Mexican American vote was in its numbers and not in its discriminatory approach.

For Mexican Americans the Democratic Party became "our party." Democratic loyalty had existed for years in the barrio, but this time the Mexican American reformers were expropriating the party in a public manner. The reason? In the view of the four signers of the open letter, the Kennedy-Johnson ticket had been the first one to formally recognize the plight of the Spanish-speaking community and the first to offer solutions. The letter went on to promote the view that there was no hierarchy between the Clubs and the candidates themselves. How could that be if the Clubs were going to deliver the determining vote? This perceived relationship made it unnecessary to negotiate, since it stood to reason that appointments and spoils would be merit-based. Thus Mexican Americans were going to get something big. "Never has there been such an important recognition of us," wrote the authors. "Thus we have to be faithful to our leaders and our responsibility," they concluded. The letter then called for a "house-by-house, name-by-name, and precinct-by-precinct" effort.[44]

Another García also proved significant in the effort in South Texas. Cleotilde García, Hector's sister, led the effort of the women in the G.I. Forum to muster votes and endorsements. Cleotilde was, like her brother, a successful doctor, and the economic status derived from her profession allowed her to host important campaign functions in her grand home on the waterfront in Corpus Christi. She personally hosted a social event for every major campaign personality that came to South Texas.[45] These exclusive parties allowed the campaign elite to mingle with the Mexican American elites and solidify a relationship that would prove beneficial to both. Cleotilde's medical practice and her interest in genealogy also gave her access to many people who were potential voters. Even Hector and Cleotilde's more conservative brother, a dentist, joined in the campaign effort by endorsing the ticket even though he feared Kennedy's interest in socialized medicine. The trade-off was "recognition of our people."[46]

The Bonillas became another reformist family that involved itself in the campaign effort in Texas. The Bonilla brothers, William and Tony, as well as their father, had previously been involved in state and national LULAC activities. Tony Bonilla assumed the directorship of the Texas

Viva Kennedy effort, though he mostly dealt with South Texas. His correspondence with local leaders indicates that there were three major functions for the state organization. The first involved the distribution of campaign materials and the coordination of campaign events that included more than one county or city. The second function was fund raising for advertising, radio announcements, the printing of literature, and for receptions for the national campaigners. Each chapter had a designated fund-raising goal, but few were ever able to consistently meet it. The third function involved assisting with major rallies for the presidential candidate and other national leaders.

This third function, more than any other, provided Tejano elites with the publicity they sought and the forum they believed they needed. In these major events, they rubbed shoulders with important leaders, sat in the important places, and had their concerns become part of the campaign rhetoric. The more successful they were in rallying large numbers of people, the more integral to the campaign they became. Consequently, there was always an implied urgency in the request for numbers, fervency, and loyalty. In reality, there was no significant change in the approach to electoral politics at the grassroots level, only a heightened sense of urgency and a larger sense of expectation.

A statewide Viva Kennedy Club structure would finally be established by the last month of the campaign, but its main function was to advertise the major rallies and to plead for funds. Most of those chapters that seemed beholden to the state structure and its leader, Tony Bonilla, came from rural South Texas communities. Most of these clubs were composed of members of the G.I. Forum and the LULAC councils that had been mainstays of reform activity over the previous decade or more. In the bigger cities, organizations of a more political nature served as the basis for the Clubs. In Houston, the Civic Action Committee led the effort, while in San Antonio, Peña's progressive coalition provided the labor.[47]

There were a number of duplicated positions in the Viva Kennedy Clubs of Texas. There were committee chairs, state advisors, directors, and local chapter directors. Having many leadership offices was a tactic that got many people involved in the effort and provided greater excitement by giving people important titles. The Viva Kennedy leadership, which grew from the original three to more than a dozen, traveled not only to their localities but also to other regions, neighboring states, and even far-away places where they could get an audience. In their efforts to boost the enthusiasm and fervor of the Viva Kennedy supporters, the leaders reminded them of the promises that had been made.

If the Mexican American community could deliver the vote, then they could request the payback. All the major leaders promoted this line of thinking, particularly Peña, Chávez, and García. González also articulated this concept, though he and Roybal emphasized Kennedy's liberalism and his commitment to fair housing, senior citizens' rights, and civil rights. Mexican Americans would benefit from a Kennedy victory both because of his promises to them and because of his liberal agenda. The image of a future Kennedy administration as a panacea for the resolution of all Mexican American problems grew stronger as Kennedy, Eleanor Roosevelt, and Franklin Roosevelt, Jr. constantly reminded them of the New Deal and anointed the Catholic candidate from Massachusetts as the heir to the leadership of the progressive wing of the party.[48]

García wrote letters and pamphlets telling the Mexican American voter not only of the public promises made to them by the Kennedy campaign but also of the "personal" assurances of the candidate and his brother. For Mexican American leaders, who tended to play politics at a very personal level, these private assurances carried much more weight. They stood as honorable agreements between friends. This public image of friendship and honor became a way to drive home the importance of the campaign to those Mexican Americans who had no particular affinity for the issues of the campaign. In the fervency of the campaign, the Mexican American leadership and many of its followers continued to reaffirm in their own minds an image that they had created themselves.

The formation of Viva Kennedy Clubs continued to almost the last week of the presidential campaign. This constant coming together throughout the nation meant that a new group of Mexican Americans had bought the Kennedy image and connected it to a developing consciousness of a national people, with national aspirations and a still-nonexistent national influence. The fact that so many Clubs arose toward the end of the campaign meant that little significant political groundwork could be performed. But it did mean a mass number of volunteers who were going to canvass the barrio for votes on election day. It also meant that these volunteers and new adherents were sustained by emotion and imagery rather than any specific political agenda. The momentum of the Kennedy campaign became strong enough to lure people to the campaign who had no particular attraction to Kennedy.

The campaign in the barrios also crystallized a new Mexican American politics that sought national attention, that sought to connect itself to national leaders, and that saw its problems and dilemmas as being national rather than local or regional. This nationalization of the Mexican American community set the foundation for what would later become the concept of Aztlán, although that was surely not the intent. Without fully realizing it, these Viva Kennedy reformers had begun connecting the barrios into a national community, even if this connection was still mostly among the elites and mostly illusory when it came to political networks beyond the very top. This nationalization became a way to create a future network of individuals who had committed themselves to this new politics. When the Chicano Movement later brought that connection down to the barrio level, these reformers would rise to be truly national leaders. Thus by the process of naming themselves Viva Kennedy Club members or Kennedy Democrats, they created a future constituency for national politics. The number of Clubs established became a symbol of strength. The enthusiasm they exhibited became the symbol of power.

Hector P. García (left) and
Ed Idar, Jr., pose in front of an
American G.I. Forum banner at
a Forum convention in California
in the 1950s. *Courtesy García Papers,
Special Collections and Archives, Bell
Library, Texas A&M University–
Corpus Christi.*

Congressman Henry B. González (left) and Hector P. García pose with Miss
Missouri during the American G.I. Forum convention in Pueblo, Colorado, in
1962. *Courtesy García Papers, Special Collections and Archives, Bell Library, Texas
A&M University–Corpus Christi.*

José Alvarado (left), chairman of the American G.I. Forum in Illinois, pins a Forum emblem to the lapel of Senator Kennedy. Kennedy joined the Mexican American veterans' organization in 1959. *From* Forum News Bulletin. *Courtesy García Papers, Special Collections and Archives, Bell Library, Texas A&M University–Corpus Christi.*

This miniature gold pin of a PT boat was used by the Viva Kennedy Clubs to promote the presidential campaign among Mexican American veterans and others who remembered Kennedy's heroics during World War II. *Courtesy García Papers, Special Collections and Archives, Bell Library, Texas A&M University–Corpus Christi.*

Senator John F. Kennedy riding on a burro and wearing a Mexican sombrero served as the symbol of the Viva Kennedy Clubs during the 1960 presidential campaign. *Courtesy García Papers, Special Collections and Archives, Bell Library, Texas A&M University–Corpus Christi.*

Carlos McCormick, executive director of the Viva Kennedy Clubs, poses with Betty Maravilla (far right) and two other unidentified members of the American G.I. Forum Women's Auxiliary of East Chicago, Indiana. The women's auxiliary formed the backbone of the Indiana Viva Kennedy Clubs. *Courtesy García Papers, Special Collections and Archives, Bell Library, Texas A&M University–Corpus Christi.*

Senator Kennedy and Latino leaders pose for a "unity" photo at the Waldorf Astoria Hotel in New York City during the early stages of the campaign. *(From left)* Ralph Estrada, president of Alianza Hispano-Americana; Felipe N. Torres, New York Assemblyman; Henry B. González, Texas State Senator; JFK; Hector P. García, founder of the American G.I. Forum; Henry Lopez, Los Angeles attorney; José Ramos, New York Assemblyman; and an unidentified supporter. *From* Forum News Bulletin. *Courtesy García Papers, Special Collections and Archives, Bell Library, Texas A&M University–Corpus Christi.*

Tony Bonilla (far right), state director of the Texas Viva Kennedy Clubs, and two unidentified supporters stand in front of a Kennedy-Johnson campaign poster announcing the opening of Viva Kennedy Club headquarters in Corpus Christi. *Courtesy García Papers, Special Collections and Archives, Bell Library, Texas A&M University–Corpus Christi.*

Numerous Viva Kennedy Club signs are visible at a presidential rally welcoming
Senator John F. Kennedy during his visit to Chicago. *From* Forum News Bulletin.
*Courtesy García Papers, Special Collections and Archives, Bell Library, Texas A&M
University-Corpus Christi.*

Vice president candidate Lyndon B. Johnson and Lady Bird at an airport rally with
Hector P. García, one of the national coordinators of the Viva Kennedy Clubs. *From*
Forum News Bulletin. *Courtesy García Papers, Special Collections and Archives, Bell
Library, Texas A&M University–Corpus Christi.*

(From left) Ed Idar, Jr., Carlos McCormick, and Robert "Bob" Sánchez clown around during a Viva Kennedy Club function in Texas. *Courtesy García Papers, Special Collections and Archives, Bell Library, Texas A&M University–Corpus Christi.*

(From left) George I. Sánchez, Albert Peña, Jr., and Hector P. García display their John F. Kennedy Memorial Award plaques from the State PASO during the 1965 convention. Roy Elizondo (right) from Houston accompanies them. *Courtesy García Papers, Special Collections and Archives, Bell Library, Texas A&M University–Corpus Christi.*

5. Election Results:
Appointments and Disappointments

 The end of the campaign saw major rallies in Los Angeles, San Antonio, Chicago, and numerous other key places for the Democratic Party. At each event, the Viva Kennedy contingency stood out in its intensity and with its idiosyncratic paraphernalia.[1] Because the national and state Viva Kennedy organizations lacked any substantial, integrated structure, nothing particularly significant came out of them during the last days of the election. The final days' effort amounted to locally initiated pushes of varying intensity and varying purpose. The only overarching themes of the final days were proving the power of the Mexican American vote and ensuring a payback after the election.

With the election almost upon them, the Viva Kennedy people exhausted all their resources and stamina. With tenuous financial underpinnings, the Viva Kennedy campaign leadership in Texas and the Midwest began to complain of economic hardships. Hector García would write the national office for assistance in paying a telephone bill because he had spent more than his barrio medical practice could afford. José Alvarado also worried that no one but himself would foot the bill for the Kennedy literature that he had published.[2]

The narrowness of the outcome would have a significant effect on how Viva Kennedy Club leaders perceived the election outcome. A landslide would have diminished the effect of minorities, regional groups, and issue-specific organizations. But a close vote could be interpreted as a "coming-out" of a new electoral group. The fact that the states with the largest Latino populations were also the states with some of the closest outcomes seemed to re-affirm the importance of the Viva Kennedy effort. In California the election was decided by two-tenths of 1 percent; in Illinois it was one-tenth of 1 percent; in New Mexico, eight-tenths of 1 percent; and in Texas the winning difference was 2 percent of the vote.[3] With Kennedy winning the election by less than 1 percent of the total vote, the effort of the Viva Kennedy Clubs could be appreciated more, or at least interpreted that way.

Nationally, Mexican Americans gave Kennedy more than 85 percent of their votes. In Texas, they gave him 91 percent of the vote or a plurality of 200,000 votes. This margin helped him overcome the white vote, which had Nixon ahead by about 150,000 votes. Kennedy would squeak out a 50,000-vote win out of a total vote of 2,250,000. In New Mexico, the respective figures were a 70 percent vote for Kennedy, a 20,000 vote plurality, and a winning margin of 2,000. In California, estimates ran about 85 percent for Kennedy.[4] No other state would break down the number of voters by ethnicity, though the estimates by the Viva Kennedy people would be the same.

The vote outcome in Texas, which had identifiable counties with Mexican American majorities, can serve to show the impact that the Viva Kennedy effort had on Mexican American voters. In the seventeen counties with Mexican American majorities, Kennedy carried sixteen of them, some by as many as a two-to-one margin. The only county Nixon won was, ironically, Zavala County, a place that would later become famous as the birthplace of the Texas Chicano Movement. And there, Kennedy lost by only fifty-plus votes. The margins in those South Texas counties that went to Kennedy were far greater than those in the traditional Democratic Party strongholds of the Panhandle, Central, and northern Texas.

Said the *Press,* an independent Democratic journal, "Senator Kennedy [should] be thankful that the big turnout of Latin American voters in San Antonio, Laredo, Corpus Christi, and El Paso enabled him to offset the losses sustained in Dallas, Houston, and west and parts of east Texas."[5] In the same periodical, the Viva Kennedy leaders proudly reported that they had been able to "bridge" the differences of the Mexican American organizations in South Texas and unite them behind the senator.

McCormick also credited the Viva Kennedy effort for the win. Kennedy's edge, said McCormick, "can be traced to the overwhelming one-sided votes in precincts inhabited by persons of Mexican or Puerto Rican descent."[6] Only days after the election, García congratulated Peña for "assuring a great victory for the Kennedy-Johnson ticket." He went on to share with the county commissioner a telegram from Senator Kennedy that congratulated García and other Club leaders for the "magnificent job turned in by the national Viva Kennedy Clubs."[7] For García, the clubs had made history. At no other time in the past had the Mexican American community come out for one candidate as they had done for Kennedy. The Kennedy telegram would be followed by more recognition from Robert F. Kennedy, who would tell a Mexico City reporter that it had been the "votes of Mexican Americans and other Latin Americans in the United States that elected" his brother. He then added that the new administration would be paying greater attention to the republics of Latin America.[8]

Mexican American leaders celebrated what seemed the first acknowledgments of their value in the campaign. They were also heartened by Robert Kennedy's comments about the new importance of the republics of the south, the arena where Mexican American leaders believed they could be of most assistance. They believed that this discussion set this Mexican American electoral effort apart from any in the past. No one had ever identified them as key to a national election, much less implied that they would be important in the process of governance; Robert Kennedy had promised them ambassadorships while campaigning in New York. At the time, the remarks seemed to be a last-minute effort to spur the troops. Having the campaign manager say this did not compare with having the candidate say it, but the post-election comments seemed so encouraging that they were reprinted in the G.I. Forum's newsletter.[9]

Shortly before the election, José Alvarado had received a letter from Manuel Avila, a State Department employee who resided in Venezuela at the time. "Now that there are so many Viva Kennedy Clubs working for his [Kennedy] election," wrote Avila, "he can't deny us those things which we need and want . . . having Carlos in Washington, Kennedy can't forget us."[10] Alvarado, having conducted a very intense Viva Kennedy campaign in Chicago, received an invitation to attend the inauguration.[11] The optimism reflected in Avila's letter would be re-emphasized just days after the election. Senator Chávez would assure his New Mexican constituency that the state would fare well with a Democratic administration and a Democratic Congress. He reminded his followers that he had worked nonstop for the Massachusetts senator and believed his work had been fruitful for the Democratic ticket.[12]

The Viva Kennedy people had many reasons to rejoice. They had been courted by a presidential candidate who had, through his brother, implied that there were going to be distinct benefits for the support given.[13] They had developed a national organization composed of hundreds of clubs throughout the country. This was a historic first for Mexican Americans in the political arena. The Viva Kennedy effort had made a number of leaders national personalities. During the campaign, many party leaders had recognized the Mexican American and Latino vote as a legitimate new force. And the campaign had provided a forum in which to articulate the problems of the barrio. More important, the jubilation over the victory made the Viva Kennedy leaders more assertive and confident of their ability to negotiate for their people. With the victory, with their strong showing, and with this new assertiveness, they expected compensation in the form of presidential appointments.

By early January, 1961, however, Viva Kennedy leaders began to worry about the fact that few if any Mexican Americans had been contacted by the administration for appointment. Even the rumor mill in the nation's capital had not identified any Mexican American as having any chance to be named to the administration or the federal bureaucracy. On January 11, García wrote the president, "respectfully" recommending Vicente Ximenez, a G.I. Forum leader from New Mexico and a college professor, to be assistant secretary of state for Latin America. García enumerated Ximenez's qualifications and told the president-elect that he was well known to Sen. Dennis Chávez and Rep. Joseph Montoya. He then alluded to some published articles which mentioned that Latin American countries were feeling "slighted" by the new administration in its appointments. García suggested to Kennedy that he make more use of Mexican Americans in the administration. "This will also help us to feel that we can be useful to our country both in time of peace and in time of war," wrote García. He sought to remind Kennedy that Mexican Americans had served proudly and bravely in the country's wars. García also reminded Kennedy that he had promised to use Mexican Americans in his government.[14]

Three days later, García received a letter from McCormick expressing some frustration over the lack of appointments and the growing disappointment of some that he was not doing enough within the Kennedy circle of advisors to remedy the neglect. McCormick acknowledged that he knew García had asked for an audience with the president-elect and wished him well. Then he reiterated an earlier telephone conversation in which he told García that he needed some understanding and appreciation. "I'm doing all within my power to secure top positions for our people," wrote McCormick. He advised García to have patience, which he described as a virtue. He also told García that if he had a better method for getting appointments, he would appreciate knowing about it.[15]

The letter clearly revealed the precarious position in which McCormick found himself. As head of the national Viva Kennedy Clubs and advisor to the president, it was his job to do what other leaders could not. Viva Kennedy supporters assumed he had the president-elect's ear. In reality, McCormick did not have direct access to the president. Even during the campaign, he had worked through the nationalities division of the Democratic Party and had not sat in on any of the high-level meetings of the campaign staff. Yet, as the top man of the Viva Kennedy organization and a representative of the Kennedy administration, McCormick faced pressure of various types from Mexican American leaders. Some Viva Kennedy leaders were not beyond criticizing McCormick's work and his lack of influence. Wrote Juan A. Flores of Washington D.C., "we have found Carlos to be most ineffective and inexperienced." Flores, a G.I. Forum leader in the nation's capital, also accused McCormick of taking too much credit for the Viva Kennedy effort.[16] Having identified their most important candidates for presidential appointments, Viva Kennedy leaders bombarded the president's staff with letters of support for these candidates, and they put pressure on other elected officials to do the same.

Senator Chávez and Representative Montoya called their colleagues on the Hill for support, and Mexican American leaders outside of Washington conducted a letter-writing campaign. They also sent the résumés of individuals interested in working for the federal government. These individuals were not people of any prominence. In fact, Viva Kennedy leaders seemed to call for résumés without taking heed of the necessity of strategic political pressure or leverage.[17] Mexican Americans leaders initially seemed to believe that the president was open to wholesale suggestions. Given that they had created in their own minds a closeness to the presidential candidate that bordered on friendship, it seems only natural that they sought to help him fill the holes in the federal bureaucracy. The fact that most of these individuals had little experience, if any, in government jobs only meant that the Viva Kennedy leaders would also serve as advisors. When the Kennedy administration ignored their advice, the Viva Kennedy leadership's frustrations mounted.

In early February, President Kennedy re-affirmed his intention of making Mexican Americans a part of his government. This assertion came in response to a reporter's question of how Kennedy would compensate the efforts of the Viva Kennedy Clubs. Kennedy acknowledged the great reservoir of talent among the "Latin Americans" and then told the gathering that Hector P. García had been sent to Jamaica as part of a delegation to negotiate a mutual defense and aid treaty with the Federation of West Indies Islands. He also added that he had offered a position of high responsibility to another Mexican American who did not accept. But the president assured the reporters, and Mexican American leaders who might be listening, that "we will continue to see if we can . . . associate them with our administration more closely."[18]

The position of "high responsibility" was an ambassadorship to a small Latin American country, and the person who turned down the job was Henry B. González, who wanted to run for Lyndon Baines Johnson's soon-to-be vacated U.S. Senate seat. The Forum's *News Bulletin* revealed that García had also been offered a similar job but had opted to stay home in Texas.[19] Others who had been considered for a federal appointment were El Paso mayor Raymond L. Telles, Jr., Los Angeles city councilman Edward R. Roybal, and New Mexico academic Vicente Ximenez, all for assistant secretary of state. The position, however, went to a Puerto Rican, Arturo Morales Carrion. Though he was Latino, Mexican American leaders were not impressed.[20]

Senator Chávez became one of the first to criticize the new administration for its appointments. He accused the president of dragging his feet on the ambassadorships and other federal appointments. The fact that

García and González had been offered ambassadorships did not deter the criticism.[21] Whether Chávez knew about the proffered ambassador posts is uncertain, though it is likely that if he did, he was not impressed by the host countries. When Viva Kennedy leaders had discussed foreign-policy postings, they mentioned Mexico and other major Latin American countries.

By spring, frustration was becoming anger and disappointment. In a letter to Vicente Ximenez, García disclosed McCormick's frustration and thoughts of quitting the job which he held on the Kennedy staff.[22] The Viva Kennedy leaders' bitterness resulted from their belief that the president had violated the "clear assurances" made by his brother before the Democratic Party convention and in his own campaign speeches. Roybal publicly accused the new administration of having "failed almost completely to recognize Viva Kennedy leaders or supporters in patronage appointments."[23] Mexican American leaders complained that even after Kennedy had re-emphasized in February his desire to bring them into the administration, he had made no major appointment since then. Of those Latin Americans he had appointed, two were Puerto Ricans who had not been part of the Viva Kennedy effort, and one was a Mexican American who had supported Eisenhower in the 1950s.[24] Only Raymond L. Telles, appointed ambassador to Costa Rica, had participated in the Viva Kennedy Clubs, but only peripherally.[25]

Mexican American leaders warned the president that he was jeopardizing his future support among Mexican Americans by ignoring their importance to his campaign. They reminded him that his "slim margins in Texas and New Mexico, and his near-win in California were all fruits of Viva Kennedy grass roots activity."[26] Failure to recognize this effort, they argued, would make Mexican Americans and other Spanish-speaking groups lean toward a liberal Republican such as Nelson A. Rockefeller. Given that most Mexican Americans tended to vote Democratic, the warning implied not only a passivity toward future Democrats but possibly a campaign effort on behalf of the Republican alternative.[27] This militancy grew out of the euphoria of an intense and highly successful campaign and because the Viva Kennedy leaders believed that they spoke for a unified bloc of voters who could be crucial in tight elections.

This sense of empowerment gave them the confidence to suggest to the president that they could have helped him avoid even his foreign-policy challenges such as the Bay of Pigs fiasco, the first major crisis of the new administration. The reasoning went that a highly placed "Latin American" in the State Department would have warned the president that the planning, timing, and leadership of the invasion were not adequate for the undertaking. They claimed that their contacts in Latin America had assured them that the southern neighbors wanted Castro gone but were extremely hostile to the way Americans sought to do it.[28] The Viva Kennedy leaders audaciously declared that the Kennedy administration would continue to have problems in Latin America if it failed to engage Mexican Americans in foreign-policy decisions.

In a letter to Manuel Avila, Jr. García pointed out the bad treatment that Teodoro Moscoso, a Puerto Rican, received as U.S. ambassador to a Latin American country. "I think that by now Kennedy would be realizing—like you said—that the only people that they respect in Latin America are the Mexicans."[29] This comment reflected both an ethnocentricity among the Viva Kennedy leadership and a recognition that Mexican Americans were the core of the Viva Kennedy rank-and-file support. While the concept of Latino unity was often in the rhetoric, Mexican American leaders in the Viva Kennedy movement were most concerned about the patronage coming to their people. In their minds, Mexican Americans constituted the real Latino political force.In the letter to Avila, García pointed out that the Democrats were not open to the demands of the Mexican American leaders. "They want us to help them, but they don't want to give us a break. *Estos desgraciados no nos quieren dar ni agua,*" wrote García. "We are going to have to buck the Democratic Party real hard."[30] By this time, the Viva Kennedy leaders had established another political organization, but more will be said in the next chapter about this new direction.

In an editorial in the Spanish-language newspaper of McAllen, Texas, *El Quijote,* the editors called Kennedy's Mexican American appointments "grains of sand in the desert of federal employment."[31] The newspaper claimed that the federal bureaucracy was now full of Kennedy's *consentidos* (favorites), some of them holding important positions in Mexico and in Central and South America. These appointments, declared the editorial writers, had no knowledge of the language, did not understand the idiosyncrasies of the region, and lacked exposure to the customs and habits of those regions. The editorial argued that it took more than money to make the Alliance for Progress (Kennedy's major anti-communist economic bail-out program) work in Latin America. The writers also chided the president for trying to cover his dismal appointment record by appointing García to be a member of the negotiating team that went to Jamaica.[32] José Alvarado, in an editorial in the Forum's *News Bulletin,* agreed with *El Quijote*'s assessment of García's trip: "Others point to Dr. Hector P. García's recent *junket* to the West Indies on a presidential mission as evidence that the Mexican Americans have not been ignored. It is well known that Dr. García hesitated a long time before accepting this mission . . . because he was fearful that it would jeopardize appointments for others. . . . One still hears about the good doctor who spent his free time visiting and encouraging the humble people of that country, assuring them of our friendship and interest. But this was merely a *junket* (author's italics)."[33] Alvarado then castigated the innocence of Mexican American leaders. "Our traditions have led us to believe that if someone says he will do a thing, it can be dismissed as accomplished. Our patience and courtesy have been interpreted as ignorance and weakness."[34] Alvarado spoke to the frustration that Mexican American leaders felt for not having negotiated more forcefully in the beginning. The fact that they had not been in a position to do so made them even more bitter. The appointment debacle even became humiliating to some Viva Kennedy Club supporters. V. G. Roel, an attorney from Laredo, Texas, had been considered a sure bet to become ambassador to Samoa. On January 8, 1962, Carlos McCormick called to inform him that an announcement was eminent. Roel began reading all that was available on the island and even put his house up for sale, only to find out that the administration had changed its mind. This reversal left Roel with ambivalent feelings toward Kennedy, and it embarrassed McCormick.[35]

The Viva Kennedy leaders had hoped to acquire for their people jobs in the federal bureaucracy, positions in the foreign-policy area, and ambassadorships to the major Latin American countries. Instead, they got almost no federal jobs, a few low-level positions in the State Department, and an ambassadorship to what they considered an insignificant country in Central America. More disappointing for them, their people had been bypassed in favor of two Puerto Ricans who had not been an integral part of the Viva Kennedy effort. As if that was not enough, Kennedy had set aside their nominee for a federal judgeship in South Texas and given the post to Reynaldo G. Garza, a moderate Mexican American who had been only lukewarm toward Kennedy. Garza had, in fact, been an Eisenhower supporter throughout the 1950s.[36] Of all the appointments for which the

Viva Kennedy people, particularly the Texas contingency, had fought, none had been as important as the one for district judge in South Texas, and no other action by Kennedy so clearly revealed the progressive Mexican Americans' lack of influence. The nomination of Garza happened despite a nearly two-year campaign to get District Judge E. D. Salinas of Laredo appointed to the federal bench.

Only days after the 1960 election, García had broached the subject with the president-elect in a congratulatory letter. "I sincerely hope that we are given the opportunity to serve under your administration," wrote García, "and it would be encouraging to have Judge E. D. Salinas appointed to the present federal judgeship vacancy."[37] Before Kennedy took office, several Viva Kennedy leaders drafted a letter supporting Salinas's candidacy. It is unclear whether they actually sent it, but the sentiments expressed within it summarized the feelings of many of Salinas's supporters. The signees were to be Hector P. García, Henry B. González, Albert Peña, Jr., and El Paso mayor Raymond L. Telles.

The letter seemed to have three purposes within the larger purpose of getting Salinas appointed to the bench.[38] First, it sought to head off other "prominent Texans" who might have had their own candidates for the position. While the undersigned had good relations with Vice-President-elect Johnson and Ralph Yarborough, also a U.S. senator from Texas, they believed that neither of the two elected officials supported Salinas wholeheartedly. There were also others who did not support the appointment of a Mexican American judge in an area where long-time Anglo American Democrats still controlled local politics and expected patronage for their election-time services.

The second purpose of the letter was to emphasize the importance of this particular appointment. "In our considered opinion," declared the letter writers, "this appointment is the most vital single action that you can take . . . to confirm, strengthen, and re-invigorate the tremendous trust . . . that our citizens of Spanish-speaking descent . . . displayed toward you." The letter then stated that Salinas had been endorsed by both the national and local leadership of various Mexican American organizations, including that of the predominantly Mexican American counties in the judgeship's area of jurisdiction. "Never has the Spanish-speaking population of the Southwest been so united behind one single aspiration as they are in this case," the letter stated. It then refuted any notion that other appointments could compensate for failure to appoint

Salinas, or that future legislature expanding the federal courts would be adequate recognition of the Mexican Americans who had worked so hard for Kennedy. The letter writers emphasized that the appointment represented not patronage but recognition for the "last major ethnic group that still has to fight to attain first-class citizenship."[39]

Lastly, the letter served notice to Kennedy that there were serious consequences for the Democratic Party if this appointment failed to materialize. One of those consequences would be that a devoted Democrat would withdraw completely from political action on behalf of the party. "While this may sound overly emotional, it is but a means of stating how deeply we look upon this as a matter of principle and justice, which goes to the very root of the attainment of first-class citizenship in every respect by the ethnic group which we represent."[40] The person threatening to quit Democratic Party politics was García. Of all the Viva Kennedy leaders, none had made the campaign such a personal issue as he. Known for his no-holds-barred commitment to his chosen crusades, García had developed a personal relationship with the Kennedy image and had staked his reputation on Kennedy's promise to use Mexican American talent in his administration. What he and others had seen as a Kennedy commitment to Mexican Americans was in reality the reflection of their own intense campaigning. García had simply projected his reformist agenda onto Kennedy and interpreted campaign rhetoric and the moderately liberal Democratic platform as an endorsement of that agenda. While García— and most of the other Viva Kennedy leaders—would remain a "Kennedy Democrat," he perceived early that Kennedy would have to be pressured to do anything for Mexican Americans. García and the others made it clear in the letter that failure to select Salinas for the federal bench would have lasting repercussions.

The Salinas episode began in the latter part of 1959 when Judge James V. Allred died, leaving a vacancy on the federal bench that had jurisdiction in South Texas. Immediately upon his death, Mexican American leaders began pushing for the promotion of one of their own. Quite quickly, they united behind Ezequiel D. Salinas of Laredo, who was the first district judge of Mexican descent to be elected in Texas.[41] The American G.I. Forum, in particular, pushed Salinas as the most qualified candidate. While there were other contenders, Salinas seems to have sailed through the political selection process without a major glitch. When

President Eisenhower received the recommendation, it came with the endorsements of the state Democratic committee and Secretary of the Treasury Robert Anderson. Anderson had been a law school classmate of Salinas's and had a fairly positive view of the South Texan.[42]

Salinas, born in Laredo, Texas, came from a politically prominent family in that very political town. A graduate of the University of Texas law school, he had also attended the National Autonomous University of Mexico for graduate work. He had a law practice in Laredo until World War II, when he joined the war effort, serving as a special assistant to the American ambassador to Uruguay. After the war, he returned to Laredo and to private practice until 1950, when he won election for judge of the 111th Judicial District Court of Webb County, Texas. Salinas would also serve as president general of LULAC in 1939 and 1940.[43]

The Salinas nomination had special importance to Mexican American leaders in Texas. The man he sought to replace had been extremely well liked by Mexican American reformers because of what they termed a "humane attitude" with which he tried the thousands of cases that came to him involving Mexican Americans. In a state where judicial hostility often meant long prison terms and humiliating treatment for Mexican Americans, Judge Allred's court had represented an island of civility and fairness in a sea of discrimination, segregation, and violence. In a letter to García, Idar, who practiced law in South Texas, wrote, "With the number of 'raza' that are involved in civil [and] criminal litigation in the . . . Federal District Court for the Southern District of Texas, it is of the utmost importance that we try to get a man appointed who understands the general situation of our people." He added that based on his own trial experience in Salinas's court, the judge from Laredo came closest to approaching Allred's judicial attitude.[44]

Salinas's candidacy seemed to gather momentum from the start. As mentioned before, he was recommended to President Eisenhower by the secretary of the Treasury Department. The recommendation had received the endorsement of the Democratic Party of Texas, the state attorney general, all members of the Texas Supreme Court, and a number of district judges. Not one major politician, Democrat or Republican, had raised any objections. The Mexican American leaders in Texas had left nothing to chance. They engaged in an all-out effort to flood the White House and a number of key senators with letters of support for Salinas.

The reception to his candidacy seemed so positive that Salinas phoned Idar in late October to tell him things were "going well."[45]

In a letter to García a few days later, Salinas thanked the Forum leader for the support and reiterated to him the importance of that support. "Even if God had made me the best judge in the world, I would not, under our system of Democratic government, have any chance at the appointment without public support and public opinion. That, only people like yourselves can give me. I must depend largely for . . . support on my friends with like origins and Spanish names who, like myself, wish to enjoy the full privileges and opportunities as well as the full duties and obligations [of] American citizenship," Salinas wrote. Salinas told García that while the appointment only dealt with one person, it, in fact, had larger ramifications than one person's personal achievement. "We either get recognition from Washington or we do not through this appointment," he wrote.[46]

When the Eisenhower administration did not move to appoint Salinas by the end of 1959, Mexican American leaders decided to intensify the pressure. On January 10, 1960, the Forum passed a resolution endorsing Salinas's candidacy. The resolution emphasized Salinas's qualifications in the legal and diplomatic arenas and then reiterated several themes that would be repeated often during the Viva Kennedy campaign. There were millions of Mexican Americans in the United States who had served faithfully in the country's wars; there were few Mexican Americans serving in government posts; Latin American nations would see Mexican American appointments as a goodwill gesture toward them; and the appointment of Salinas was a way to recognize the Mexican American community for its patriotism. Another letter-writing campaign ensued to disseminate the resolution to the president and other political figures.[47]

Eisenhower would ultimately decide to leave the appointment to his successor. Frustrated that no appointment had been made by the spring of 1960, Mexican American leaders changed the focus of their pro-Salinas campaign. Led by García, they began to emphasize appointments as an important Democratic Party issue in the upcoming elections. When the actual presidential campaign began, appointments became of the utmost importance. Salinas himself would tell the G.I. Forum state convention at the start of the election season that they "must bombard, pressure, cajole and persuade our leadership in Washington to use . . . Latin American citizens to extend the bonds of friendship between [the United States] and the Latin American nations. We must prepare ourselves . . . and be willing and eager to help our country."[48]

As the Democrats began to look forward to a Democratic administration, some of their priorities changed. There would be spoils to be given and received, and who got whose support for the future became more important than when Eisenhower made any further appointments. Support for Salinas had come when there was considerable doubt that an active Democrat could get the appointment. But after Kennedy's victory, support from the major players in Texas, namely Vice-President-elect Johnson and Senator Yarborough dissolved or turned into hostile resistance to Salinas's candidacy.

Whereas Democrats had put forward no significant alternate candidates for the judgeship while Eisenhower was in office, party members became very interested in the vacancy on the federal bench after Kennedy's election.[49] At the local and regional level Democratic leaders began lobbying for the position, and South Texas county politicians followed suit. Even Mexican American leaders, though less blatantly, began to formulate strategies to get the appointment. In Salinas's hometown of Laredo, there were those who were less than supportive of his candidacy. One of the major families in the border town, according to a letter from Idar to García, had shifted its support away from Salinas. The reason: Salinas's appointment meant that one of the family members seeking another federal post would be bypassed, since no president would appoint two people from the same county to important regional posts.[50]

Regional rivalries also reappeared. Rio Grande Valley Mexican American leaders—outside the Viva Kennedy leadership—reverted to being suspicious of those from the border area. Since Laredo Mexican American politicians had been much more successful in their integrationist politics, they were seen with some hostility by those in rural communities of South Texas. Many also believed that the Laredo group was much more conservative and elitist. This lack of unity allowed the Anglo American political leadership in South Texas to re-affirm its place in the region's political hierarchy. The initial fear of a Mexican American solid front gave way to an aggressive effort to keep Mexican Americans divided and dependent on Anglo American leadership.

For those politicians who understood their minority status in the region, the appointment of a Mexican American at federal judge level would reveal a shift in political power—from the traditional county and local groups of Anglo American and Mexican American *politicos* to Mexican American liberals and reformers. The 1960 election had indicated that a force outside of the traditional political coalitions could deliver the vote for a major candidate. This situation threatened to redistribute the patronage and to redirect the loyalty of Mexican Americans who had always voted according to their instructions. Even those Anglo American politicians who had been "friendly" believed that the status quo had to be maintained.[51]

As disruptive as the local and regional schisms were to Salinas's candidacy, the lack of support from the top made his appointment impossible. Senator Yarborough initially supported Salinas, though his support had been lukewarm at best.[52] After the election, Yarborough became noncommittal, indicating several times that he really had no say in the selection process. He found ways not to meet with Viva Kennedy leaders, even though they made an effort to see him in both Washington, D.C., and South Texas. While continuing to deny any influence, he privately sought alternate candidates.

In a private memo, Idar accused the senator of seeking conservative support for future political races and also of believing that Salinas had not been a consistent supporter.[53] This was a charge Viva Kennedy leaders refuted. It is also probable that Yarborough did not like Salinas's campaign to get the appointment. He considered it improper that anyone would campaign for a federal judgeship. Yarborough's attitude reflected either ignorance or disdain for the circumstances that Mexican Americans faced in trying to get appointments. Anglo American hopefuls also lobbied for positions, but they often did it through their campaign contributions or through supporters who were in a position to put pressure on the administration. Few Mexican Americans could claim to have either.[54]

Vice-President-elect Johnson remained publicly aloof from the process, but he also revealed indifference to Salinas's candidacy. Whether to spite the Viva Kennedy leaders or to keep his other supporters happy in South Texas, Johnson privately told Salinas supporters that he would play no role in the selection process.[55] As he would soon resign from the Senate to become vice-president, he would no longer have senatorial courtesy. The fact that one of the South Texas groups lobbying for an alternative to Salinas was strongly identified with his rise in Texas politics made the Viva Kennedy group doubtful that Johnson would be on their side. This must have been a bitter pill for García, who had been one of Johnson's most loyal supporters. To their credit, Johnson's supporters did indicate that Salinas was one of their top six candidates for the federal judgeship.

By early 1961, the heat on Yarborough intensified. On January 13, Dennis Chávez chided Yarborough on the Senate floor for failing to support Salinas. That chastising was followed by a letter from Idar and R. P. Sánchez, a South Texas Viva Kennedy leader, expressing displeasure with the senator's attitude toward the Salinas appointment.[56] On February 12, García, Peña, and Virgilio Roel met with Yarborough in Washington, D.C., but the discussion resolved nothing, and García stormed out of the meeting. Later that day, Salinas met with Yarborough, and the senator chastised the judge for campaigning for the position and for having his friends lobby so openly. He also criticized him for helping García establish a political organization. Later, the senator would be accused of telling one of his supporters that Salinas should not have made the trip to Washington.[57]

By March, the alternatives to Salinas had increased several-fold and even included prominent members of the G.I. Forum and supporters of Salinas. In a process akin to political musical chairs, the following names were thrown into the pool of potential appointees: District Judge H. A. García of Brownsville; Judge Fidencio Guerra of McAllen; J. C. Looney of Hidalgo County (a Johnson supporter); Cecil Burney of Corpus Christi (a Johnson supporter); Judge Roberto Benavides of Laredo; attorney Jimmy De Anda of Corpus Christi (a Salinas supporter); and District Judge Reynaldo G. Garza.[58] By the middle of month, Garza had emerged as the top candidate despite the total lack of support from the Viva Kennedy leaders. They had dismissed Garza's candidacy back in December because he had not supported Yarborough before and had been only lukewarm toward the Democratic Party's national candidates. They could not believe that as the senior senator from Texas, Yarborough would support Garza's nomination. In the end, it did not matter who Yarborough supported because on March 23, President Kennedy announced the appointment of Garza for the federal bench. On April 13, the full Senate ratified the nomination.[59]

One day before the announcement, García and others had been contacted by Yarborough, who told them that the appointment rested between an Anglo American attorney and Reynaldo Garza. García and Jimmy De Anda both believed that the senator wanted them to block Garza's nomination. But García and others believed that Garza, as a Mexican American and a distant acquaintance, would better serve the needs of Mexican Americans in South Texas. They both expressed their support for Garza to, they believed, a very surprised Yarborough.[60] Thus ended any chance that Viva Kennedy leaders had to deliver on the promise of significant appointments. While Garza was a Mexican American, their all-out effort for Salinas diminished any immediate euphoria that they might have had over the new Mexican American federal judge.

The appointment of Garza also rubbed Viva Kennedy leaders the wrong way as it frustrated their efforts to bring a new type of leadership to the Mexican American community. While Garza was a good judge and a respected member of the South Texas community, he was too moderate and accommodating for the likes of those pushing for more militancy. Garza came across as being more anxious to do what was "appropriate" than in helping his own people.[61] He represented well the elite families of South Texas who fought against racial stereotypes but who were content with the class distinctions so common in the predominantly Mexican American communities that were governed by Anglo American politicians.

Garza, like other Mexican American elites in Texas, had gained his status through friendships and political alliances. A college mate of John Connally and a strong supporter and campaigner for Johnson and Yarborough, Garza was considered less militant and more acceptable to Texas moderates and conservatives. In many ways, he shared the same values of most Viva Kennedy leaders, but he did not share their enthusiasm for public politics that might undermine his respectability. In the end, his respectability and his connections had more leverage than the support of the Viva Kennedy leaders for Salinas.

Failure to get the appointments they had envisioned at the beginning of the campaign represented a bitter repudiation of the Viva Kennedy efforts. The bitterness would eventually subside and Kennedy would again become a hero to Mexican Americans, but the experience would be a constant reminder of *la raza*'s political anemia. Failure to gain significant appointments, however, resulted more from the circumstances in which the Mexican American community found itself than from mistakes by Viva Kennedy leaders or any blatant insensitivity by the Kennedy administration. Disadvantages that Mexican Americans had made it easier to ignore them and harder for them to take advantage of the American political system. When Viva Kennedy leaders joined the Kennedy campaign without any concrete promises, they did so because they knew they had little bargaining power.[62] Given that beginning, they were lucky to have been consulted the few times they were.

With the election being as close as it was, every group that participated in the Kennedy effort could claim to have made the difference. This claim was followed by intense lobbying for the spoils that come with political victories. For the Viva Kennedy people, their only representative was Carlos McCormick, the law school student whose only Washington "experience" before the Kennedy campaign had been as a low-level aide to a Republican congressman. The fact that he had been a paid campaign staffer meant that he had little independence and even less status as a voice for the Mexican American community. When Kennedy sought advice on appointments, he turned to party veterans and influential Democrats.

The limited pool of eligible and qualified Mexican Americans further hampered the appointment process for the Viva Kennedy people. There were few Mexican Americans with any type of federal government experience or even experience in state government. Other than Dennis Chávez, there were no significant Mexican American Democratic Party leaders to whom the president could turn for advice on filling the important posts. The fact that Viva Kennedy leaders had bypassed the state party structures indicated that they had little connection and even less influence at the state and regional levels. All of this may have been overcome if Viva Kennedy leaders had had powerful friends willing to fight for them. The debacle in Texas emphasized that they had neither strong personal relationships with important politicians nor the influence to pressure them in any significant way.

The few appointments they did receive were probably significant considering their powerlessness. To Viva Kennedy leaders, however, their snubbing by the Kennedy administration represented one more instance of Anglo American insensitivity. After all, they had done everything asked of them. Without funds from the national campaign and without the assistance of the state Democratic Party organizations, they had mounted a successful national campaign. They had established hundreds of Viva Kennedy Clubs not only in the Southwest but also in the Midwest, the Rocky Mountain region, and the East and Southeast. They had mobilized hundreds of volunteers and had delivered their constituency's vote.

In their minds, they had put to a test the democratic creed. They had participated in the electoral process and they had won. Rewards were supposed to follow.

Viva Kennedy leaders saw their middle-class constituency as highly prepared to assume leadership positions at the national level. Their confidence in their abilities may have been exaggerated, but the bigger problem revolved around their naivete. They believed that college degrees, successful careers, patriotism, and intelligence were the prerequisite for serving their country. Since democracy meant that government was open to all, they believed they merited consideration as much as anyone else. Their own politics had been played out in the open. Thus, they were not prepared to be undermined by under-the-table negotiations or private lobbying by groups higher up on the political totem pole. In particular, they did not expect a "friend" in the White House to forget them after the election.

Undoubtedly, the White House had a different perspective on the matter of appointments. The president wanted to surround himself with bright, successful, well-placed individuals who had experience in economics, business, the academy, and foreign policy. While McCormick would eventually make it to the peripheries of the president's outer circle, none of the others in the Viva Kennedy constituency fit the mold.[63] They were neither technocrats nor economic, political, or social elites. And since they had no other leverage, they remained in the periphery of national politics and federal policy-making. Viva Kennedy leaders would learn an important lesson that would lead them to another phase of their political socialization. In an important way, this disappointment would lead them to a political partisanship that stressed their ethnicity and promoted their native sons and daughters as leaders of the *raza*.

They would become politicians rather than reformers. Politics would replace all other forms of activism as the primary approach for these Viva Kennedy leaders and their constituencies until the rise of the Chicano Movement would again legitimize social reform. These individuals did not abandon other reform activities, but they did place them within the context of their ability to win elections, influence candidates, and motivate their communities to become political. Dependence on "friends" produced limited results, so they set out to become power brokers and candidates themselves.

6. A PASO Forward

 Even before the Salinas debacle Viva Kennedy Club leaders surmised that they needed to remain together. On March 16, 1961, McCormick wrote to García inviting him to a meeting in Phoenix, Arizona, to discuss the organization of a national political group. He added that the idea came from Viva Kennedy leaders and members who wished to keep up the momentum of the presidential election. "We have evidenced the tremendous desire our people have to participate in their government and its political process," wrote McCormick. "We have seen the . . . results of their concerted action. We need now to consolidate our force."[1] In March, the Texas contingency of the Viva Kennedy leadership came together in Victoria to establish the Mexican Americans for Political Action (MAPA) organization. The group selected Albert Peña, Jr. as

the state chairman and Hector P. García as the national organizer. As its first action, the group endorsed District Judge E. D. Salinas for the federal bench vacancy in South Texas and committed support for Henry B. González's run for the U.S. Senate.[2] The meeting attracted most of the leadership of the South Texas Viva Kennedy movement. Aside from rallying the Texas reformers into a new organization, it also prepared the local leadership for the national MAPA meeting later that month in Phoenix.

The meeting in Victoria signaled a magnification of the decades-long local and regional efforts to give Mexican Americans a political voice. Politics had always been important in the barrio, even when the elections themselves resulted in few changes for the barrio. In South Texas and San Antonio one or more Mexican American politicians had held elected office or provided a serious challenge to the entrenched politicians. In the Rio Grande Valley, where the Mexican American population predominated, there were some local organizations that controlled local politics.[3] But there were no statewide political organizations for Mexican Americans. Most Mexican American middle-class reformers shied away from creating this kind of organization because of the hostility it would attract from Anglo Americans voters and party officials.[4] They mostly settled for alliances with Anglo American reformers or participation in voter registration and get-out-the-vote campaigns.

Another reason for the lack of such organizations was the absence of political unity among Mexican American politicians. Since politics was mostly played out in small localities, there had been little effort at creating strategies that dealt with anything beyond local issues. Also, political allegiance was divided between liberal reformers who sought state government intervention in resolving the barrio's problems and the local politicians who believed that solutions came from patronage and political favors. The two sides were both a testament to the insensitivity of Anglo American politicians in Texas. The liberal reformers sought to circumvent most elected officials by putting pressure on the very top. Local officials avoided insensitive officials by concentrating on those things they did control.[5]

This gap between the two groups had been bridged by the Viva Kennedy campaign. Both sides had seen the benefit of jumping on a national bandwagon. Recognition, patronage, muscle-flexing, experience, and future political office were the positive consequences of the campaign. Inter-action among the different groups generated the hope that the factions could work together to bring recognition to Mexican American leaders and solutions to the problems of the barrio. This political unity thus had the making of a dual class strategy. Recognition, patronage, and political appointments would come to the middle-class reformers, while working-class Mexican Americans could see government efforts to eliminate seg-regation, police brutality, bad education, and high unemployment. This dual strategy became possible because of the demise of working-class mili-tancy. Political reformism now stood as the philosophy of the Mexican American activist.

McCormick, serving as chairman pro-tem in Phoenix, opened the na-tional MAPA meeting by providing an assessment of the status of the Mexican American population in the area of politics. He summarized population percentages and voting totals and gave examples of the lop-sided support that Mexican Americans gave Kennedy. He also explained that there were many—including "people in the Democratic Party"—who did not want Mexican Americans coming together. He added that while lack of sophistication was a problem for the Mexican American leadership, there was, however, enough toughness, intelligence, and im-agination to create a strong political force.[6]

Since most of those who attended were either lawyers or organizational leaders, Robert's Rules of Order were adopted, and committees were quickly established. They also pledged allegiance to the flag and structured the discussion into five-minute speeches by the participants.[7] Rather than creating a dialogue, the rules led to a series of opinion-sharing presen-tations. Most presenters discussed the great work of the Viva Kennedy Clubs, the neglect of Mexican Americans by politicians, and the need for Mexican Americans to be united. Roybal and García were particularly incensed over Kennedy's failure to keep his promise to appoint Spanish-speaking persons to high positions. "We find no consolation [in Ken-nedy's actions] and for that reason we must do something concrete about it," Roybal told the conference participants. García went further and ac-cused the national politicians of "collusion" to keep the Mexican Ameri-can down.[8] He told McCormick that he had been used for the benefit of politicians who were threatening to be the same as those elected in the past, who sought support, promised patronage and understanding, and delivered neither. García urged the delegates to see themselves as one with other Spanish-speaking peoples despite their geographical dispersion and different national origins.

Roybal, Gene Marín of Arizona, Lino López of Colorado, and García called for unity among the delegates and among Mexican American reformers nationwide. Marín told the delegates that in the Phoenix metropolitan area, there were twenty-one organizations for the Spanish-speaking that had similar goals but which could not agree to work together. "They all stand for the same thing basically, but they are bidding for the same members, for the same monies, [and] for the same effort," said Marín. López told the delegates that failure to create a national organization that would bring together all Mexican Americans would be "failing our duties to some five to six million Americans." García added that no one wanted Mexican Americans to organize, but they had to despite the opposition, "or else the [raza] will perish." Roybal told the delegates that the jealousies among them had to end and that unity had to be promoted. He recommended that the organization send a letter to the president stating that Mexican Americans were united.[9]

Beyond the discussion of election results and calls for unity, the narrative report of the meeting reveals very little discussion of philosophy, strategy, or goals, only a re-affirmation of discontent. Without establishing any philosophical foundation, the morning session ended for lunch and for committee work.[10] After lunch, the participants quickly voted to accept the organizational structure presented by a committee headed by García. The structure reflected that of numerous existing Mexican American organizations. It called for a national president, four vice-presidents, a secretary, a treasurer, and an executive secretary. It also established a board comprised of the above mentioned officers and two representatives from each state who would meet twice a year. The structure was a top-heavy hierarchy that could best be described by the delegates' own words as a "vertical-type organization."[11] The number of elected officers reflected two aspects of existing Mexican American organizations: it provided positions for the elites within the membership, and it kept the decision-making at the top by putting the most articulate and passionate members in leadership positions. Thus, while the organization was based on mass participation, much of the discussion and decision-making remained the domain of a numerically enhanced but still small group of men. García would be named president and Roybal vice-president.

The naming of the organization would take up most of the rest of the meeting time. Roybal later remembered that the delegates could not agree on an organizational name because they could not agree on what to call themselves. During the election, they had been Kennedy Democrats or the Spanish-speaking, or they had simply referred to themselves according to the state in which they lived.[12] Coming together required them to find a name that was inclusive of their diversity. The difficulty arose from the fact that Mexican Americans in the United States had lived regionally segregated, and thus large numbers of Mexican Americans had little contact with others of the same origin. The uniqueness of each state combined with the immigration patterns, economic conditions, political circumstances, and cultural traits to promote a regional identity that often highlighted differences among Mexican Americans. The reaction of Mexican Americans to their political powerlessness, economic deprivation, and discrimination as well as to their political empowerment or economic success made Mexican Americans cling to a regional ethnocentrism. Mexican Americans in Colorado were called Spanish Americans, in New Mexico they were Hispanos, in Texas they were Latin Americans or Spanish-speaking, in California they were Mexican American, and in other places they might be Latinos or Americans of Spanish descent.[13] Over time these names, often imposed from the outside, had become self-assumed and a way to promote regional distinction. Whatever the name, it seemed a way to avoid being called a "Mexican." Chicano activist Carlos Guerra would later say that identity ambivalence came only when English was spoken. Everyone was a *mexicano* in Spanish, but a Latin American, Spanish American, Hispano, and so on, in English.[14]

When the delegates came together they struggled to find unity in what Rudolfo Anaya calls the most important ritual that a people could perform, that of finding a name and an identity.[15] Compounding the search for a name was the political capital that came with the name. Californians, led by Roybal, wanted the national organization to be named Mexican American Political Association, the same as their state organization. They were the most adamant in seeking to promote the idea that they were Mexican, thus empowering the term and eliminating its stigma. While the delegates in Phoenix tentatively agreed on Political Association of Spanish-speaking Organizations (PASO), the decision resolved little.[16]

The next meeting took place in Las Vegas, Nevada. At that meeting, there were fewer delegates, and one significant person was missing.

Edward R. Roybal, the organization's vice-president, joined González, Peña, Chávez, and Montoya in being a no-show. There were also others who had been in Phoenix that had chosen not to or were unable to attend. The minutes indicate that the meeting again became bogged down over the same issues that plagued the meeting in Phoenix.[17]

Three major issues took up much of the meeting, and they reflected the character of the individuals and their major concerns. The least political issue revolved around the constitutional and organizational structure. As in Phoenix, the delegates spent more time discussing vice-presidencies, state representatives, protocol, and voting procedures than they did developing a mission statement or ideology. The concern over structure towered over any discussion of goals or political philosophy. The minutes of the meeting go on page after page detailing organizational changes and modifications.[18]

Following behind structure-building came the discussion of the name. Delegates again took up the issue of what to call the organization. Several delegates took issue with the name chosen in Phoenix. Particularly opposed were those who did not want to use an ethnic designation. They wanted to emphasize their Americanism. Joining them against the name PASO were those who believed that there should be an emphasis on the fact that Mexican Americans would constitute most of the membership and possibly all the leadership.[19] This debate highlighted the profound differences the leadership had on how best to pursue reform politics in the national arena.

There were those who did not want to separate themselves from the American mainstream. After all, separation only meant accentuating their cultural differences, their economic subjugation, and their political powerlessness. By being simply American, they could then be seen as equals and be permitted access to all aspects of American society. Their color-blind language sought less to deny their ethnicity than it did to deflect any prejudices from mainstream society.[20] Ethnic labels, they believed, would play into the hands of those who discriminated. Also, playing the ethnic card might limit their service to dealing only with the issues of the barrio. Most of the proponents of a non-ethnic name wanted to become involved in national and international issues. Unlike some of their colleagues, they were not as interested in being Mexican American "leaders" as they were in becoming "American" leaders. Leadership in the barrio had its limitations. Leadership in the most powerful nation in the world promised endless opportunities.

Those who sought a greater identification with community had a different problem with the generic or nebulous name. To them, PASO failed to distinguish the Mexican American focus of their efforts. They argued that the organization would attract mostly Mexican Americans as other Latino groups were either too small or had their own organizations and issues with which to concern themselves. Among the California group there was the feeling that too many reformers were unwilling to face up to their Mexican heritage. Mexican was what they were and what they should call themselves.[21]

The third compounding element to the name problem was the existence of the Mexican American Political Association organization in California that Roybal headed and which had an impressive track record in its first two years.[22] The California MAPA members were not interested in changing their name or subsuming their efforts to be part of a larger national umbrella group. With California being the state with the most Mexican Americans, PASO's recruiting efforts would be significantly affected. Some California reformers wanted to challenge MAPA for the loyalty of Mexican American leaders statewide, but the PASO leadership was not willing to engage in a recruiting war with MAPA or Roybal.

The convention delegates resolved none of the issues though they affirmed the name by a small margin. They did, however, give themselves the option of changing their mind at the next meeting, but there would not be another major gathering to build on the Phoenix and Las Vegas foundations. Instead, the California group went back to continue MAPA in its own way, the Arizona reformers established their own organization, and the reformers from other states either became affiliates of the Texas PASO or joined other organizations.[23] The Texas group would keep the name and for a few years retain the guise of a national group, but their concerns would be focused on the Lone Star state. New Mexico, with its two congressmen, would play almost no leadership role. Any chance that this would happen ended when Chávez died in 1962.

The three issues simply created a major obstacle for organizing a national entity. A fourth factor would magnify the problems. There were no funds available to establish a functioning entity. During both conventions delegates had discussed fund raising and money for day-to-day operations. Although delegates talked about putting together some literature to use in attracting interest and contributions to the newly formed group, they did not have the funds to produce even a pamphlet. McCormick pleaded with the delegates to provide funds for daily operations, but few could promise more than small personal contributions.[24]

Still another problem compounding the obstacles to national unity was the absence of some of the major figures of the Viva Kennedy movement. Except for Roybal, none of the other elected officials that were prominent in the Kennedy campaign attended any of the meetings. By the second one even Roybal was absent. The value of these men lay in the fact that they had contacts and political experience. They had always been good fund-raisers and could attract a cross section of followers. Not having Montoya and Chávez meant that they had no legislative or political presence in Washington, D.C., nor two politicians who could travel at government expense to organize for PASO. Without Roybal, González, and Peña, they lacked three of the most articulate, passionate, and inspiring speakers in the reformist community. The five major political figures represented the body of nationally known Mexican American leaders. Others, such as García, Sánchez, McCormick, and Ralph Estrada, head of the Alianza Hispano-Americana in Tucson, were either just becoming known or fading from the limelight. Since they were not politicians, they could not claim a large constituency. Only García could make such a claim, but outside of South Texas his influence was limited to that of G.I. Forum activities. Since Mexican American reformers were moving toward electoral politics as the most significant avenue of reform, the five elected officials loomed as the most important individuals in the struggle for civil rights.

There is no one reason why these officials stayed away from the creation of the organization. Political battles at home—and for some political ambitions—kept them occupied.[25] While all of them were secure in their elected office, they were so because they were vigilant, and that took time and resources. Another reason for their absence may have been that organizational leadership required a collective approach to leadership and reform. Though some of them were both politicians and organizational leaders—particularly Roybal and Peña—they tended to be rather independent, making individual choices about issues and political campaigns. For men who tenaciously protected their spheres of influence, the struggle to build an organization from scratch did not seem overly appealing. There is no doubt that they all wanted PASO to succeed, but all had also proven that they could go it alone. Finally, all—except for Peña—had outgrown organization-based politics and were committed to playing politics in the larger national arena.

Without national leaders, without funding, without unanimity in a name, without California, and with only half-hearted support in New Mexico, a national PASO became an impossibility. After the Las Vegas meeting, no PASO gathering of national significance took place. Within a short time the dream of a national organization had succumbed to the reality that Mexican Americans were fragmented in their politics, goals, and leaders. Said a frustrated García, "Our Raza always think of their individual problems first, and they believe what they do with themselves is [more] important to them than what they do for the people, and this is wrong."[26] They also lacked the resources and sophistication to resolve those issues before they derailed national unity. The respect that each leader had for the other is underscored by the fact that there was little criticism of each other for the demise of the national effort.[27] Used to working in their own states, most reformers seemed to have taken the failure of the national organization in stride as they prepared to continue working on their statewide agendas.

Even before the situation with the national organization had been resolved, however, the Texas PASO leadership jumped onto the campaign trail again, this time in the race for the U.S. Senate. The effort proved to be futile; on July 10, García sent out a letter telling the national PASO membership that the Texas chapter had decided not to support the Democratic Party's candidate for the U.S. Senate.[28] Their strategy was to prove to state Democratic leaders that they could not win without the active support of the Mexican American leadership in Texas. This action had been partly the result of González's failure to capture the party's nomination for the seat Lyndon B. Johnson vacated. Without an organizational structure or funds, the former Viva Kennedy people had set out to work for González's candidacy. At the time, Viva Kennedy leaders had already met to keep the network together. Some had envisioned a permanent Viva Kennedy organization, but that had not proved feasible.[29] But during that meeting, the gathered had committed to the state senator. It is doubtful that they had any choice. In a now-customary style, González made the decision to run on his own. As a political lone wolf who had the propensity to run for whatever position was available, González forced the leaders to commit themselves to another electoral effort even before they could rest from the previous one. This sudden jump into the political frying pan without organizational strength would become a common occurrence for the former Viva Kennedy troops. González, who had little money and no major endorsements, never had much chance.[30] He had also not received any Democratic Party officials' support.

As a result of González's defeat, PASO chose not to endorse the Democratic senate candidate. PASO leaders felt betrayed by the Democratic Party leadership, which used González to campaign for them during the presidential election but which saw no need to repay the effort. Without strong Mexican American support for the Democratic nominee, John Tower won the race by nine thousand votes, making him the first Republican to win a U.S. Senate seat in Texas in the twentieth century. Said García, "We had to prove to the Democratic machinery that they could not win without our work and help. . . . This took guts but we proved it."[31] García had threatened to resign from the Democratic Party if it won without PASO support. A Democratic victory would have been devastating and an indication that the new organization had little clout with the voters of Texas. The Forum's News Bulletin. claimed that García's endorsement alone would have meant at least thirty thousand votes for the Democrat in Corpus Christi alone. This estimate seems exaggerated, but its tone was consistent with the political bravado that permeated Viva Kennedy pronouncements.[32] This bravado troubled not only conservative Democrats but also those with a liberal persuasion.

The PASO organization, despite its liberal leanings, posed a threat to Texas liberalism which depended on the Mexican American leaders' hearts and the rank-and-file's votes. While Texas conservatives shunned any association with Mexican American reformers and were usually supportive of any measure that kept Mexican Americans from gaining power, liberals represented an even greater challenge. Texas liberals were condescending and paternalistic.[33] While they often criticized the Mexican American community for its lack of civic participation, they rarely provided support for Mexican American candidates and almost never raised issues that were of particular importance to Mexican Americans. For many liberals, what was good for them and for liberal politics was good for Mexican Americans.[34] While often bemoaning the harsh conditions under which Mexican Americans lived, they were more likely to be concerned with civil rights issues that focused largely on African Americans. Their liberalism was defined not by their involvement with Texas' largest minority group but by their stance on national civil-rights issues. PASO leaders found it hypocritical that Texas liberals wanted them to toe an ideological line that liberals often violated when it benefited them. Several months after the formation of PASO, George I. Sánchez would re-affirm the organization's hostility to liberals in a letter to Idar. "I personally no longer give a damn what the liberals think," he wrote.[35]

In a letter to Ronnie Dugger, editor of the *Texas Observer*, the state's most liberal political magazine, Idar chastised Texas liberals for trying to decide what was good for Mexican Americans since they had rarely committed themselves to supporting Mexican American candidates and legislative issues of importance to the barrio.[36] Idar reminded Dugger that in 1958 Texas liberals had a chance to support Henry B. González for governor but chose to endorse someone else. Though the *Texas Observer* had declared González the best liberal in the race, they had chosen to "set the needs of the organization ahead of liberal principles."[37] Idar also pointed out Dugger's endorsement of Maury Maverick over González in the race to fill Johnson's seat in the Senate.[38] González had waited to see if Maverick would run. When Maverick let his supporters know that he was not running, González declared himself a candidate. Maverick then reversed himself and declared his candidacy. The action split the Mexican American and liberal coalition and both lost badly.

Revealing deep disenchantment with Texas liberals, Idar took issue with Dugger over the importance of Ralph Yarborough's re-election. Yarborough was engaged in a tough re-election battle, but to some PASO leaders, the race did not seem that important. "After all," wrote Idar, "of twelve liberal issues on which Yarborough was tested, he voted right in all except the one with which Latins were primarily concerned." Idar added that the "biggest political story" of the past year had been the manner in which the liberal senator had alienated the Mexican American leadership by not supporting Salinas's candidacy for the federal bench. He reminded liberals that without Mexican American support, Yarborough would never have risen to be the "anointed of the liberals." He further chided the *Texas Observer* for not having considered the issue important enough to cover. Idar declared that Mexican Americans could not be blamed for the demise of Texas liberalism. The liberals had done it to themselves by not supporting Mexican American candidates and by doing what was expedient rather than principled. "Latins have been taken for granted once too often," wrote Idar, "and [we] are no longer tied to anyone's apron strings—be they liberal, moderate, or conservative."[39]

Idar's stinging letter revealed how frustrated PASO leaders had become over liberals' ambivalence about Mexican American political power. They believed that liberals saw Mexican American voting strength only as a mechanism for getting liberals elected and liberal legislation passed. In a political version of trickle-down economics, liberals believed that their empowerment would eventually result in gains for Mexican Americans. PASO leaders rejected that view. All progressive activity in Texas had to have the full participation of Mexican American reformers, and they could take that stand because they believed that liberals could not recruit too many more Anglo Americans to their side. In conservative Texas, liberalism would grow only if Mexican American voters became involved in the political process. The assumption was that most Mexican Americans would vote liberal.

In trying to find its own political creed, PASO adopted an article by Sánchez, "The American of Mexican Descent," as its organizing document.[40] Sánchez remained the one reformer who could provide an intellectual foundation to the organization's activities. He knew the history of his people, and he had long experienced the indifference of government to the plight of the Mexican American. Sánchez began his article by providing some background and then distinguishing Mexican Americans from the traditional immigrants. "As an Indian, the Spanish-Mexican was here from time immemorial; and his Spanish forebears were in this region long, long before John Smith and his followers pioneered Virginia," wrote Sánchez. He then detailed most of the points he had already introduced in the Texas Viva Kennedy Club manifesto about government indifference, health and educational problems, migrant worker exploitation, and lack of political appointments. The importance of this re-statement was the fact that it was being presented to a broader audience and as a prelude to a political "coming out" by Mexican Americans. This time, PASO was not supporting a candidate but promoting itself to the Mexican American and Anglo American communities as the "new" and legitimate reform organization in Texas. The point that drew the greatest attention, particularly among liberals, was the statement that "only *mexicanos* can speak for *mexicanos*."[41] Dick Messkill, columnist of the *Alamo*

Messenger, the newspaper of the liberal-leaning Catholic diocese of San Antonio, attacked the statement as discrimination in reverse.[42]

Peña took exception to the criticism, and he argued that membership in PASO remained open to anyone who had the interests of the Mexican American in mind. He added that the Mexican American viewpoint had been ignored for years, and some of their problems remained unique to them. He also pointed out that PASO favored coalitions with liberals "as long as we are treated with mutual respect." As to the accusation that PASO would support only Mexican Americans for office, Peña remarked, "we will recommend them based on the basis of their performance—regardless of race, creed, or color."[43] Sánchez also took exception to the charge of reverse discrimination. He explained that few Anglo Americans understood Mexican American culture, and so they tended to make decisions that were either detrimental to the interests of Mexican Americans or which simply ignored them. "I may be wrong in saying that only the *mexicano* can speak for the *mexicano.* Up to now there hasn't been any evidence that the contrary is so. . . . I can't help but take a completely cynical, pessimistic view of Anglo politics and Anglo politicians."[44]

Sánchez spoke from experience. As a professor who for nearly thirty years had served on numerous educational committees, published extensively in the field of Mexican American education, and been a politically active reformer, Sánchez had grown progressively more frustrated. Like many other Mexican American reformers, he believed that a golden opportunity had passed to improve the lives of Mexican Americans through government action. Now, Sánchez believed that changes would come only through the practice of political hardball. In responding to liberal criticism, Sánchez revealed a slight disappointment with Henry B. González that would later have profound consequences in PASO. In describing politicians' failure to understand Mexican Americans, he told the *Texas Observer,* "there is a submerged [Mexican] culture there that . . . few . . . understand . . . except Henry (González) and I have some doubts about him."[45] Sánchez's views were privately endorsed by others who questioned González's commitment to any organization of Mexican Americans. Even among his most ardent supporters, there were few who truly knew what González would do next. His independence threatened to remain outside a collective approach to reform. Ironically, González's independence was only slightly more blatant than that of other leaders, who themselves would be uncorrallable. Sánchez himself would prove to be as independent as the rest.

The first statewide convention of PASO met in San Antonio on February 9, 1962. The purpose of the convention was to interview the candidates who were running for state office that year and to try to obtain a consensus on whom to endorse. Once the endorsement was given, delegates would return to their communities and work for the candidates. Hoping to strengthen the infrastructure, the convention had strict guidelines that PASO chapters had to meet to be able to vote. The number of delegate votes depended on the size of the chapter, its payment of fees, and its attendance at the convention. No social functions were scheduled; delegates would instead spend the two days—and possibly a night—hearing the candidates, discussing their merits, and deciding on whom to endorse. The convention leaders were conscious that they were staging an important first in the state of Texas. They emphasized the unprecedented nature of the event in the call to gather: "This convention is going to be a historic occasion because this is the first time in the history of Texas as a state that the people of Mexican descent have been able to organize a strictly political organization which has been needed for a long time to insure that persons in public office pay attention to the problems that affect all of us." Idar, who sent out the call to the chapters, ended the memo with the handwritten comment, *"Paso a Paso para Adelante,"* which meant "step by step forward."[46]

The PASO convention sought to create an informed unity after delegates heard the candidates, discussed the issues, and voted on endorsements. Strength through political independence served as the underlying theme of the conference. Said Peña, "[for] too long have Mexican Americans voted blindly for candidates—Democrats for the most part—who have taken them for granted."[47] In the memorandum inviting the different chapters to the convention, Idar had admonished the delegates not to make commitments to any of the candidates until the meeting in San Antonio, where they would "act together in deciding who to endorse."[48] Idar's plan for a consensus endorsement proved to be overly ambitious, given that a number of delegates were political veterans who were constantly being wooed by Anglo American politicians for support. There were many others who were new to the process and came with the idea that delegates would vote their conscience without regard to the needs or wishes of the organization's leadership. There were still others who represented groups which had their own agenda. When Peña announced that the delegates were expected to support the endorsed candidate, Paul Montemayor, a well-known labor activist, walked out, saying that as a union organizer he had to support the candidate endorsed by the union.[49] His departure was a friendly one, and his situation was understood by most of the delegates who knew his commitment to the Mexican American community. The fact that no consensus had been sought beforehand by the PASO leadership meant that the convention would be a wide-open affair.

Yet there had been some serious wooing before the convention, and some that stretched into the opening day. Price Daniel, the incumbent governor, had called Sánchez to Austin to provide a briefing on the issues of importance to the PASO delegates. While Sánchez supported the liberal challenger, Don Yarborough, some PASO members believed he had left a door open to Daniel's campaign if Yarborough lost. In fairness to Sánchez, he had written Idar a four-page letter indicating why he thought Yarborough represented the best choice for Mexican Americans. In the letter, he had also blasted Daniel for his failure to do anything for the Mexican American community.[50] Yarborough had also been busy acquiring support, particularly in South Texas and the Rio Grande Valley. His efforts had paid off in Hidalgo County, where PASO leaders Leo Leo, Bob Sánchez, and Ramiro Cassas had endorsed him. This put Idar, a resident of Hidalgo County, in a predicament because he refused to endorse the candidate before the convention. After all, his memo would plead with the delegates not to make pre-convention commitments.[51]

The two major candidates were not the only ones seeking support early. John Connally, the third candidate in the race, was also seeking to overcome his opponents' advantages by making inroads into their Mexican American support. Connally had some very important Mexican American help in the person of Carlos McCormick. The former Viva Kennedy Clubs coordinator rented a hotel room in San Antonio and from there lobbied the delegates on behalf of the dark horse in the race. The lobbying would be seen by some as a favor to Vice-President Johnson.[52] The vice-president, who kept a close watch on what happened in Texas, supported the Connally constituency as a way to maintain political control in the state.

While no solid consensus existed on any particular candidate, there did exist a strong resentment against Texas liberals among a number of PASO leaders. Peña, in particular, but also Idar and García, were anxious to let liberals know that the Mexican American vote had to be won. They were no longer in anyone's pocket. Yet coming into the convention, Don Yarborough, a moderate liberal from Houston, seemed the most likely to win the support of the delegates. Sánchez had privately sent PASO leaders a letter that described Yarborough as a "sincere and practical liberal committed to helping Mexicans."[53] Also, Yarborough came in with a strong organization in South Texas and confidence that he best represented the interests of the Mexican American community.

Working against him, though, was a growing resentment over liberals' lack of support for Mexican American candidates dating back to the González run for governor in 1958 and for the U.S. Senate only months before. The lack of liberal support to get Salinas appointed to the federal district court bench remained fresh in the minds of PASO leaders. Finally, desire for political independence worked against the traditional liberal. Mexican American leaders wanted PASO to become the voice of *la raza*. It could become so only if it could gain the loyalty of Mexican American voters. Given that a number of PASO leaders were liberal, they found it difficult to differentiate themselves ideologically. They found that the real difference came in the area of priorities and ethnocentricity. Texas liberals had an agenda that emphasized liberalism in the state government and "sensitivity" toward the needs of minorities. But often they continued to see civil rights in terms of black and white. Mexican Americans were simply not dark enough or oppressed viciously enough. There was also a condescending paternalism that revealed itself in the competition for political office, where white liberals always saw themselves as better candidates. Liberals also questioned the liberalism of the Mexican American leadership because it remained focused on local issues. For their part, Mexican American reformers found it difficult to distinguish between conservative and liberal neglect. In the end, some Mexican American leaders saw their oppressors as simply white.

The convention attracted twenty-four Democratic and Republican candidates. Most came with the recognition that Mexican Americans seemed on the verge of becoming a political force in Texas. James Thurman, a candidate for lieutenant governor, called the gathering "a new political era in Texas." And Les Proctor, candidate for attorney general, admitted that he came "with my hat in hand, asking your backing."[54] This is exactly how PASO leaders wanted the candidates to come. For years, the situation had been reversed, with Mexican Americans always having to plead their case with the hope of finding sympathy among Anglo American politicians. Rarely had their supplications been answered affirmatively. By having candidates of both parties woo them, it presented them with an opportunity to become election brokers, and to do so independently. The Democratic Party candidates' presence at the convention indicated that Mexican Americans were not to be taken for granted as they had been for years by Democrats. Republican attendance signaled that conservatives recognized that they could not make Texas a two-party state without Mexican American support.

Had the convention ended with the candidates' plea for support, PASO leaders could have proclaimed victory. They wanted to be seen as an independent political force, and they were. They wanted to set the ground rules for endorsement, and they had. They wanted to grill the candidates and reveal their true feelings, and they got their chance during the screening committee session of the first evening. And they wanted to be able to disqualify candidates, or at least let them know that they had fallen from the good graces of Mexican Americans. They did this when they gave John Connally—Johnson's choice for governor—a bad review and almost no votes when endorsement time came. But the convention did not end with the candidates' plea for support nor the tough screening session. Once the candidates had their say, the PASO delegates set out to find a consensus, and that proved to be quite difficult. The most important and heated debate would revolve around the endorsement for governor.

After the screening, a number of the delegates met in the evening to discuss the candidates. According to Idar, six or seven key people led by García met and decided to support Daniel as the best candidate. "We did not think Yarborough could win and Connally had done badly [in the screening]," Idar remembered. Daniel, on the other hand, had won his last election by a million votes, and his presentation had been sympathetic. "We always supported liberals and they lost. It [was] time to change our approach—to try to get what we wanted instead of just supporting liberals," Idar would say years later.[55]

Once the decision was made to support Daniel, Idar was assigned to tell the Connally campaign. Connally told Idar that he understood. The Yarborough people, however, reacted quite differently. They "hit the ceiling" and accused García, Idar, Peña, and others of selling out. Sánchez, when he heard of the decision, called Idar in the middle of the night and told him in no uncertain terms that PASO could not endorse Daniel. "Yarborough is our kind," he told Idar. For Idar and others, that attitude smacked of martyrdom, and they went ahead with their efforts to endorse Daniel.[56]

Among the delegates the choice quickly came down to incumbent Price Daniel or Yarborough. As noted before, Yarborough had some major obstacles to overcome, but he was also the one whose views were closest to those of the PASO leadership. Daniel also had major handicaps, the most significant being that he led a state government that had proven time and time again its insensitivity to Mexican American issues. Just as important was his strained relationship with González, who did not attend the convention. González had, in fact, challenged Daniel for the governorship and in the process had engaged him in a heated war of words. While the relationship had improved since 1960, many delegates still had doubts about Daniel. Given the two candidates' problems with Mexican Americans, Connally had initially been seen as a possible alternative. He was moderate, had held federal appointments, and had strong support in South Texas. But his poor showing in the screening eliminated his chances.[57]

The endorsement process became an open battle that revealed profound differences among the delegates. While the debates often made reference to experience, prior performance, and political philosophy, on the whole they revealed a split over appropriate strategy and political integrity. The goals for both sides always remained empowerment for Mexican Americans through political appointments, employment opportunities in government and the private sector, the elimination of the poll tax, and vigorous prosecution of civil-rights violations. The conflict arose over the quickest way to attain those goals. The faction led by García and Idar favored Daniel because he was the incumbent and ready to promise anything to retain his job. Daniel promised another district judgeship, this time in San Antonio, the largest Mexican American community in the state. He also promised more Mexican Americans in the state highway patrol and other state agencies. He admitted to having been "sleeping" and not knowing about the problems that Mexican Americans faced. But as governor, he told the delegates, he had the power to fulfill promises and to begin doing so even before the election. He reminded the PASO delegates of his support for the Good Neighbor Commission and that as attorney general he had ruled that segregation of Mexican Americans was illegal.[58]

Favoring Yarborough was a faction led by Idar's law partner, Bob Sánchez, as well as George I. Sánchez and labor leader Paul Montemayor. They distrusted Daniel, some considering him a "revolving hypocrite" whose five years in office had been ones of "mediocrity and indifference."[59] Yarborough promised that he would consult PASO on appointments and find solutions to the problems of the *bracero* program, migrant workers, and other poor Mexican Americans. He also fully endorsed President Kennedy's legislative program, something PASO had done in the first year of the organization's existence. "We have a great opportunity to win with real Democrats," said Yarborough, "and we don't have to compromise to do it." Sánchez would echo the sentiment when he declared, "Principles rather than petty patronage must dictate our political choices."[60] For Yarborough supporters, Daniel had had ample time to prove his sensitivity to the concerns of Mexican Americans and had done little. Also, during the screening, Daniel had implied that Mexican Americans were partly to blame for their scarcity in government agencies because they did not apply or were not qualified. Pro-Yarborough delegates also believed that re-electing incumbents did not signal a "change," and PASO had been created to bring change to the state of Texas.

For Daniel supporters, Yarborough represented the self-righteous liberal who expected Mexican American support because of his progressive rhetoric. Said one pro-Daniel delegate, "What did Yarborough promise us? All he did was wave his hands and say he was with us." Another delegate resented the fact that Yarborough had told him that he had "90 percent of the Latin vote in the bag regardless of what the organization [PASO] did."[61] To Idar, Yarborough was promising things that he could not deliver. During the screening, an exasperated Idar had asked, "where is your authority?" when Yarborough had promised to resolve issues dealing with the international border.[62] In the minds of many PASO delegates, Yarborough had acted in the typical condescending manner by coming to the convention with the idea that he would let PASO become part of his progressive campaign. He did not come with "hat in hand" or with the idea that he could not win without them. As far as Daniel supporters were concerned, supporting Yarborough meant practicing politics as usual: Mexican Americans supporting liberals in return for vague promises of "sensitivity" toward minority issues.

While the fervency for both candidates seemed equally divided, one other criterion shifted the uncommitted delegates toward Daniel. PASO delegates saw it as imperative that they endorse the candidates who were likely to have a chance of winning the general election. Said a PASO spokesperson, "From 1950 to 1960 we supported candidates for governor and lost every time. From past defeats we have learned that we must (1) have a candidate that offers a positive program with respect to our group, and (2) that also has a chance to win."[63] Many delegates believed that Daniel, as the incumbent, had the best chance to win. Expediency then became important. Victory by an endorsed candidate meant that PASO had made a difference, even if it did endorse the candidate most likely to win. This attitude of expediency alienated Sánchez so much that he walked out of the convention before the endorsement vote and then publicly repudiated the selection. "I am terribly disappointed at the endorsement of candidates who have done nothing for our people," Sánchez told a reporter as he left.[64] Later, in a letter to a friend, Sánchez justified his refusal to support Daniel, "I was, and still am, under the conviction that if we are to operate successfully in the interest of our people, we are going to have to operate simply, sincerely, and unequivocally as a moral force."[65] In the final vote, Daniel received 51-1/2 votes to Yarborough's 41-1/2.[66]

The split at the convention made it difficult to promote a united front in public. But more devastating to the organization proved to be the inability to get all the PASO chapters to unite behind the endorsement. In San Antonio, the Bexar County Democratic Coalition, an organization with strong PASO influence, endorsed Yarborough. Other chapters would do the same.[67] The pro-Yarborough delegates would continue their support despite the organization's vote. Worse, Yarborough supporters lashed out at García and other Daniel supporters, revealing a split that would later become almost unbridgeable. Leo J. Leo, leader of the South Texas Yarborough supporters, would send García a stinging three-page letter rebuking him for using his influence to manipulate the convention endorsement process. "You did wrong in using the tremendous . . . influence that you have . . . to turn the convention for a man that has never been our friend. Don't fool yourself, doctor, he will not be our friend for long; he is not our type, he has never been," Leo wrote. Leo reminded García that it was the G.I. Forum leader who constantly preached "*no se vendan por un pedazo de tortilla, barbacoa, o por una miserable chamba,*" and now he had sold out PASO for political appointments.[68] Leo went on to express his support for the liberals in Texas, re-affirming Peña and Idar's view that some Mexican American reformers would follow the liberal politicians over their own leaders.

The governor's supporters sought to counter the attacks by outlining their reasons for supporting Daniel. It was Idar who would lead the counterattack. In an open letter to voters, Idar argued that Mexican American reformers had lost too many times in the past for not supporting a winner, and they believed that Daniel had a very good chance of winning. He also asserted that as attorney general in 1949, Daniel had campaigned against the poll tax, he had named a Mexican American as an assistant, and he had declared unconstitutional the segregation of Mexican Americans in schools and public places. He had also appointed numerous Mexican Americans to state boards and agencies.[69] Idar was tenacious in the defense of Daniel's endorsement, but in the long run neither he nor Leo was able to change any minds.

The failure to keep its local chapters in line revealed a structural weakness in PASO. But more importantly, it revealed an ideological flaw in the organization. From its beginning, PASO's leadership assumed that most Mexican American reformers put unity above politics. In fact, unity seemed often to be the ideological, or at least philosophical, base of most actions by middle-class reformers. They believed that if only they could unite, they would be able to eliminate discrimination, strike down segregation, and gain political power. Unity represented an all-encompassing state-of-being which incorporated the humanitarian desires and political ambitions of the reformers. But this middle-class concept of unity lacked coercive powers to keep the troops in line. Since PASO leaders were usually leaders in their own communities or headed particular organizations, they never subsumed their individuality for the greater good of PASO.

PASO's own name indicated a confederation rather than a tightly knit political association. Their allegiance to American individuality and their belief in personal integrity made it difficult for any leader or any issue to amalgamate the members into a solid bloc that subsumed individual preferences or political orientation. Nothing in PASO's organizing principles called upon members to sacrifice their personal beliefs or their public persona for an organizational cause. Because of this, PASO could maintain unity only through the leaders' personalities or through organizational victories.

Several months after the convention and after the first round of primaries, Sánchez attempted to smooth things over with those who had supported Daniel. He wrote to Idar and told him that all was forgotten and that he was prepared to join "you and other leaders to make PASSO work." But then, in a style customary to him, Sánchez told Idar it was a mistake to make PASO a political machine. Instead, he added that PASO would function best as a political club, endorsing candidates when unanimity prevailed but allowing the members to go their separate ways when no agreement existed. Idar, still smarting from the split and the first round of the primaries, made the following notation at the bottom of the letter: "You must be kidding! Like all liberals you assume your judgment is the only one that is infallible. You and I know that you were intellectually dishonest in certain statements regarding Price Daniel and civil rights. . . . You helped . . . PASO fall flat on its face and now you think it can be made to work. How many candidates do you think we will have at another state convention?"[70] Idar did not send those comments to Sánchez but did later sent him a more formal letter.

The split may have caused the loss of some of the leaders' popularity, but the loss of the endorsed gubernatorial candidate rattled the organization to its foundations. Daniel lost in the primaries, leaving Yarborough and Connally in the run-off. While Daniel carried the majority of the South Texas vote, PASO could not corral the larger bloc of Mexican American voters, who went for Yarborough and Connally.[71] Following the defeat of Daniel, PASO endorsed Yarborough, but the Houston liberal fared no better as Connally won a sizable number of Mexican American votes and won the run-off. Johnson's old cronies in South Texas were able to deliver in a two-way race better than in the earlier primaries.[72] The second defeat left PASO in danger of being left out of the general election. To avoid that possibility, PASO then endorsed Connally for the general election.[73] By then, PASO's endorsement did not carry much weight. In a four-way race, the endorsement had represented a significant advantage. In the run-offs liberals needed all the support they could muster. By the general election, the PASO contingency became just another part of the Democratic bloc. The fact that Connally won the Mexican American vote over the endorsed Yarborough meant that he was less open to negotiation. He had no reason to be. Johnson's political machine had proven that it could deliver the votes and that it had strong ties to many more moderate Mexican American leaders.

When the state Democratic Party platform committee met in September to prepare for the fall election, they failed to support a more liberal voter registration law, which was one of PASO's demands. The committee also rejected a PASO-supported endorsement of the Kennedy administration. Peña's lobbying went for naught at the convention as conservative Democrats blocked the PASO initiative.[74] The failure of the PASO forces to be a significant player attracted ridicule from those unhappy with PASO's election brokering. The *San Antonio Evening News* accused Peña of leading an organization that "obviously doesn't speak for very many Spanish-speaking people." It further accused him of staging a "caboose-grabbing act" for calling a meeting of the PASO membership to reconsider its endorsement of Connally. "In what telephone booth will you meet, Mr. Commissioner?" asked the editorial writer sarcastically.[75]

Peña responded to the editorial by calling for a meeting on October 7, at a telephone booth on the corner of Houston Street and Soledad in San Antonio, with the main session to take place at the hotel nearby. Said Peña in issuing the call, "PASO is a moving vital force in Texas politics or it isn't. PASO is an independent thinking, tied-to-no-one's apron strings organization or it isn't. PASO is the conscience of the aims and aspirations of the Mexican American . . . or it isn't." The call attracted five hundred delegates from twenty-one counties, two hundred of which first met at the telephone booth.[76]

In a three-hour marathon, the delegates voted almost unanimously to withdraw the endorsement of Connally for the general elections. They did, however, leave open the possibility that local chapters could re-endorse Connally or his Republican opponent. The delegates blasted Connally for his arrogance and his unwillingness to listen to the voice of the people. Albert Fuentes, an up-and-coming PASO delegate from San Antonio, told the gathered, "If there is any man who thinks he is too big to take orders from the people, then he is too big to be governor." Said another, "If Connally doesn't want to make any deals with us, let's tell him to forget that vote he thought he had in his pocket."[77] State representative John Alaniz of San Antonio told the delegates that PASO needed to let out the word that anyone who "runs for political office . . . [must] know the *Americano* is to be reckoned with."[78]

The defiant voices in the San Antonio meeting expressed anger over the unwillingness of the conservative state Democratic Party to integrate a more Mexican American–friendly platform. Anger also boiled over because of PASO's inability to make inroads at the top of the political ladder. The success in bringing out the voters for the Democratic Party in the presidential election had earned them little clout among the party leaders. The PASO leaders were also angered by the lack of support among state liberals who seemed more comfortable with an unorganized mass of Mexican American voters from among whom they could find support as needed. García lamented that PASO suffered from "historical prejudice." There were few politicians, said García, who wanted an organization of Mexican Americans to succeed.[79] Peña, in his call to meet, had written, "Is PASO a figment of our imagination? Your absence will prove it a fact."[80]

Though they rescinded the endorsement, Connally's victory in the general election re-affirmed PASO's lack of impact on the election. While they had not worked against Connally, PASO leaders had expected some backlash. None seemed to have occurred, though. His victory only affirmed that in one election season, PASO had gone to defeat three times because they had not rallied Mexican American voters to their side. PASO leaders quickly realized that the defeat had its beginning at the first convention when PASO members decided to act as individuals, chapter leaders, and regional power brokers rather than as members of a single organization. The defeat caused widespread discontent among the membership. Defeat was a bitter pill to swallow, but external ridicule was even more painful for individuals who constantly sought legitimacy. The inability to rally solidly behind a candidate revived the feelings that Mexican Americans could never be united.

The year had begun on a positive note. The liberal state representative Jake Johnson of San Antonio declared, "The Latins are no longer a sleeping ethnic group. They're on the march." With six members in the Texas House of Representatives, a growing participation in the electoral process, and Henry B. González in Congress (he had won the seat with a strong endorsement from the Kennedy administration), Mexican Americans seemed ready for a breakthrough. "The Latin is getting interested," said Representative Alaniz, "not only in city councils but in justice of the peace races [and] school trusteeships—all over."[81] The assumption was that PASO would accelerate the process, taking democracy to communities where the Mexican American still had no leadership and where they normally did "what they're told."[82]

The campaign debacle had, however, dampened enthusiasm and caused some of the PASO members to declare that the Mexican American was poorly equipped for political activity.[83] This type of criticism was often a veiled evaluation of the people's character. That the Mexican American lacked the resources, knowledge, and at times motivation to participate in the electoral process was an accepted fact. But often the criticism implied that somehow the Mexican American had to "outgrow" such circumstances and beliefs. The criticism did not take into consideration PASO's failure to help the Mexican American voter make better choices. They brought no new resources, they were seen as jumping from one candidate to another for no real reason, and they could promise little to the mass of working-class voters in the barrio. Political appointments and two or three new openings in the highway patrol were simply not much motivation to vote. The people were supposed to get excited because the PASO leaders had extracted a few concrete promises from one candidate, a commitment of liberal sensitivity from another, and almost nothing from a third. Without any grassroots organization and without a track record, PASO did not have the influence to stop the division of Mexican American voters.

PASO leaders realized, even before the November statewide election, that they had to regroup and prove to the membership, to Mexican Americans in general, and to Texas Anglo Americans that the organization remained viable. But there were no more statewide races or major issues in which to become involved. They then looked to the local areas to find important issues over which to organize. It was there, after all, where most of the reformers had proven their abilities. The community of Crystal City, located in a rich agricultural area known as the Winter Garden, 150 miles southwest of San Antonio, presented PASO a great opportunity to finally prove its viability as a force in Texas.

The story of Crystal City's "revolt" has been the subject of a number of important studies, thus a detailed history will be avoided here.[84] There are, however, several important aspects of the Crystal City revolt that shed light on the politics of PASO and Mexican Americans in the early 1960s. It is important also to know a bit about the rural town and its Mexican and Mexican American citizens and their relationship to the town's Anglo American community. Mexican and Mexican Americans constituted almost 80 percent of the population, and many of them were migrant farm workers who traveled throughout the state and to the Midwest for a large part of the spring and summer. They were poor, and their median education was less than three years.

Since Crystal City had been founded as a company town, it was governed by Anglo American politicians beholden to the agricultural interests of the county. Some of these Anglo politicians, such as the mayor, had served for decades in their posts, rarely challenged by other Anglo Americans, much less by Mexican Americans. These politicians maintained their power because few Mexican Americans registered to vote, even fewer voted, and those that did vote could easily be threatened with the loss of their jobs or law enforcement violence. Mexican Americans could not count on much native leadership. There were almost no elected officials of Mexican descent, few Mexican American business leaders bold enough to challenge Anglo American hegemony, and few with more than just a semi-skilled job. Only the Mexican chamber of commerce and the Mexican American–dominated local of the Teamsters union could be seen as potentially important community organizations. Neither had been involved in Crystal City politics before the 1960s. That, however, would change in 1963.

In that year, a voter registration drive was initiated by a disgruntled Anglo American who felt that the city was being unfair in evaluating his property for tax purposes. He recruited the Mexican American business agent from the union local at the Del Monte packing plant, thinking that a Mexican American urging his people to follow his lead could threaten city officials with a potential electoral challenge. Initially the state Teamster leadership saw the voter registration drive as a way to enhance the union's influence in the South Texas area. But as the drive progressed, they saw the need to become more circumspect since the anti-union feeling among Anglo Americans in the area might become an obstacle to the registration drive. Seeking to find another group to assist them and take the focus off of them, the Teamsters approached PASO leaders about helping with the registration drive.

Moses Falcon, a union member from Crystal City, asked PASO to become involved and to help them with the logistics and the possible legal obstacles they might face once the Anglo Americans discovered what was happening. This did not happen immediately, however. Since voter registration drives were a common activity among Mexican Americans in

South Texas, few Anglo Americans took notice. After all, other than electing a few Mexican Americans to the school board the drives had rarely presented a threat to the entrenched politicians. By the end of January, 1963, the registration drive proved so successful that 1,139 out of a total of 1,681 registered voters were Mexican Americans.[85]

When those leading the registration effort realized what they had done, they quickly moved to create a slate to challenge the incumbents in the spring election. PASO sent Martín García, a law student and member of the organization, to assist the new voters. The Teamsters also sent several of their organizers. Together, they set out to find candidates, help them file for office, and prepare them to respond to the numerous legal challenges they would face. The presence of PASO members and Teamster organizers helped to keep the pressure off five Mexican Americans who chose to run for office. They were particularly able to keep the Texas Rangers from using their traditional intimidation tactics. This was crucial because the candidates and their followers were quite vulnerable to intimidation. The five were, for the most part, working-class individuals who depended heavily on the Anglo American community's goodwill to make a living. Only Juan Cornejo, the Teamster business agent, could claim independence from the local Anglo elite.

With a large advantage of registered voters, legal assistance, and protection from law enforcement violence, the Mexican American candidates swept all five city council seats in the spring elections. The victory stunned the Anglo American population of Crystal City and many other places in Texas. It also sent waves of jubilation through the barrios of South Texas. Nothing like this had happened in Texas in the twentieth century, and it seemed to represent a new phase in Mexican American politics. While individual Mexican American politicians had been elected, never had the barrio taken control of a community.[86]

While some liberals saw it as only right that the Mexican American majority should rule, for many other liberals and conservatives the victory smacked of reverse discrimination. Conservatives realized that there were more than a dozen counties where Mexican Americans were the majority of the population. If Mexican Americans decided to challenge them, they could be swept out of office. For the state conservative Democratic leaders, a loss of South Texas meant that they could not count on the votes that had kept them in power and the liberals at bay for most of the twentieth century. For liberals, always uncertain of the liberal credentials of most Mexican American reformers, a new political force in the barrio meant fierce new competition for a constituency that had the potential to put them on top.

The Crystal City victory also represented a potential dilemma for moderate and conservative Mexican Americans in the middle class. Most of them had worked hard to reach an acceptable accommodation with their Anglo American neighbors. By proving themselves to be "good citizens" and avoiding the ethnic politics of the barrio, they had avoided conflict. By the 1960s they found more elbow room to become involved in business ventures and occasionally in politics. By maintaining clear class distinctions, they had managed to differentiate themselves from the working class which often found disfavor among Anglo Americans. A Mexican American revolt then represented a potential disruption of the accommodation and a return to earlier perceptions that all Mexicans were alike and should be treated as such.

For the more militant members of PASO, Crystal City represented a breakthrough of major proportions. Both Fuentes, now PASO executive secretary, and Peña declared that there would be many more of these revolts in South Texas. "The Mexicans have learned all South Texans are equal," said Fuentes. Peña added that the once-sleeping giant had awakened.[87] For both of these PASO leaders, Crystal City proved that hard work, good planning, and coalition politics could bring positive results at the ballot box and make it possible for Mexican Americans to control their own destiny. In some ways, Crystal City had surpassed their expectations. Confronting many difficult obstacles and winning meant that Mexican Americans had the potential to make significant inroads into the political structure of Texas. In a pamphlet titled "What Is PASO?" Peña boldly declared, "The five members of this winning ticket . . . stand as a beacon to all others like them, struggling in the morass of discrimination and equality. For the first time in South Texas the true majority ruled."[88]

Shortly after the victory in Crystal City, PASO leaders went out on the offensive. They sent Fuentes, now the state director of the organization, to Washington, D.C., to testify in support of President Kennedy's civil-rights legislation. In his testimony, Fuentes pointed out that Mexican Americans were denied even basic accommodation, referring to a controversy over the city swimming pool in Kenedy, Texas. Rather than integrate the facility, city officials closed the pool, and local business leaders built a private pool that was closed to Mexican Americans. The same was true in Crystal City and in Kingsville, where the local country club refused to admit non-whites. "[Governor] Connally said he is proud of the progress made so far in civil rights in Texas . . . the governor may be proud but we are not," said Fuentes.[89]

Fuentes pointed out that there were no "Latin Americans in any of the state's law enforcement agencies, in the state government, or in the state commissions. In 1961, there was not a single state employee of Latin American descent in the state capital." He recited county after county and major corporations which had no Mexican Americans on staff above the level of unskilled laborer. "In San Antonio, no law firm with more than six employees has any Latin American employees. . . . One third of the lawyers in San Antonio are Latin American [but] not one Latin American lawyer is retained by the city of San Antonio or any board of the city," he continued. Fuentes told the congressional committee holding the hearings that the city public service company in the Alamo City even discriminated in the recreational facilities for their employees. The Live Wire Club, composed of Anglo Americans, met in the principal building, whereas the Latin Club met in an old building across the maintenance yard. When questioned about the situation, the board had responded that the "Latins preferred it that way." Fuentes responded that they were afraid to protest for fear of losing their jobs.[90]

The victory in Crystal City emboldened PASO leaders throughout the state and led to a more intense drive to organize chapters and plan potential challenges to the existing power structures in Texas. A number of local PASO chapters set out to plan electoral challenges in their own communities. These efforts, however, had no overarching strategy. While discussions of the Crystal City takeover and some of the techniques involved did take place, no major meetings were held to discuss statewide strategy. Nor were there any coordinated efforts with the Teamsters or other outside groups to help in the local organizing. In some of the local chapters coalitions were sought because the Mexican American population was simply not large enough to do it the "Crystal City way." Also, some local PASO leaders were more committed to the local Democratic Party structure than were the five Mexican American officials elected in Crystal City, and those individuals thus hesitated breaking ranks.

The euphoria over the victory would prove to be short-lived as opposition soon arose within PASO to the idea of more Crystal City–type political victories. The opposition hinged on two major issues. First, a number of PASO leaders believed that the choice of candidates in Crystal City had been disastrous. The candidates had limited education, lacked political refinement, and had no history of legitimate reform activity. These individuals were not the type of role models that some Texas reformers believed could inspire others to political participation. They were in fact representative of the stereotype that Anglo Americans used to denigrate Mexican American participation in politics.[91] As early as one month after the victory, Martín García wondered aloud if the choice of candidates had been a good one. He believed that teaching them to win was the easy part. "We didn't teach them how to be politicians," García told the *Dallas Morning News*. This oversight would come to haunt PASO as *los cinco* (as the Crystal City elected officials were known) would eventually fight among themselves, get into legal problems, and then be roundly defeated by an Anglo/Mexican American coalition in 1965.[92] There were others, like Bob Sánchez of McAllen, who felt uncomfortable with the idea of a racial political war. "One Crystal City is all we need and we don't want to repeat it if we can help it," Sánchez told a reporter. "We don't envision or entertain the idea of a takeover of any kind. I would regret such a move." Sánchez echoed the sentiments of those who believed bloc voting was a necessary evil that should be discarded as quickly as possible. "When a man is elected to office for what he is—no distinction on race or anything else, I will be the first to ask that PASO be disbanded," he said.[93] Given the conditions in the Rio Grande Valley of Texas at the time, Sánchez's views seem rather naive and wishful. But Sánchez represented the view of many reformers who believed that Anglo Americans would vote for Mexican American candidates if they only knew them better.

The second major reason for opposition to Crystal City revolved around the Teamsters' participation in the election. Two things worked against the Teamsters' image. First, they were considered enemies of the Kennedy administration, and second, they were seen as trying to manipulate PASO. The one PASO leader most hostile to the relationship with the Teamsters proved to be García. Interestingly, the Teamsters were basically on good terms with the American G.I. Forum. In fact, the San Antonio chapter of the Forum gave Ray Shafer, head of the Texas Teamsters, a plaque shortly before the PASO convention to honor him for his "outstanding effort on behalf of Democracy and for being a 'great American.'"[94] Three months after the Crystal City affair, however, García had written to Virgilio G. Roel and told him that he was never really against the results in Crystal City, "but I was really against the fact that the Teamsters used their money and their manpower to work in Crystal City."[95]

It is difficult to assess why García so adamantly opposed the Teamsters. It may have been their hostile relationship with the Kennedy administration and the fact that they were by then perceived as a union wracked with corruption and mob influence. Yet in Texas they were considered more liberal and friendlier to reform than other unions. It may also be that the Teamsters were seen by García as threatening to co-opt the Mexican American reform agenda. Never in the past had Mexican Americans united with a group as large or as economically powerful as the Teamsters. With their organizers, lawyers, and rank-and-file members, they were seen as already being in a stronger position than anyone else to make inroads in the barrio. This perception of them was more image than reality. The Teamsters had not done much organizing in South Texas, and the lack of major industry in the area precluded any major organizing effort. García, however, was never one to closely look at the facts, and he may not have realized the Teamsters' limitations. A final reason may well be that in local affairs, García was much more nationalistic than other Mexican American reformers. While he had often created coalitions with non–Mexican Americans, they had always been temporary relationships. García and the American G.I. Forum preferred to work alone among Mexican Americans.[96]

By the time the PASO state convention took place in June in San Antonio, the differences between those who supported the Crystal City approach and those who opposed it became irreconcilable. As the national president, García quickly called for a severance of the relationship with the Teamsters, reminding the delegates that Mexican American reformers had always been self-sufficient in performing their work. "Is PASO going to be run by ourselves or will the Teamsters do it for us? García asked the delegates. "We have won our battles with our own money, our own talent, and our own guts." William Bonilla, a long-time reformer and a candidate for PASO's leadership, concurred with García. "It is my opinion that PASO as a political group should fight its own battles freely and independently of any organization, especially the Teamsters who have no respect for the rights of others . . . and who have a . . . reputation of using . . . unlawful tactics."[97] Peña and Fuentes led the opposition. They told the delegates that "anytime PASO thinks it can get the job done by itself, it is dead." Others agreed, adding that PASO was in no position to be too discriminating in picking its allies.[98] There was simply too much to do and too much opposition to exclude such a potentially powerful ally as the Teamsters. Peña and Fuentes, however, did emphasize that they had not received one cent from the Teamsters. Instead, the relationship was based on the mutual desire to see Texas become more liberal.

Carlos McCormick would join the debate by calling for independence from "outside groups," causing the *Texas Observer* to question whether McCormick was speaking for himself or stating a concern that Attorney General Robert F. Kennedy had about PASO's relationship with the Teamsters.[99] The debate led to recrimination on both sides. García and, on particular issues, the Bonilla brothers matched up against Peña, Fuentes, and an aging George Sánchez, who had by this late stage in his life given up on the soft and conventional approach to activism. Having already chastised González for his accommodationist views, he proceeded to question García's commitment to true reforms. As delegate after delegate rebutted García, he danced in the aisle possibly with the belief that PASO was finally going to stand up in a more militant posture.[100] Sánchez had confided to a pastor friend that he was worried about García's "irrationality," believing the G.I. Forum leader to have become, momentarily at least, "virtually incoherent."[101]

The majority of those gathered in San Antonio supported the Crystal City effort, but for the second time in the history of the PASO meetings a prominent reformer walked out, unwilling to accept the predominant view. García stormed out of the convention and declared "I cannot be a member of any organization that has Ray Shafer as one of its members."[102] Martín García mockingly asked if García had forgotten that Shafer was a dues-paying member of the San Antonio chapter of the American G.I. Forum.[103] The split over the Teamsters, however, was not the only point of contention at the convention. Just as divisive was the question of who would head the organization. With Peña's term as state chairman ending, the delegates sought to elect someone who could lead them for another two years.

Coming into the convention, Albert Fuentes, one of the masterminds behind Crystal City, had cast eyes on the chairmanship, but his association with the Teamsters and his enmity with Congressman González soon derailed his candidacy. Even his position as executive secretary of PASO seemed in danger until Peña resolved to run again and, after winning, re-appointed Fuentes. The eventual opposition to the Peña-Fuentes coalition came from the García and Bonilla forces, with William Bonilla as the chief challenge. The Bonillas did not approve of Crystal City but were not as anti-Teamster as García. They nevertheless represented a much more conservative constituency. Said Bonilla, "many of our professional and business people feel that PASO has received unfavorable publicity because of the Crystal City election, and they do not know if it's worthwhile for them to give of their time to work for the organization."[104] The Bonilla candidacy represented an attempt by the LBJ and Connally forces to gain influence in PASO, while Peña and Fuentes were aligned with Sen. Ralph Yarborough and gubernatorial candidate Don Yarborough. The four had patched up their differences after the gubernatorial election of the previous year. The divisions caused a number of delegates to leave disillusioned with the direction of PASO. Peña would be re-elected by a 41-to-20 margin, and Crystal City would be recognized as a legitimate strategy. At the same time, delegates voted to bar any outside interference and send a strong message that Fuentes had little future as a leader of PASO. The delegates would also endorse a two-party system in Texas and repudiate the work of the state legislature. These two resolutions were, in essence, a rejection of the Johnson-Connally influence in PASO.[105]

While not all the Forum members took García's side, PASO quickly faded from the limelight at the Forum meetings and from its publication.[106] Any chance of conciliation quickly died as the split grew wider and wider. There were also attempts by those who split with Peña and Fuentes to compete with PASO. William Bonilla made an effort shortly after the convention to establish a LULAC council in Crystal City, and this was seen by some as a way to undermine PASO in that community. In Hidalgo County, whose PASO delegation had been key to Peña's re-election, a new group calling itself the Hidalgo County Progressive Citizens League was formed. "We're not anti-PASO," declared its chairman, "but we don't like some PASO ideas."[107]

Despite the splits, Peña, Fuentes, and others saw the opportunity to engage in more "Crystal Cities" and to develop coalitions with blacks, labor, liberals, and anyone else willing to buck the system. Their new militancy had been heading toward a collision course with now-Congressman González, who had by this time abandoned the collective approach to leadership and had become aligned with mainstream politicians and the Johnson people. González also took the attitude that as congressman he could not side with one constituency or another. He continued to pursue a liberal course—with Cold War strains—and remained very good at resolving local problems for the people in his district. He would, however, steer clear of becoming a "Mexican American leader." This aggravated many PASO leaders who believed that González had won because of their support and because their criticism of the administration had forced Kennedy and Johnson to support González's candidacy. García, in his letter to Roel, revealed the rift and acknowledged that "this is going to be very hard to correct."[108]

García, whose quick temper got him in trouble but who usually did not keep a grudge, also contributed to the alienation by taking the conflict outside of PASO. Shortly after the convention, he wrote Robert F. Kennedy a report of the proceedings. In it, he accused the Teamsters of trying to take over PASO and accused Peña, Fuentes, and Shafer of trying to embarrass González and of preparing a challenge to the congressman. "I put up a good fight, but in the end I had to walk out," wrote García. Making the internal conflict something much larger and the Peña faction almost sinister, he told the attorney general that he and McCormick were "awaiting any suggestions that you may give."[109] Having lost influence in PASO and among a number of Texas reformers, García sought to transcend his political limitations by inviting presidential intervention. By so doing, he violated his own "go-at-it-alone" creed and set in motion the creation of a godson-to-godfather relationship with national Democratic leaders that would cement the already asymmetric relations between Mexican Americans and Anglo Americans. From here on, Mexican American reformers would use Anglo Americans to help wage battle against those in the barrio who opposed them. This approach would leave them open to charges of *vendidos* by those in the soon-to-rise Chicano Movement.

For García, and what would become a growing number of reformers, the Viva Kennedy Club movement became a nostalgic past that brought memories of unity and victory. Years later the conflicts would pass from memory, and the Kennedy campaign would again become a highlight of their political careers. The death of President John F. Kennedy would immortalize the campaign of 1960. But in the summer of 1963, their differences on political approaches and coalitions divided them and led to the demise of the organization.

Initially, however, PASO reformers who believed in the Crystal City approach, or who at least were willing to follow Peña's lead, launched an all-out effort to organize chapters, recruit new members, and highlight the problems of the barrio. They also sought to make politics the predominant reform strategy. "We are convinced that the only way to remedy problems particular to Latin American people in Texas is through participation in government," said Peña to a reporter for the *Fort Worth Star-Telegram*. "The only language politicians understand are votes. We are strictly a political action organization."[110]

By April, 1963, only a short time before the conflict arose over Crystal City, PASO leaders claimed chapters in about seventy Texas counties and membership of about twenty thousand.[111] These numbers were more likely to reflect Mexican American sympathizers of PASO rather than actual members. The fact is, many of the chapters had few active members, so a number of the twenty thousand were likely to be dues-paying but non-participating members. Lack of membership records makes it impossible to know the real strength of PASO. The conventions, which were the major PASO events annually, never attracted more than several hundred members.

The political approach was particularly advanced by those who lived in communities where elections promised to shift political power toward Mexican Americans. The 1960 census revealed the potential for a successful electoral revolution in South Texas and the Rio Grande Valley. In an article titled, "Census Shows Latins Hold Power in Valley," a journalist declared, "U.S. Census figures make the fear of a Latin American political takeover in the Rio Grande Valley a naked possibility."[112] This possibility represented a change of tremendous proportions for Mexican American reformers. Winning political power meant that they would have the force of law behind their efforts to desegregate schools and other public facilities and to confront discriminatory bureaucrats and business leaders. In vying for this electoral power, PASO members were looking to unseat not only Anglo American politicians but also long-time barrio *politicos*. "Latin *jefes* (bosses) have profited from selling our people out down here," said Leo Leo, chair of PASO in Hidalgo County. But he added that PASO was undermining the power of these bosses by engaging in grassroots political education. "We tell [the people], these are the candidates PASO has endorsed. Talk to them, listen to them, and ask them questions."[113]

PASO leaders were confident that Mexican Americans would support PASO candidates even when the candidates were Anglo American because they would see the difference in quality and in the platforms. In this, they were at times naive. Since their major philosophical contribution was liberalism, they often seemed not to distinguish themselves too much from other Mexican American candidates, at least when it came to practicing politics at the local level. Most barrio politicians also promised protection from Anglo Americans and jobs in the bureaucracy, and they promoted pride in their ethnicity. While they actually did little to protect Mexican Americans from discrimination and the promised jobs went mostly to relatives, they did promote a barrio nationalism that kept Mexican Americans dependent on them. What urban historian Alan Lessoff has said about Corpus Christi, Texas, applies to much of South Texas: "In Corpus Christi the rich get richer and the poor get self-esteem."[114] This situation may have been a reason why PASO reformers promoted a more assimilative orientation in the barrio even as they practiced a politics of ethnicity outside of the barrio. Their only hope of breaking the *jefes'* hold on the Mexican vote was to discredit them by highlighting their ties to racist Anglo American candidates and by presenting candidates who represented a link to a more progressive American society. Said Leo of the *politico*–Anglo American coalitions that opposed PASO, "they're the same old guys who have been running this county for years and years."[115]

The PASO approach seemed, at the peak of the organization's political strength, the right alternative for fighting the problems that afflicted the barrios. These reformers offered a link to a more "progressive" political world outside of the barrio that did not require Mexican Americans to give up their ethnic identity. The residents' participation in the electoral process was an affirmation of their citizenship and their commitment to Americanism. This participation in regions that were predominantly Mexican American promised to integrate them further into the mainstream. With electoral victories, a new order would come to Texas. The approach also promised to raise the ceiling for Mexican American elites. They could now aspire to regional and statewide political office as well as appointments to office at the state and federal levels.

Political empowerment also meant the ability to eliminate media and other stereotypes. New role models would also be available to young Mexican Americans. PASO could promise all this by its triumphs in Texas politics. But despite all the optimism and initial success, PASO's momentum quickly dissipated. The most important ingredient for PASO or any middle-class reform group was unity, and this was the one thing that most eluded them. The challenge for PASO to succeed in Texas politics required that all the organizational parts work together and with tremendous intensity. But by the end of year PASO had alienated its major office holder and a large chunk of its rank-and-file and had depleted its leadership. The "PASO forward" had occurred somewhat philosophically and even electorally, but organizationally and politically the group had been running in place.

7. Demise of Camelot: The Search Continues

The split at the PASO convention became a permanent one. García never returned to the fold, and within a short time the Bonillas and many of their followers also abandoned the organization. Idar, who had left South Texas for San Angelo before the split occurred, did not return to PASO and neither did many other PASO members.[1] Most found themselves pressured to choose sides between leaders and strategies. Those who were reformers before joining PASO chose to leave the political association and return to non-partisan reform activities. There, they had found more unity and fewer schisms. Justifying his departure, García would write later, "I was never against . . . Crystal City, but I was . . . against the fact that the Teamsters used their money and their manpower to work in Crystal City."[2] This difference in strategy was, for García, an indication that the PASO leaders were drifting apart. "Every

day within PASO I feel there is more and more division of our people without any expectation of ever achieving any unity," he would tell his friend Virgilio G. Roel.[3] The departure of those leaders and their followers weakened the ranks of PASO, both in terms of numbers as well as energy and experience. More important, the conflict over PASO had caused division among a number of reformers who had worked together for years. The recrimination and backbiting would carry over into other organizations, particularly the G.I. Forum. In a letter to Bob Sánchez shortly after the PASO convention, Idar wrote that PASO was dead and that he was glad of it. "All that PASO has done is ruin friendships and tarnish leaders," said Idar, adding that *la raza* was not ready for the concept of PASO.[4]

The departure of those leaders created problems that PASO could not completely overcome. García's leaving meant that the organization had lost its most tenacious advocate, the one person who remained a "national" leader. García also took with him most of the Forum leadership and the rank-and-file members who had been the backbone of the Viva Kennedy Clubs and PASO. His fellow reformers were the most experienced in voter registration, get-out-the-vote drives, and in the electoral process. They were known in their communities, and many were veterans of numerous desegregation and anti-discrimination battles. The Forum newspaper had served as the one consistently published medium that publicized and promoted PASO. García and other Forum leaders were also good at getting positive media coverage. They did not seem to threaten the Anglo American mainstream as much as PASO now did. Also, García had an amiable relationship with the president and particularly the vice-president.

Losing Congressman González's empathy meant that PASO would not have the highest-ranking Mexican American politician in the state supporting its agenda. In fact, with the Peña-González feud, the potential for a strong backlash against PASO existed. Those who had clashed with González in the past knew him to be an a unbeatable foe. And González would prove quite quickly that he tolerated no opposition.[5] The fact that he was extremely popular among Mexican Americans statewide and also could garner significant Anglo American support meant that PASO had an opponent who could undermine their efforts. González's defection also meant that another political option existed for Mexican Americans not ready to endorse PASO's direction.

The congressman from San Antonio was an integrationist who opposed ethnic politics and articulated a pluralist philosophy that down-played racial and ethnic barriers to full citizenship.[6] Throughout his career, González had run as a liberal, not as a Mexican American. Without playing the ethnic card publicly, he had still managed to become a hero to many Mexican Americans seeking racial and ethnic pride. PASO's efforts to define a Mexican American political agenda without the major Mexican American politician in the state undermined its credibility by implying that a tireless reformer like González could not stomach the new militancy.

Without Idar, PASO lost one of its most prolific writers. His ability to analyze the issues affecting Mexican Americans was something that PASO needed badly. Peña was not a writer. He was more the orator who could rally the troops. Fuentes was much like Peña, though he lacked the latter's ability to form alliances. George I. Sánchez, whose writings were a strong foundation for PASO, never assumed a leadership role in the organization, being too independent to be limited by PASO's decisions. Though one of the most radical of the PASO members, he was more a product of an earlier age when reform activity among Mexican Americans did not require such organizational loyalty. While he was the prototype for PASO, he was quite spent by the early 1960s. By the second PASO convention his health was declining and he was less able to articulate the new militancy with the fervor of earlier years, though in many ways he was more militant than ever. Without his intellect and his scholarly background, the organization lost the one reformer who could provide historicity and a philosophical, if not ideological, context to PASO's reform activities. Sánchez's liberalism, like that of Peña, was intellectual and philosophical, whereas liberalism for many others was a political and tactical focus. He was the one reformer aside from Peña who remained committed to both his liberalism and his membership in PASO.

The loss of the Bonillas meant that along with the American G.I. Forum, PASO would also lose supporters from LULAC, which was greatly influenced by the Bonilla family.[7] The loss of the two major national organizations robbed PASO of the human resources and organizational experience that it needed as a new group. It also meant that the loyalty of the Mexican American community would be split between the organizations. That split also diminished the potential leadership. One consequence turned out to be that Peña would be the only real leader PASO had until its death in the early 1970s.

The loss of those strong personalities and their followers meant that PASO would take the characteristics of its two main leaders, Peña and Fuentes. There would be several consequences to this situation. With such strong personalities, the organization became top-heavy in influence. PASO also stopped developing structurally as both Peña and Fuentes were more adept at using the organization as a forum than they were at using it as a collective force. They both had electoral battles to contend with, and they both spent a lot of time building coalitions with African Americans, labor people, and liberals.[8]

Both, while popular among some liberals and many Mexican Americans, were not well received by the media and mainstream Anglo American politicians. They were too bombastic and confrontational, and they often enjoyed shocking their opponents and sometimes their followers. Interestingly, neither man was as popular with working-class Mexican Americans as with the militant middle class. Both leaders came across as being too Americanized. Peña, particularly, spoke his Spanish with a Texas accent and tended to use rhetoric devoid of nationalist symbolism.

Unlike some of the other reformers, Peña came from a middle-class family, so he lacked a personal knowledge of what "Corky" Gonzales would years later call the "mud . . . dirt . . . and blood of the urban [working-class] experience."[9] This class-constricted experience meant that Peña's concerns for his people grew out of his liberal politics, his ethnic pride, and his perceptions of the problems of the barrio and not from personal experience. His middle-class background would sustain a cultural gap between Peña and the working-class *raza* that rarely followed his middle-class crusades. Ironically, it would be the Chicano Movement leaders that enhanced his status among working-class Chicanos because of his support for them and his willingness to suffer politically for that support, while others of his generation turned against these new militants.[10] Interestingly, with the slow demise of PASO, Peña was freed to become the wandering reformer, speaking to all the important issues of the barrio and calling for Mexican American unity among those who would listen.

Another dilemma for the new PASO resulted from the fact that the leadership emphasized victimization based on statistics and constitutional rights rather than on ideology or morality. As a political organization, PASO saw solutions to the problems of the barrio coming through the ballot or through the leadership of Mexican Americans. Since PASO's political views were mainstream, with a touch of militancy, there were no fundamental solutions other than electing "liberal-minded" Mexican Americans. The Crystal City fiasco had revealed PASO's reliance on traditional American-style politics. The overwhelming concern in the election of 1963 had been to win. But once *los cinco* won, no more assistance came from PASO. After all, victory had been the ultimate goal. Martín García, PASO's front man in Crystal City, would later lament this strategy, saying, "We taught them how to win but we did not teach them how to govern."[11] PASO leaders did not know how to lead any other way; they simply did what they had seen Anglo Americans do. Their "deviation" from traditional politicians' practice meant giving Mexican Americans more jobs, firing Anglo American racists, and seeking federal intervention in the barrio.

In none of their political statements did they outline a political approach that differed much from traditional American politics. They could not, for by Idar's own admission, they were liberals rather than radicals.[12] In neither the Texas Viva Kennedy Club statement nor Sánchez's article, "The American of Mexican Descent," did they present a vision of governance. Rather, they identified problems, placed blame, and then sought redress from government or the American people. Given that situation, it is not difficult to see why they often reiterated their status as "subject-people." In the minds of more radical nationalists or leftists, the concept of "subject-people" would have been the basis for a profound critique of American society. But for the PASO leaders, subject-people remained a descriptor of the present condition. While based on the military conquest and past violence and discrimination, the term subject-people represented no ideological interpretation of the American political or social past. Even Sánchez's efforts to provide the term historicity did not enhance the ideological meanings of the word because its historical context did not fundamentally differ from traditional American history.[13]

PASO had been an attempt to go beyond simple integration and upward mobility. The organization sought empowerment by uniting Mexican Americans under an umbrella that could control hundreds of thousands of votes and dozens of elected officials. Through this unity, they could negotiate for concessions; they could coalesce with other groups; and they could elect their own to public office. PASO spoke to more than a hundred years of seeking unity. But in the end PASO failed to unite Mexican Americans into a political force that would stay together on the issues and on the candidates. One of the reasons for this failure was the lack of an ideological base. The Viva Kennedy Club movement had been successful for three major reasons. It was short in duration, there were no divisive issues, and each locality had been given a free hand to conduct the campaign as it wished. A fourth important reason was that Kennedy stood outside the community of reformers and thus was not part of any faction nor did he represent a particular strategy that might cause conflict.[14] He also represented power and national prominence, something most reformers admired and desired for their communities.

Chicano activists of later years would accuse the reformers of "hero-worshiping" powerful and charismatic Anglo American politicians. This criticism is probably inaccurate, since those Viva Kennedy people were often fierce critics of Anglo American politicians, including Kennedy. They were often unrelenting in their criticism of rural town bosses, urban political machines, and both conservative and liberal party officials. But the criticism did touch on the irony that these reformers' fiercest battles often developed over which Anglo American politician to support or whether to support one at all. Loyalty to their preferred non–Mexican American politician often seemed to take precedence over group solidarity. This resulted from the lack of an ideology and the pursuit of political strategies that were often connected to one Anglo American politician or another. Without a firm base of political beliefs, they were forced to choose from a variety of approaches that were initially meant to resolve problems or empower interest groups outside the barrio.

PASO could not function as the Viva Kennedy Clubs had. The crusades in which they sought to involve themselves were not going to be of short duration. Even the gubernatorial campaigns were long-range affairs as the reformers sought to work closely with the elected candidates in order to make changes in those laws and practices which adversely affected Mexican Americans. To work toward long-range goals, one needs a vision for the future. PASO, however, could not develop any vision beyond some general observations of their people's status and abilities. Without a comprehensive and profound vision of ethnic solidarity, they could not keep their ranks united when divisive issues came along. There were simply no profoundly held beliefs and no enforcement mechanism to keep the membership together.

The long tradition of each locality being autonomous played into the hands of those politicians who sought to keep Mexican Americans from uniting into a powerful political force. Local, regional, and state boundaries had grown rigid over the years. And so had philosophical and political boundaries. Mexican Americans were not only separated from their brothers and sisters to the south, they were also divided from those outside their areas of activism. Isolated from each other and dependent on the issue of what they could get for their communities, some Mexican American leaders were forced to play *cacique* politics—that is, they served as power brokers by offering their small constituencies to the statewide coalitions that vied for power at the state level. Over time, politics became personalized, and thus outside politicians had a link—in the person of the community leader—to whatever part of that community did participate in electoral politics. In this sense, some PASO leaders would become the new *politicos* in the barrio.[15]

The unity over the Kennedy crusade had provided a false illusion of ethnic solidarity. This illusion had evolved on the false premise that the Viva Kennedy campaign had been a campaign of reform, a tying-in of all the disparate efforts that had been going on in the barrio for decades. The reality was that the Kennedy Democrats had not engaged in any real reform movement. They had mostly preached to the choir. By campaigning among their people, most of whom were Democrats, and promoting an agenda that did not fundamentally question American society, they avoided major debates among themselves and with established Democratic Party leaders. By declaring their needs but not demanding solutions, they became part of the pool of victims which the Democratic Party used to point to bad Republican government and insensitivity. Had the Viva Kennedy reformers participated in the primaries or in choosing the nominee, they would have had to negotiate with the candidates and taken stronger positions on the issues. But having the candidate thrust on them, they were forced to integrate the Kennedy platform into the context of the barrio's needs. This interpretation had no competing parts; Viva Kennedy leaders could thus claim unity of purpose.

When the PASO leadership sought to become more than just a Democratic Party constituency, they confronted some new problems and revived old ones. They quickly ran afoul of the party establishment, with both conservatives and liberals undermining any potential power that PASO could accumulate. The unity-at-all-cost approach quickly revived divisions that had existed for years and challenged the autonomy that most local reformers had long cherished. In becoming power brokers rather than supporters, these reformers and their followers were choosing the political players instead of confirming one over the other. Power brokering was a new experience for which many were not ready. Idar would lament years later that "many who had never worked together" were brought together too quickly and without training to make important decisions.[16] Without a clear vision and without any indoctrination, each reformer brought his or her experiences as the basis for their choice of candidates to endorse or political strategy to follow. PASO simply became a forum for competing interests and a place to debate ideas on reform.

It is important to note here that the concept of ethnic politics was a difficult one for many Mexican American reformers. Some, like Bob Sánchez (see preceding chapter), were supportive of bloc voting only as a way to crack barriers to Mexican Americans political participation, not as a long-range strategy. There were others, however, who shunned the ethnic strategy because they believed Mexican Americans were neither ready for nor capable of leadership. Said reformer Roman Barrera of Robstown, Texas, in a letter to García, "If a Figueroa announced for a position, I think our people would be better off to defeat him, than to be embarrassed later by incompetency and lack of integrity." Barrera believed that with time and because of "newspapers, radio, and television," the people of Robstown would progress and become good citizens. Unlike Chicano activists of a few years later, Barrera believed that Mexican Americans would be better off the more they Americanized.[17]

It is possible that with resources and a united core of leaders some of the problems might have been overcome and the organization might have attracted even people such as Barrera, but PASO had neither. Unlike the American G.I. Forum and LULAC, which could sustain their activities on yearly membership fees and local fund raising, PASO required a more generous flow of funds. PASO leaders were always hesitant in calling for more than a few dollars in membership fees, and any local fund raising placed them in competition with the large number of clubs and organizations that competed for the limited resources in the barrio.[18] Without a big name such as Congressman González, PASO could not attract much Anglo American money. The expansion of the PASO agenda meant an increased need for funds, and in the early 1960s the barrios did not have resources to give. Much of the cost of PASO fell on the shoulders of those who were professionals and had some economic stability, and there were simply not enough of them. This may be one other reason why Peña remained the only leader of PASO. As a county commissioner, he had the schedule flexibility and financial stability needed to be politically active.

The lack of a core leadership, as discussed before, made PASO less an organization and more a following of reformers, as Peña and Fuentes became the primary and secondary statewide leaders of the group. The strength of the Mexican American reform movement had depended on the fortitude of a few individuals willing to put all their efforts and resources into civil reform. To sustain a civil-rights or political organization without finding a new alternative to this individually based reform became extremely difficult, and in the end PASO succumbed to the leadership of one man. Coincidentally, while Peña remained the *caudillo* (strong leader), his arms-length approach to directing the statewide organization meant that few local PASO chapters ever received the necessary training. Peña was an organizer who could rally people effectively around important issues, but his own political battles and political style prevented him from being a sustainer of organizations. Like a Chicano Johnny Appleseed, he planted many a Chicano revolution but left the structuring to others.

At this moment, it would be appropriate to recognize that PASO did not simply self-destruct as much as it fell victim to two powerful forces, which it was partly responsible for creating. First, PASO's militancy brought a backlash from those in power who feared a Mexican American challenge to the political status quo. Their response to PASO ranged from disdain to mockery to outright electoral or political challenges to remove PASO leaders from power.[19] The most effective way for Anglos to discredit the group was to question their "appropriateness" and legitimacy. Since appropriateness and legitimacy were important to PASO members, this strategy proved effective in creating factions within the organization and in driving out of the group those who did not want to be seen in that negative light.[20]

The second force that helped to marginalize PASO was the emergence of the Chicano Movement. This new force in the barrio had been, in part, the result of heightened expectations created by PASO activism. Once many realized that the legitimate, jockeying-for-position approach of organizations like PASO did not create change quickly enough, they looked toward other groups for leadership to combat Anglo American intransigence. The Movement organizations, unrestrained by moderate rhetoric or alliances with Anglo Americans, attracted many who were ready for confrontation. The Movement recruited some of the more militant PASO members; more important, it co-opted future members by organizing the youth in the barrio, something PASO had failed to do because it placed a premium on professionals and on citizenship.[21] The new militancy also shifted media attention away from PASO reformers as Chicano activists became better copy and a more ominous enemy to the political establishment. This shift would eventually open up the political doors for the Viva Kennedy constituency and other Mexican American Hispanics. But by this time, some of the fire had diminished as they sought to dissociate themselves from Chicano radicalism.[22]

When Chicano activists began attacking them for being *vendidos,* many of the long-time reformers were forced to cooperate with some of the same politicians they had fought against in the past. They had to reevaluate their own perception of American society. The Chicano Movement activists' questioning of the fundamental goodness of American society meant that those reformers who were loyal Americans were supporting an immoral society. These attacks forced many of the old militants to choose or reject the political status quo. Politicians like Henry B. González, Raul Castro, and others chose to fight the new militants. Reformers like García and the Bonillas found themselves in competition with the new militants, and their responses varied from disdain to open hostility.[23] While many continued to engage in their reform activities, the new challenge destroyed any hope they had of creating a united Mexican American community that fought for inclusion in American society. Their hopes of a social and political Camelot succumbed to the schisms of the barrio.

PASO, however, should not be dismissed as a do-nothing organization. While it did not win many races at the statewide level, it did serve as a catalyst for Mexican Americans to take control of a number of small communities.[24] It also served as a training ground for Mexican American reformers, some of whom became Chicano Movement radicals or joined the liberal wing of the Democratic Party. In the end, the Viva Kennedy movement and the formation of PASO profoundly affected the course of Mexican American politics.

There were three major effects of this political reform movement: it made Mexican Americans more dependent on Anglo American national leaders even as it promoted grassroots leadership; it nationalized Mexican American political activism; and it politicized the Mexican American reform agenda. These three changes would differentiate Mexican American political thought from that of the past. The Viva Kennedy people would not necessarily initiate those changes, but they certainly would accomplish them more thoroughly than any political generation before them. These changes would serve to move Mexican Americans, particularly those in the middle class, closer to American society. If they did not necessarily open new avenues for them, they at least provided them with higher expectations about what they could attain outside the barrio.

Becoming more dependent on national Anglo American leaders for the progress of the barrio and their own careers was a double-edged sword. The Viva Kennedy Club campaign allowed a number of Mexican American leaders to meet, associate, and correspond with politicians outside their states. These opportunities proved beneficial in that Mexican Americans could promote their agenda among Anglo American political leaders who were not competing with them for the votes of barrio residents. These national leaders then had an opportunity to meet the best and the brightest that the middle-class sector of the barrio could provide them. Since most were loyal Democrats who claimed to represent a united constituency, they were seen as valuable resources. The fact that these individuals did not have much experience in negotiating meant that they really demanded little. Even the clamoring for appointments was done in the public arena where it could be dismissed as public posturing. In private meetings and in correspondence they were cordial and accommodating. Mexican American leaders on the whole remained timid and reverential toward the president and other national leaders even as they fumed over their neglect.[25]

For Viva Kennedy leaders the association with national leaders served a purpose. It made Mexican Americans a permanent part of the pool of potential appointees for federal jobs and foreign-service appointments. As few as the Kennedy appointments were, they were the first by a presidential administration, and they would not be the last. In time, the Republicans would also look toward the Mexican American community for potential appointees. For the Viva Kennedy people, this was a major victory, and while it remained a point of contention with each succeeding administration, it did show that the political ceiling had risen because of their electoral efforts. At the national level there was finally recognition that Mexican Americans could serve in positions of authority and prominence.

The Viva Kennedy campaign and PASO and MAPA's efforts made Mexican Americans a national constituency that could not be completely ignored. After Viva Kennedy would come Viva Johnson, Viva Humphrey, Viva Mondale, and on to Adelante Clinton.[26] Mexican American endorsements and votes would become an important part of any Democratic Party constituency and eventually even that of the Republicans. Even a staunch conservative like Barry Goldwater would have a highly devoted campaign support group of Mexican Americans.[27] This recruitment effort by the established parties meant campaign jobs, low-level as well as cabinet-level appointments, and a forum in which to discuss the problems of the Mexican American community.

The second effect of the association with national leaders was that certain Mexican American reformers would be anointed as the "national" leaders of the community, and these individuals would receive the benefits of that identification. Reformers such as Roybal, González, Peña, Montoya, García, and others received support in their electoral efforts, were provided a national forum for their reform activities, and were included in discussions pertaining to the Mexican American community. This relationship affirmed their leadership in the community and, for some, guaranteed that they would not confront serious Anglo American Democratic Party challenges to their re-election. Their relationship also had the effect of legitimizing reform activities as individuals such as Peña, García, and others regularly placed their efforts under the umbrella of the national liberal Democrats. For a community with few elected officials, the nationalization of their leadership was a great accomplishment.

Association with national leaders, however, led to dependence on them, and many of the major schisms among these reformers were over which leader to follow. Many Mexican American reformers moved from seeing grassroots organizing as the key to resolving the problems in the barrio to depending on the right politician at the state level and the right administration in Washington, D.C. While the American G.I. Forum and LULAC would renew their activist efforts in the mid-1970s, many of their leaders would continue to clamor for government assistance. They became susceptible, as had the barrio politicians of the past, to the wooing of any Anglo American politician who invested time and money and who could call upon the memory of the late John F. Kennedy. The more charismatic or the more liberal these politicians, the more successful they were in gaining Mexican American leaders' endorsements. This situation would make it difficult for Mexican American candidates to win races against charismatic liberal or moderate Anglo American candidates. Not until Mexican American candidates began emulating the Kennedy style would they start winning statewide or regional races.[28]

Another dilemma of this dependence would be a short collective memory among Mexican American leadership. For those who promoted their national ties, few Mexican Americans measured up except those who played their politics at the national level. That is why González, Roybal, and Montoya became the most successful and prominent leaders even as their national responsibilities often took them away from the issues of the barrio. And that is why many grassroots leaders would not be "rediscovered" until the Chicano Movement's scholars began to look away from state houses and national politics and to the barrio for its heroes. The dependence on Anglo American politicians by low-level Mexican American politicos and reformers made them vulnerable to the nationalism of the barrios in the 1960s and 1970s. It would also create a schism between the nationalistic working class/student alliance and the accommodating, moderately liberal middle-class reformers. Only Peña, Sánchez, and to some extent Roybal would bridge the gap.

The concern with national links did serve to make the Mexican American reform agenda a national one. There had been numerous efforts before at organizing national structures, but they had all succumbed to red-baiting, lack of resources, ideological schisms, and lack of communication. The national PASO would succumb to the same problems, but the legacy of the Viva Kennedy movement, the political appointments, and the recognition that Mexican Americans were now an important electoral constituency made the national links stronger. It would take the Chicano Movement to truly promote the sense of nationhood at the barrio level, but for many politically active middle-class Mexican Americans, the connection now existed. They could point to Roybal in California; Montoya in New Mexico; González, Peña, and García in Texas; Raul Castro in Arizona; and the Mexican communities in the Midwest as evidence that Mexican Americans were "everywhere" and that they faced the same challenges. Mexican American leaders of each state and locality became leaders for all the communities. Even the federal government recognized this national agenda when it called a national meeting of Spanish-speaking leaders in El Paso in 1967 and established the Inter-Agency Committee on Mexican American Affairs.[29]

The third major effect of the Viva Kennedy, MAPA, and PASO efforts was to politicize the Mexican American reform agenda. Politics became the most important part of the reform strategy. While desegregation campaigns continued to attract much support and many individuals, political campaigns became more important because of the increasing number of victories by Mexican American candidates. The most articulate and educated began to look toward the political arena, and their rhetoric became the language of political solutions. This meant that mass participation became less important and individual leadership became more significant.

As Mexican Americans politicized the reform agenda, they de-moralized it. In the past, Mexican and Mexican American reformers had argued for a moral alternative to their situation. Anglo Americans had been immoral in their treatment of Mexicans and in denying them their basic rights by using legal loopholes. Since Mexicans and Mexican Americans were human beings, workers, and often citizens, they merited respect on those counts. As early as the 1920s, however, Mexican American reformers had begun moving away from the moral approach toward constitutional and legal challenges.[30] The Viva Kennedy movement would add the political to the constitutional and legal approach, formulating a strategy based on citizenship or residency and on ability to vote. In doing this the Viva Kennedy reformers created a sharper dichotomy. While they recognized their ethnicity in order to create a voting bloc, they endorsed an Americanism that depended on a lessening of ties to their country of origin. In promoting their own for foreign-policy posts, they were aligning themselves with a political strategy that proved unpopular in Latin America over the next two decades. Interestingly, the anti-American movements in Latin America would provide fuel for Chicano nationalism that attacked American foreign policy as imperialistic.[31]

In moving toward politics, Kennedy Democrats also abandoned any intent some of them might have entertained of making fundamental changes in American society. The American political system in the early 1960s was a system still embroiled in the Cold War. Many political decisions were made with one eye focused on the conflict between the United States and the Soviet Union. Those reformers who had seen combat were very conscious of the conflict and firmly committed to the American side to the extent that they sought integration into society and not a repudiation of it. Thus, political rhetoric which was more accommodating than accusatory became the language of the Kennedy Democrats. In many ways, it was a language devoid of history. It was a language of loyalty, of accommodation mixed with frustration and righteous indignation. In that sense, it was a rhetoric that contextualized activism into reform and away from fundamental change.

At this point, the Viva Kennedy effort might well be seen as a failure or even a political fantasy in which the search for a Mexican American Camelot proved to be as flawed as the one of English folklore. That is not the case, however. The Viva Kennedy movement and its subsequent off-shoots played a significant role in both American politics and in Mexican American reform efforts. The Viva Kennedy Clubs in 1960 forced the two major parties to expand their rhetoric of inclusion to Mexican Americans. Over the next three decades both political parties added Latinos to their staffs, fielded more Latino candidates, and engaged in public discussions over the problems affecting Mexican Americans and Latino barrios nationwide. While American politics have traditionally been the politics of black and white, political discussion since the 1960s has grudgingly been opened up to issues important to Mexican Americans and Latinos. Politicians have had to consider language, religion, and national-origins diversity as important, something which had not been previously been possible in the black/white dichotomy.

The Viva Kennedy Clubs and the PASO and MAPA reformers also forced American leaders to see Latin America in a new light. While these reformers may not have had a great influence in developing Kennedy's Latin American foreign policy, they did remind him that actions taken south of the border had political ramifications in the United States.[32] Their electoral participation also provided Kennedy the proof he needed to persuade Latin American countries that his administration represented a departure from those of the past. In the battle against communism, Mexican American participation re-affirmed American democracy's superiority to the Soviet Union's totalitarianism.

In the barrio, the Viva Kennedy movement provided an alternative to barrio politicians and labor and nationalist activism. For those Mexican Americans who sought integration—not necessarily assimilation—into the national mainstream, the new reform activism proved inviting. These reformers were better educated, articulated barrio concerns to Anglo American society better than previous politicos, and they were more in tune with the American political scene. Their political activity, although often militant and controversial, was not truly radical and did not usually bring the backlash that labor and nationalist activities did. The Viva Kennedy people may have criticized the status quo, but they were more than ready to join the mainstream if allowed. They presented no ideology that caused any ambivalence about loyalty to American society. For the majority of Mexican Americans who had been in the United States several generations, this new political orientation meant that they could seek to be part of the American mainstream without giving up who they were. Their militancy was rejected by some but welcomed by others who saw it as part of the larger American liberal constituency.

The new emphasis on ethnicity, while often used as a political tool (e.g., the threat of bloc voting), kept the nationalist fires smoldering in the barrio. Peña, Fuentes, and to a smaller extent Roybal, García, and Montoya continually emphasized national origins in the context of their Americanism. By the end of the 1960s, the organizations they headed or the issues in which they became involved promoted ethnic consciousness. The Kennedy Democrats, through their political activities, educated a new generation of young leaders who would follow them. José Angel Gutiérrez and Juan Patlán, two of the founders of the Mexican American Youth Organization, were involved in the Crystal City revolt of 1963.[33] Rodolfo "Corky" Gonzales, founder of the Crusade for Justice, headed the Viva Kennedy Club efforts in Colorado.[34] César Chávez, as a young social reformer for the Community Service Organization, also participated in a limited fashion but would be influenced greatly and remain a personal friend of the Kennedys. There would be countless others who became involved through the Viva Kennedy Clubs or through subsequent activities of former Club members. While most of these individuals radicalized their politics beyond the comfort level of the Kennedy Democrats, they would owe much of their early political awakenings to them.

These statements do not imply that the Viva Kennedy reformers were a transitional or precursor generation. Their value is not limited to creating the climate for the Chicano Movement. This was not their intent, and for some of them, the Chicano Movement represented a contradiction of their goals. Their intent was to integrate Mexican Americans into American society, but an American society that respected cultural pluralism and provided leadership opportunities for those seeking to serve their country. The integration would be not only social and political but also historical. After all, Mexican Americans had been "here" first, had helped build the railroads, mine the minerals, gather the crops, and fight in the great wars.[35] Americans of Mexican descent had always been loyal—Mexican American insurgency, labor unrest, nationalist-oriented reform, and so forth, had no place in the Viva Kennedy public historical record. Viva Kennedy reformers saw past injustices not as evidence of institutional or historical racism but as evidence of discrimination based on ignorance of Mexican American loyalty and contributions.

The Viva Kennedy constituency articulated a vision of America much more in step with the American historical narrative. They saw themselves as Americans and injected their diverse historical experience into the American narrative. Like Carlos Castañeda years earlier, they did not see their history as incompatible with the history of other American groups. They saw their future connected to the American future. They were not just satisfied with their citizenship and accessibility to American prosperity as had been the older Mexican American generation. They saw themselves as critical to the future of the United States. They believed that they represented a loyal constituency that could be counted on during times of war and one that could play a determining factor in national elections. They also perceived themselves as able to save American foreign policy in Latin America because they could speak the language and understand the culture. They could be America's best Cold War warriors south of the border.

These individuals defined their identity through their American experiences rather than through their Mexican origins. For this reason they should best be seen as intellectual precursors to the Mexican American/Hispanic Generation than to the Chicano Movement. This Mexican American/Hispanic Generation constitutes the most integrated Mexican American generation in history and one of the most ambitious in its search to gain the full benefits of American society. Its members are elected officials in the traditional Southwest as well as in such places as Kansas, Oregon, Washington, Illinois, and other nontraditional areas. Their ambition transcends the federal bureaucracy as they seek statewide political office and appointment to the Supreme Court and the president's cabinet. They have established lobby groups in Washington, D.C., and a Congressional Hispanic Caucus. And throughout the areas where they are a solid majority, they have won most of the elected offices. Finally, their leaders and organizations are watchdogs seeking to ensure that no racist stereotypes go unchallenged.[36]

These Mexican Americans are tenacious in promoting their Latino agenda. No doubt they are a hybrid of the two preceding generations, sharing similarities with both.[37] They mingled the politics of ethnicity with the language of inclusion. They are Chicanos, Latinos, and Hispanics, but they cling to their Americanism as it provides them the one qualification that the Chicano Generation—at least its most militant sector—did not celebrate. Yet, their ethnicity provides them their distinction, making them an electoral constituency that must be wooed in its own language and within its own political culture and which must be promised something more than the traditional political spoils. In a time of high-powered, well-financed special interest groups, Mexican American Hispanics are just learning the lobbying game as part of their national politics. They still lack the money and the political clout of smaller but more powerful groups, but their increasing numbers make them an "awakening giant" that grows larger every day.

In many of its fundamental characteristics, the Mexican American/ Hispanic Generation owes its agenda to the Viva Kennedy reformers. It was the Viva Kennedy constituency that more successfully developed the idea of a fully integrated Mexican American community, one whose sons and daughters would serve at the highest appointed levels, run successfully for political office, and represent American policy to the rest of the world. This integration would be political, social, economic, and historical but not ideological. Mexican Americans can be good citizens, and they can bring their music and food to the American fold but not their ideology. For that reason much of the Hispanic militancy is based on its search for inclusiveness, its ethnic pride, and its promotion of a welfare state that seeks to resolve the problems Mexican Americans face in such areas as employment, health, and education.

In this context, the Mexican American/Hispanic Generation retains the limitations of the Viva Kennedy generation. This generation has yet to develop an impetus for historical interpretation, cultural renaissance, or political ideology. Mexican American Hispanics, much like their Viva Kennedy counterparts, see historical integration as critical to Mexican American acceptance by the larger society. While they promote Chicano scholarship, they often fail to understand its alienation from traditional American historiography and simply use it to bolster their claim that Mexican Americans have been victims of American prejudice. They either do not know or choose to ignore that Chicano historians have sought to construct a counter-narrative to American history, and until recently the intent has rarely been to integrate Mexican Americans into U.S. history.[38]

The same situation applies to the arts. Mexican American Hispanics may use them to promote their ethnicity, but in reality Chicano arts are working-class-focused, and thus their historical artistic narrative usually excludes the history of the middle-class reformer. As Chicano writers and artists move toward the mainstream, the class consciousness of their work diminishes and becomes less ethnic and less historical. This shift is not a permanent phenomenon, but it is the present situation.

As for political ideology, that of the Mexican American/Hispanic Generation remains constricted by its concern with legitimacy and acceptability. It is also limited by the lack of a conceptual ideological landscape which sees Mexicans as more than immigrants lining up at the INS office waiting for citizenship, then moving through college and into suburbia. While Mexican American Hispanics might harbor grandiose dreams of a president who grew up in the barrio, they have yet to discern what this president might bring to the White House that is different from the person who grew up in a ghetto, in the suburbs, or on a reservation. Their promotion of the now-obvious fact that Latinos will become a major part of the U.S. population over the next two or three decades does not disguise the fact that they have yet to discuss profoundly what this would mean in socio-economic or geo-political terms. In fairness, this is a young generation, and there is much more intellectual and political development to take place. Also, this generation of Mexican American leaders must be accommodating toward other Latino leaders in developing political agendas, and that is a challenge unique to this generation of Mexican American reformers.[39] But recognizing this generation's non-ideological foundations—and those of the other Latino groups—the Mexican American Hispanic Generation will be hard-pressed to offer new ideas for the twenty-first century.

This should in no way, however, minimize the efforts and accomplishments of the Viva Kennedy reformers. We have dealt with their collective contributions, but there is much to appreciate in their individual efforts, and there is also much legacy there for future biographers. Hector P. García was a medical doctor who remained in the barrios of Corpus Christi, providing medical attention to many who would otherwise have gone without. He delivered thousands of babies, cured thousands others of untold ills while maintaining a reformer's agenda that would have been inconceivable for others. He was unrelenting in his battle to desegregate the public schools, promote Mexican Americans to positions of leadership, and support scholarship on Mexican Americans. He also served as a bridge to those in the Anglo American community interested in the welfare of Corpus Christi and South Texas barrio residents. The fact that he never gained economic security demonstrates his commitment to others before himself.

Albert Peña, Jr. fought Anglo American political bosses, Mexican American power brokers, and economic elites in San Antonio and South Texas, and he almost single-handedly sustained democracy in the barrios. His eventual loss of what would have been a "secure" political office in the barrio indicates how much he sacrificed. And even out of office and at great personal cost he continued speaking out against injustices to his people.[40] Of the Viva Kennedy generation, none will stand out as a more faithful friend of political democracy in the barrio than Peña. His commitment to defend the constitutional and legal rights of the *mexicano* earned him the respect of not only his own G.I. Generation but also that of the Chicano Movement and the current Hispanic Generation. When others of his generation sought to minimize the contributions of the Chicano activists or feared associating with them, Peña remained their advocate and at times their advisor. While other reformer friends retired and moved away from politics and reform, he has continued to work with new Hispanic reformers. While forever a "Kennedy Democrat," he was first, and still is, a Mexican American committed to his community.

Edward R. Roybal, once elected to Congress, remained a voice and a defender for *la raza*, helping to found the Congressional Hispanic Caucus to defend Hispanic interests in Washington, D.C. Joseph Montoya remained a progressive lone voice in Congress and initially welcomed the emerging Chicano Movement when he saw the intransigence of the American system. María Urquides became one of the precursors of bilingual education in the United States and a much beloved high-school teacher in Tucson, Arizona. The Bonilla brothers fought hard to rejuvenate LULAC and make it a legitimate reform organization in the late 1960s and 1970s, when most middle-class organizations had been eclipsed by the more militant Chicano Movement groups.

Henry B. González, though he parted company with many of his Viva Kennedy colleagues, remained a "Kennedy Democrat" throughout his life. He kept his commitment to American liberalism and to his *raza* constituency. In some ways he lost step with both Mexican American reformers and Anglo American liberals, but he remained a powerful symbol of Mexican American achievement. Over time, most of his Viva Kennedy opponents learned to accommodate his maverick politics and again honored him as a great Mexican American leader.

There were many others who left a personal legacy in the barrios of the Southwest, Midwest, and every other place where Mexican Americans lived. These men and women joined preceding generations in fighting for others who could not articulate their oppression. With varying degrees they again disproved two prevailing notions about Mexican Americans. First, they re-affirmed that Mexican Americans had not been nor were they now passive in the face of discrimination and oppression. Like individuals and groups of the past, they refused to accept second-class citizenship because of their ethnicity, and in the process they affirmed their ethnic pride. Second, they again proved that the American formula for acceptance—assimilation, patriotism, education, and electoral participation—worked for certain individuals but proved inadequate for the whole of the Mexican American community. These men and women had cast their lot with the "American way," but still their communities suffered neglect. In the end, this situation says more about American society than it does about their own abilities as reformers.

The pluralistic and inclusive America in which they believed remains a nation divided by race and class issues. Chicano history remains absent from most classrooms, bilingual education is under attack, and Mexican immigrants—both legal and undocumented—remain unwelcome in many quarters. And many Americans political leaders continue to speak in terms of black and white in spite of the fact that Latinos will soon be the largest recognizable ethnic group in the United States. This was not the Camelot that Viva Kennedy leaders envisioned. Their dream remains mostly unfulfilled, but their story is another testament to the *mexicano's* quest to find his and her niche in American society and to their tenacity in achieving it with dignity and pride.

Notes

CHAPTER 1

1. "Better Civilizations," *Life* (December 28, 1959); see also "How America Feels as We Enter the Soaring Sixties," *Look* (January 5, 1960). For a short discussion on American liberalism by the beginning of the 1960s, see Allen J. Matusow, *The Unraveling of America: A History of Liberalism in the Sixties;* Daniel Bell, *The End of Ideology: On the Exhaustion of Political Ideas in the Fifties;* see also *The End of Ideology Debate,* ed. Chaim I. Waxman.

2. The term Anglo American is used here to denote most white Americans. While the term is problematic, it is the one most likely to convey the author's intended classification.

3. For a discussion on how Mexican Americans have been treated in American historical literature, see Rodolfo Acuña, *Occupied America: A History of Chicanos,* 2d ed., 3; and Juan Gómez-Quiñones, *Roots of Chicano Politics, 1600–1940,* vii–xiii; also, see Octavio Romano's "The Anthropology and Sociology of the Mexican American: The Distortion of Mexican American History," *El Grito* 2 (1968): 13–15.

4. I heard Guerra say this during a political rally in the summer of 1972, in San Antonio, Texas.

5. Leo Grebler, Joan W. Moore, and Ralph C. Guzmán, *The Mexican American People: The Nation's Second Largest Minority.* This is still the best comprehensive work on Mexican Americans and their economic, social, and educational situation in the major urban centers of the Southwest.

6. See Ralph C. Guzmán, *The Political Socialization of the Mexican American People,* especially chaps. 5–7, for a discussion of such organizations and their efforts; see also, Juan Gómez-Quiñones, *Chicano Politics: Reality & Promise, 1940–1990,* 31–99.

7. See Mario T. García, *Mexican Americans: Leadership, Ideology and Identity, 1930–1960;* Richard A. Garcia, *Rise of the Mexican American Middle Class: San Antonio, 1929–1941;* and Guadalupe San Miguel, Jr., *"Let All of Them Take Heed": Mexican Americans and the Campaign for Educational Equality in Texas, 1910–1981,* for a discussion of Mexican American middle-class reform activity from the 1920s to the 1960s.

8. Acuña, *Occupied America,* 123–54, 299–340; Emilio Zamora, *The World of the Mexican Worker in Texas,* 197–210.

9. Ibid.; see also, Vicki L. Ruiz, *Cannery Women, Cannery Lives: Mexican Women, Unionization, and the California Food Processing Industry,* 44–57.

10. M. T. García, *Mexican Americans,* 25–61; Gómez-Quiñones, *Chicano Politics,* 53–74.

11. For a discussion of the Mexican American veterans' attitudes during the war years and afterward, see Raúl Morín, *Among the Valiant: Mexican Americans in World War II and Korea;* Carl Allsup, *The American G.I. Forum: Origins and Evolution;* and Albert M. Camarrillo, "The G.I. Generation," *Aztlán* 2 (Fall 1971).

12. Ibid.

13. See Stephen J. Whitfield, *The Culture of the Cold War (The American Moment),* 2d ed., 91–99, for a discussion of Catholic anti-communism. See also John Cooney's *The American Pope: The Life and Times of Francis Cardinal Spellman;* and Donald F. Crosby, *God, Church, and the Flag: Senator Joseph R. McCarthy and the Catholic Church, 1950–1957,* for a history of American Catholicism's most ardent Cold War warrior.

14. Jay P. Dolan and Allan Figueroa Deck, eds., *Hispanic Catholic Culture in the U.S.: Issues and Concerns,* 77–130, 281–86; see also Cassian Yuhas, ed., *The Catholic Church and American Culture,* 90–108.

15. Ibid.

16. For a discussion of the surveillance of the Mexican American community, see José Angel Gutiérrez, "Chicanos and Mexicans under Surveillance: 1940–1980," *Renato Rosaldo Lecture Series Monograph* (Spring 1986), 29–58.

17. M. T. García, *Mexican Americans,* 25–61.

18. For an outstanding analysis of these types of novels and how they depicted the barrio residents, see Marcienne Rocard, *The Children of the Sun,* 109–85.

19. Ibid.

20. Ibid.

21. See Ronnie Dugger, "Who Lay Unnamed," *Texas Observer* (February 14, 1958): 1.

22. "Let Juan Do It for You," *Desert Magazine* 19 (July, 1956): 27–28.

23. For works by scholars sympathetic to yet pointed in their criticism of Mexican Americans, see Ruth Tuck, *Not with the Fist;* Edmonson S. Munro, *Los Manitos: A Study of Institutional Values;* William Madsen, *Mexican Americans of South Texas;* and Emory Bogardus, *The Mexican in the United States.*

24. For analyses of stereotypic works written on Mexican Americans in the 1950s and early 1960s, see Romano, "Anthropology and Sociology of the Mexican American"; "Editorial," *El Grito* 1 (1967): 4; and Ignacio M. García, *Chicanismo: The Forging of a Militant Ethos among Mexican Americans,* 43–67.

25. For works that reveal some of these reformers' misgivings about their own people, read George I. Sánchez, *Forgotten People: A Study of New Mexicans;* Guzmán, *Political Socialization of the Mexican American People;* Ernesto Galarza, *Strangers in Our Fields;* and Julian Samora, ed., *La Raza/Forgotten Americans.* These books are strong advocates for Mexican American rights, but a closer look reveals that the authors accept and repeat some of the stereotypes that Anglo Americans applied to people in the barrio. The books also indicate the authors' frustration with their people's inability to overcome their circumstances. Given the conditions of Mexican Americans in the 1950s and early 1960s, the authors' frustration is understandable.

26. Whitfield, *Culture of the Cold War,* 169–70.

27. For a discussion of Mexican Americans in film, see Gary D. Keller, ed., *Chicano Cinema: Research, Reviews and Resources;* Chon A. Noriega, ed., *Chicanos and Film: Essays on Chicano Representation and Resistance;* and Juan R. García, "Hollywood and the West: Mexican Images in American Film," in *Old Southwest, New Southwest,* ed. Judy Nolte Lensink.

28. Felix F. Gutiérrez and Jorge Reina Schement, *Spanish-Language Radio in the Southwestern United States,* 4–15.

29. Robert Somerville Graham, "Spanish-Language Radio in Northern Colorado," *American Speech* (October, 1962): 211.

30. See Thomas E. Sheridan, *Los Tucsonenses: The Mexican Community in Tucson, 1854– 1941,* 93–110, for a discussion of this line of thinking in Arizona at the turn of the century. Also, see M. T. García, *Mexican Americans,* 2–22. García is not willing to concede that these individuals were assimilationists; rather, he argues that they were pluralists seeking to make the best of their situation.

31. See Vicki L. Ruiz's article "'Star Struck': Acculturation, Adolescence, and the Mexican American Woman, 1920–1950," in *Building with Our Hands: New Directions in Chicana Studies,* ed. Adela de la Torre and Beatríz M. Pesquera, 109–29.

32. In the Mexican barrios, the high school was the "American" institution. In my own high-school years, I saw many former students join the numerous social clubs for graduates that kept them involved in school activities and as role models, thus extending their high-school years. Barred from achieving much outside of high

school, the ex-students created their own Mexican American world in the social clubs, the football games, the after-school carnivals, and a host of other school-related activities.

33. See Richard Rodriguez, *Hunger of Memory: The Education of Richard Rodriguez*, 19–32. While I do not agree with the author's arguments, he is one of the few Mexican American writers who is willing to admit to the dichotomy of language experience that many Mexican Americans confront in American society. See Ernesto Galarza's *Barrio Boy* and Mario T. García's *Memories of Chicano History: The Life and Narrative of Bert Corona.* Both Galarza and Corona imply that this dichotomy existed in their own lives.

34. See Elizabeth A. Fones-Wolf, *Selling Free Enterprise: The Business Assault on Labor and Liberalism, 1945–1960.*

35. M. T. García, *Mexican Americans,* 2–22.

36. Ruiz, "Star Struck," 112.

37. Gómez-Quiñones, *Chicano Politics,* 32.

38. Ruiz, "Star Struck," 112–18.

39. For an excellent but succinct discussion of the border, see Oscar J. Martínez, *Troublesome Border.* For a more popularized view of the border, see Tom Miller, *On the Border: Portraits of America's Southwestern Frontier.*

40. Carlos Monsiváis, "La Utopia Indocumentada: La Cultura Mexicana de los Noventas," *Renato Rosaldo Lecture Series Monograph* 9 (1993): 51–60; see also Alan Riding, *Distant Neighbors: A Portrait of the Mexicans,* 42–58.

41. For years, as a child growing up watching English-language movies at the barrio theater, I saw most of the movie characters as looking more like me than the Anglo American youth I met in the east side of San Antonio.

42. San Miguel, *"Let All of Them Take Heed,"* 103–108.

43. M. T. García, *Mexican Americans,* 231–51; also, see Ralph C. Guzmán, "The Function of Anglo-American Racism in the Political Development of Chicanos," *California Historical Quarterly* 50, no. 1 (1971): 321–37, Ozzie G. Simmons, "The Mutual Images and Expectations of Anglo-Americans and Mexican-Americans," *Daedalus* (spring, 1961): 286–99; and Carlos E. Castañeda, "Why I Chose History," *The Americas* (April, 1952).

44. Castañeda, "Why I Chose History," 252–72; also, George I. Sánchez, "Bilingualism and Mental Measure: A Word of Caution," *Journal of Applied Psychology* 18 (December, 1934).

45. See Galarza, *Strangers in Our Fields,* for a short history of his work among farm workers.

46. Hector P. García, letter to Manuel Avila, Jr., September 18, 1961, Dr. Hector P. García Papers, Special Collections and Archives, Bell Library, Texas A&M University–Corpus Christi.

47. This unattributed quote can be found in Carlos Muñoz, Jr., *Youth, Identity, Power: The Chicano Movement,* 33.

48. Hector P. García, "South Texas War Dead Have Returned," open letter to Corpus Christi, dated 1947 (no month or day given), García Papers.

49. See undated *Bulletin* of the Civic Action Committee. The Committee was the main organization of Mexican American reformers in Houston, Texas. Copies of the organization's documents, including the bulletins, can be found in the archives of the Houston Metropolitan Research Center of the Houston Public Library.

50. See "A Pessimistic View," *Texas Observer* (December, 1960). This article is an excerpt from an address by Sánchez to the Austin Human Relations Commission. Date of address is unknown.

51. John R. Martínez, "Leadership and Politics," in *La Raza/Forgotten Americans*, 47–62.

52. Donald N. Barrett, "Demographic Characteristics" in *La Raza/Forgotten Americans*, 159–200.

53. For more on Roybal's campaigns, see Beatrice W. Griffith, "Viva Roybal—Viva America," *Common Ground* 10 (August, 1949): 61–70; Kathleen Underwood, "Process and Politics: Multiracial Electoral Coalition Building and Representation in Los Angeles Ninth District, 1949–1962" (Ph.D. diss., University of California, San Diego, 1992); and María Linda Apodaca, "They Kept the Home Fires Burning: Mexican American Women and Social Change" (Ph.D. diss., University of California, Irvine, 1994).

54. Eugene Rodríguez, Jr., "Henry B. González: A Political Profile" (master's thesis, St. Mary's University, 1965).

CHAPTER 2

1. M. T. García, *Mexican Americans*, 200.

2. For a discussion of Republican efforts among Mexican Americans, see Richard Santillan and Federico A. Subervi-Vélez, "Latino Participation in Republican Party Politics in California," in *Racial and Ethnic Politics in California*, ed. Byran O. Jackson and Michael B. Preston, 285–319; and Richard Santillan and Carlos Muñoz, Jr., "Latinos and the Democratic Party," in *The Democrats Must Lead: The Case for a Progressive Democratic Party*, ed. James MacGregor Burns, William Crotty, Lois Lovelace Duke, and Lawrence D. Longley, 173–84.

3. Bell, *End of Ideology*.

4. Beyond recognizing that they were "here first," most reformers had little knowledge of their history and thus tended to see their circumstances within the context of American history. This despite Carlos Castañeda's multi-volume *Our Catholic Heritage in Texas, 1519–1936* and George I. Sánchez's *Forgotten People*.

5. For the story of the American G.I. Forum, see Allsup, *American G.I. Forum*.

6. "Statement of Dr. Hector P. García, Founder of the American G.I. Forum, to be Presented to the Democratic National Committee Nationalities Division," July 12, 1960, García Papers.

7. Ibid., 1.

8. Ibid.

9. Ibid.

10. Gilbert Casarez, interview with Veronica Hayes, Corpus Christi, Tex., summer 1996. Casarez would serve as one of García's most loyal lieutenants in the American G.I. Forum. He expressed the feelings of many veterans who found the armed services a friendly place during World War II. For similar thoughts, see introduction to Raúl Morín's *Among the Valiant.*

11. "Statement of Dr. Hector P. García," 1.

12. Reformers such as Henry B. González, Bert Corona, Ernesto Galarza, Ed Idar, Jr., and others recall conversations of the Mexican Revolution in their early years.

13. "Statement of Dr. Hector P. García," 2.

14. Ibid.

15. Albert Peña, Jr., interview with author, San Antonio, Tex., July 4, 1996.

16. "Peña Is Not in LBJ's Club," *Texas Observer* (December 15, 1959).

17. Peña quoted in "The Only Way I Want to Win," *Texas Observer* (July 4, 1959): 5.

18. Peña interview.

19. Ibid.

20. Ibid.; "The Only Way I Want to Win."

21. Peña interview; "The Only Way I Want to Win."

22. Peña interview; "The Only Way I Want to Win."

23. "Confidential Report for Senator Lyndon Johnson by Dr. Hector Garcia," June 10, 1960, García Papers.

24. Ibid., 3.

25. Edward R. Roybal, telephone interview with author, August 12, 1997.

26. Ibid.

27. "Carlos McCormick Named Coordinator of National Viva Kennedy Clubs," *Forum News Bulletin,* August, 1960.

28. Peña interview.

29. Ibid. The elimination of the poll tax was an important issue for Mexican American reformers. See Henry B. González, "Poll Tax Primer: The Behead Tax," *Texas Observer* (October 18, 1963).

30. "Senator Joins G.I. Forum," *Forum News Bulletin,* May, 1960; "Senator Kennedy Sends Warm Message to G.I. Forum in Los Angeles," *Forum News Bulletin,* September, 1959; see also Hector P. García, letter to J. (John Carlos) McCormick, May 18, 1960, García Papers.

31. The document containing the convention resolutions is titled, "American G.I. Forum of the US National Convention, Wichita, Kansas," dated August 5–7, 1960, García Papers.

32. César Chávez was not a member of the Forum, but as an organizer for the Community Service Organization he was initially sympathetic to this type of reform activity. See Richard Griswold Del Castillo and Richard A. Garcia, *César Chávez: A Triumph of Spirit,* 22–40.

33. "American G.I. Forum of the US National Convention."

34. Ibid.

35. Ed Idar, Jr., telephone interview with author, March 15, 1996; see also chaps. 5–6 of Robert A. Cuellar's "A Social and Political History of the Mexican American Population in Texas, 1929–1963" (master's thesis, Texas State University, Denton, 1969).

36. Idar interview.

37. Santillan and Subervi-Vélez, "Latino Participation in Republican Party Politics."

38. Idar interview.

39. Ibid. This request for appointments had been part of García's statement to the Democratic Party delegates to the Los Angeles convention, and also part of the G.I. Forum national resolutions. See chap. 2, notes 6 and 31.

40. Peña interview.

41. Even the Amigos de Wallace effort had been regional, mostly focused on California. See chap. 2, note 1.

42. Peña interview; Idar interview.

43. Ibid.

44. Idar interview.

45. Ibid.

46. Albert Peña, Jr., letter to Ed Idar, Jr., dated August 17, 1960, in Idar's personal collection.

47. "Latin Americans Organize Viva Kennedy Committee," *Dallas News,* October 5, 1960.

48. "Anyone Can Be Organization Man in Current Campaign," *Herald-Telegram* (Chippewa Falls, Wisc.), October 3, 1960.

49. Warner F. Brock, letter to William Bonilla, dated September 28, 1960. See also the response of Tony Bonilla, letter to Warner F. Brock, October 4, 1960, both in the García Papers.

50. Idar interview.

51. Ibid.

52. Ed Idar, Jr., letter to Senator John F. Kennedy, dated August 31, 1960, García Papers.

53. For a discussion of Anglo American fears, see "Voting Drive for Latins Criticized," *Texas Observer* (November, 1955); see also Ed Idar, Jr., letter to Michael G. Hernandez, dated December 1, 1966, García Papers.

54. Idar letter to John F. Kennedy.

55. For other examples of these kinds of letters, see "To All Persons Interested in Helping in the Election of Senator John Kennedy and Senator Lyndon Johnson to the Presidency and the Vice Presidency of the U.S." (undated); and "Una Carta Para Todos Los Votantes de El Estado De Texas" (undated), both in García Papers. Also, see "Carlos McCormick Named Coordinator."

56. "Forumeers Participate as Individuals in 'Viva Clubs,'" *Forum News Bulletin,* October, 1960; also, see Hector P. García letter to Salvador Olalde of Fort Clinton, Ohio

(no date available, but likely to have been in October, 1960, or some where about), García Papers.

57. "Viva Kennedy Club Is Planned," *Corpus Christi Caller,* September 23, 1960.

58. Minutes of Viva Kennedy Club, October 3, 1960, García Papers.

59. "Carlos McCormick Named National Coordinator"; "New Mexico Dems Head Drive to Corral the Spanish Vote," *Flagstaff Sun,* October 12, 1960.

60. Ibid.; see also California *Viva Kennedy Weekly News Bulletin,* no. 2, dated October 3, 1960, García Papers, for an example of Viva Kennedy Club formation nationwide.

61. *Forum News Bulletin,* November-December, 1960.

62. *Forum News Bulletin,* October, 1960.

63. Quoted in "Carlos McCormick Named Coordinator."

64. Idar interview.

65. Roybal interview; Casarez interview. Of the major reformers during the Viva Kennedy campaign, only these two were willing to admit that Kennedy's Catholicism was important in attracting support among Mexican Americans.

66. José R. Reyna, "Readings in Southwestern Folklore," *Perspectives in Mexican American Studies* 1 (1988): vi.

67. See untitled, undated open letter by Gregorio Coronado (West Texas Viva Kennedy Club), García Papers. This letter discusses Democratic Party concern for the poor, the elderly, and the worker and also reminds the reader of Franklin D. Roosevelt's efforts to end the Depression. Also, see "Kennedy's Liberal Promises," *Time* (September 19, 1960): 23, and "Kennedy's Promises for the Future," *U.S. News & World Report* (November 21, 1960): 42. For Kennedy's speech at the civil-rights conference, see the civil-rights section of the October 31, 1960, issue of the *Campaign Bulletin,* the news organ of the Democratic National Committee.

68. Peña interview.

69. Peña and García did not meet Senator Kennedy until after the election.

70. Roybal interview.

71. Kennedy's Catholicism was an important issue for journalists and pundits. See "A Catholic for President?" *The New Republic* (November 18, 1957): 10–13; "Both Sides of the Catholic Issue," *U.S. News & World Report* (September 26, 1960): 74–81; "Catholics on the Court," *The New Republic* (September 20, 1960): 13–15. A good number of newspaper editors believed that Catholicism was also an advantage for Kennedy, especially in areas with large Mexican American populations. See two articles in the *New York Times,* "New Mexico Race Is Rated a Toss-up," September 19, 1960, and "Southern California Puzzles Experts," September 20, 1960.

72. Rudy Acuña, conversation with the author, Sacramento, Calif., summer 1997.

73. It should be noted that during the campaign Kennedy spoke against aid to Catholic schools because of potential problems with Protestant ministers. See "The Enemy within Our Borders," a pamphlet distributed by the Rev. G. de Chaplain, García Papers.

74. Kennedy's image was one of his strongest selling points. See "The Kennedy Story," *U.S. News & World Report* (November 21, 1960): 46–55; and "This Is John Fitzgerald Kennedy," *Newsweek* (June 23, 1958): 29–34.

75. "American G.I. Forum of the US," 4–5.

76. Idar interview.

CHAPTER 3

1. Casarez interview with Veronica Hayes, summer, 1996; Hector P. García, interview with Tom Kreneck, Corpus Christi, Tex., July 16, 1991, 1–3, García Oral History Project, García Papers. Also, see M. T. García, *Memories of Chicano History: The Life and Narrative of Bert Corona.* All three, Casarez, [Hector] García, and Corona paint a picture of rather happy childhoods devoid of any racial or cultural traumas. The same can be said of Ernesto Galarza. See Muñoz, *Youth, Identity, Power,* 25.

2. "González," *Texas Observer* (May 30, 1958): 1.

3. "Robstown Latin Replies to Anglo," *Texas Observer* (August 1, 1959): 3.

4. Muñoz, *Youth, Identity, Power,* 31–44. Muñoz's discussion of the Mexican American Movement in California in the 1930s and 1940s reveals how some Mexican American reformers saw themselves as "new" types of Mexican Americans more interested in progressing and fighting for their rights. Their words and actions suggested that nothing had been fought for in the past.

5. See Hector P. García, letter to Manuel Avila, Jr., September 18, 1961, García Papers. In the letter, García tells Avila that most American minorities are "doing well"— that is, they are united—but he laments, "why in the Lord's name we cannot organize [unite] . . . I do not know."

6. One of the works to deal with this phenomenon is Martínez, "Leadership and Politics," 47–62. Also, see M. T. García, *Mexican Americans,* 25–61. García takes a more positive view of this generation of reformers but does provide a glimpse of this internalized Americanism. Another, but more critical view is Ignacio M. García, "El rechazo de Aztlán: la contrapolitica de los hispánicos en Robstown, Texas," *NACCS Journal* (Summer 1999).

7. García interview with Kreneck, 1.

8. Ibid., 2.

9. Ibid., 1.

10. For background on this important figure in Mexican American politics, see Rodríguez, "Henry B. González: A Political Profile," and "Henry Barbosa González: Mexican American Political and Governmental Leader, Lawyer," in *Notable Latino Americans,* ed. Matt S. Meier.

11. Ibid.

12. Maurilio E. Vigil, *Los Patrones: Profiles of Hispanic Political Leaders in New Mexico History,* and Vigil's *Joseph Montoya, Democratic Senator from New Mexico.* See also *Memorial Addresses Delivered in Congress.* These monographs have biographies on

Dennis Chávez and Joseph Montoya and a discussion of Mexican American politics in New Mexico.

13. Ibid.

14. Elizabeth González-Gutiérrez, "The Education and Public Career of María C. Urquides: A Case Study of a Mexican American Community Leader" (Ph.D. diss., University of Arizona, Tucson, 1986), 39–40.

15. Ibid., 42.

16. Ibid., 48.

17. Ibid., 74.

18. For more on Arthur L. Campa, see M. T. García, *Mexican Americans*, 273–90. See also Anselmo F. Arellano and Julian Josue, eds., *Arthur L. Campa and the Coronado Cuatro Centennial.*

19. Sánchez, *Forgotten People.*

20. San Miguel, *"Let All of Them Take Heed,"* 99–103.

21. Ibid.

22. Ibid., 103–108.

23. No major work has been written on Edward R. Roybal, but a discussion of his early work can be found in Beatrice Griffith, "Mexican Americans Enter L.A. Politics," *The Mirror*, May 6, 1949; Griffith, "Viva Roybal"; Martin Hall, "Roybal's Candidacy and What It Means," *Frontier* (June, 1949); and for an excellent study on the women who supported Roybal's political efforts, see Apodaca, "They Kept the Home Fires Burning."

24. Apodaca, "They Kept the Home Fires Burning."

25. Ibid.; see also the pamphlet by Mike Glazer, "LA CSO History" as well as "Los Angeles Community Service Organization, 20th Anniversary" (pamphlet, March 5, 1967, Commerce Hyatt House, City of Commerce) as reproduced in Gómez-Quiñones, *Chicano Politics*, 231.

26. Texas had many integrationist organizations from quite early in the twentieth century. They included LULAC, the Pan American Progressive Association, the American G.I. Forum, and a host of other smaller organizations that came and went with tremendous frequency. There were also numerous mutual aid societies that promoted integration while catering to the working class.

27. Rodríguez, "Henry B. González."

28. Ibid.

29. Ronnie Dugger, "San Antonio Liberalism: Piecing It Together," *Texas Observer* (May 27, 1966): 1–5.

30. Peña interview.

31. See Allsup, *American G.I. Forum;* also, see David G. Gutiérrez, "Ethnicity, Ideology, and Political Development: Mexican Immigration as a Political Issue in the Chicano Community, 1910–1977" (Ph.D. diss., Stanford University, 1988), 6.

32. Ibid.

33. See "The Americans of Mexican Descent: A Statement of Principles by the Viva Kennedy Texas Organization," 1. This document is a six-page typed manuscript found in the García Papers.

34. See Sánchez, "History, Culture and Education," in *La Raza/Forgotten Americans*, 1–26; M. T. García, *Mexican Americans*, 231–51.

35. "Americans of Mexican Descent," 1.

36. Ibid.

37. Sánchez, *Forgotten People*.

38. Mexican American scholars had simply not provided an analysis which contradicted the American historical narrative. Castañeda had challenged the view that Mexicans had not contributed to the progress of the Southwest; Sánchez had placed some of the problems of the barrio in the context of the military conquest; and Arthur L. Campa, Aurelio Rodríguez, and Américo Paredes had presented Mexican American folklore as a sign of the vitality of the community. But none of these scholars or the few others that existed provided a framework by which to dissociate Chicano history from the corner in which it was stuck in the American historical narrative.

39. "Americans of Mexican Descent," 1.

40. Ibid., 2.

41. Ibid., 3.

42. Ibid.

43. See M. T. García, *Mexican Americans*, 18. García does not accept an alienation, but he does differentiate the early immigrant working-class activism from that of the Mexican American Generation. While accepting García's argument that this generation sympathized with working-class issues, I would argue that in fact they moved away from working-class radicalism, away from many bread-and-butter issues, and created organizations that would not be led by anyone except by middle-class professionals. Two works that somewhat support my view are Rodolfo Alvarez, "The Psycho-Historical and Socioeconomic Development of the Chicano Community in the United States," *Social Science Quarterly* 53 (March, 1973): 920–42; and Richard Garcia, "The Mexican American Mind: A Product of the 1930s," in *History, Culture, and Society: Chicano Studies in the 1980s*.

44. "Americans of Mexican Descent," 5.

45. Manuel Gamio, *The Mexican Immigrant, His Life Story*; Paul S. Taylor, *An American-Mexican Frontier: Nueces County, Texas*.

46. "Americans of Mexican Descent," 4.

47. Ibid., 5–6.

48. Ernesto Portillo, interview with author, Tucson, Ariz., December 28, 1995. Portillo, a business leader and radio personality who participated in reform politics throughout his broadcasting career, articulated this generation's dismay with Mexican American elites of earlier years, referring to them as too accommodating and assimilative

and too satisfied with the little they had received from American society. This perception is no doubt biased by a generational gap, but it was a prevalent one. Some of this disdain is expressed in both the Idar and Peña interviews.

49. "Americans of Mexican Descent," 6.

50. Ibid.

51. Aztlán is the mythical homeland of the Aztecs. It also became the name that Chicano activists would use to denote the territory conquered during the U.S.-Mexican War. See Rudolfo A. Anaya and Francisco Lomelí, *Aztlán: Essays on the Chicano Homeland.* See also Ignacio M. García, *United We Win: The Rise and Fall of La Raza Unida Party,* 91–95, for a discussion of the political ramifications of Aztlán.

CHAPTER 4

1. Ed Idar, Jr., telephone interview with author, March 25, 1996.

2. Sánchez, *Forgotten People,* 97.

3. With few elected officials and few possibilities to influence government policies, Mexican Americans have had to depend on Anglo American politicians. Since many Mexican Americans were unfamiliar with the political system, they were willing to accept with gratitude whatever advocacy they received. See Douglas E. Foley, Clarice Mota, Donald E. Post, and Ignacio Lozano, *From Peones to Politicos: Ethnic Relations in a South Texas Town, 1900–1977;* and Evan Anders, *Boss Rule in South Texas,* for a discussion of Mexican American dependence on Anglo American leadership. Also pertinent is Simmons, "Mutual Images and Expectations of Anglo Americans and Mexican Americans," 286–99.

4. "Kennedy es Nuestro Lider," *Latin Times,* October 29, 1960, 1.

5. See "Viva Kennedy Clubs Host Senator Gonzalez," *Latin Times,* October 29, 1960, 7. In this article, Henry B. González is described as a "personal friend of John F. and Robert Kennedy."

6. For information on the meeting, see "Viva Kennedy Movement in East Chicago," *Latin Times,* October 1, 1960, 1. For more on the organizational efforts and the naming of club leaders, see "Viva Kennedy Club," *Latin Times,* October 15, 1960; "Viva Kennedy Quarters Opened in East Chicago," *Hammond Times,* October 9, 1960; "TV Talks Spur Kennedy and Nixon Activity," *Chicago Daily Tribune,* September 28, 1960; "Announce Viva Kennedy Club in Cal City," *Advertiser* (East Chicago, Ind.), October 27, 1960; and "Name Two Local Spanish Speaking Men for Kennedy," *Calumet* (Indiana) *News,* October 12, 1960. See Hector P. García, letter to Joseph Maravilla, October 12, 1960, García Papers, congratulating him and the East Chicago G.I. Forum for their Viva Kennedy efforts.

7. A number of works have been published on the Midwest. Some examples are: Dennis Nodín Valdes, *"El pueblo mexicano en Detroit y Michigan: A Social History" (Ph.D. diss., Wayne State University, 1982); Arthur D. Martínez, "Los de Dodge City, Kansas: A Mexican American Community at the Heartland of the U.S.," Journal of the West* 24 (1985); Neil Betten, "From Discrimination to Repatriation: Mexican Life

in Gary, Indiana, during the Great Depression," *Pacific Historical Review* 42 (1973); Richard Santillan, "Latino Politics in the Midwestern United States," in *Latinos and the Political System,* ed. F. Chris García; and Michael Smith, *The Mexicans of Oklahoma.*

8. "Record Registration in East Chicago," *Latin Times,* October 22, 1960. See Joseph Maravilla, letter to Carlos McCormick, October 14, 1960, García Papers.

9. Ibid.

10. Maravilla letter to McCormick, October 14, 1960.

11. Roybal interview, August 19, 1997.

12. "Senator Henry Gonzalez to Speak," *Latin Times,* October 22, 1960. See also campaign poster inviting the Hispanic community to González rally in East Chicago, in the García Papers.

13. "Viva Kennedy Clubs Host Senator Gonzalez," 7.

14. See pictures and caption on page 5 of the *Tribuna* (East Chicago, Ind.), October 27, 1960, showing State Senator González with Indiana congressman Roy Madden and Gary, Indiana, mayor George Chacharis. Also pictured is Mrs. Alfredo Vidal.

15. "Informes al Pueblo," *Latin Times,* October 29, 1960.

16. "Back Democrats," *Hammond Times,* October 16, 1960. This is a captioned picture caption of "Jack" and "Lynda," two burros donated to the campaign in East Chicago.

17. "Senator Henry Gonzalez to Speak."

18. A UPI telephoto shows Illinois Viva Kennedy Club chairman José Alvarado with U.S. senator Paul Douglas and Michigan governor G. Mennen Williams proudly holding a Viva Kennedy bumper sticker. See *Tribuna,* October 27, 1960, 5.

19. See captioned photograph in the *Chicago Tribune,* October 26, 1960, showing hundreds of Latinos with Viva Kennedy posters waiting to see Sen. John F. Kennedy's motorcade.

20. For an official history of MAPA, see Kenneth Burt, "The History of MAPA and Chicano Politics in California," pamphlet of the Mexican American Political Association, 1982.

21. For Guzmán's story of his Viva Kennedy voter registration efforts, see Louis Weshler and John Gallagher, "Viva Kennedy," in *Cases in American National Politics and Government,* ed. Rocco J. Tresolini and Richard T. Frost.

22. "Forumeers Participate as Individuals in 'Viva' Clubs," *Forum News Bulletin,* October, 1960, 2; see also, "Forumeers and Sen. Kennedy Ride into White House on the Mexican Burro," *Forum News Bulletin,* December, 1960, 1.

23. Roybal interview, August 19, 1997.

24 Ibid. See also "Viva Kennedy Campaña Goes into High Gear," in *Viva Kennedy Weekly News Bulletin,* October 3, 1960, 3, García Papers.

25. Ibid., 2.

26. Roybal interview.

27. Ibid.

28. Ibid.

29. Ibid.

30. "Chavez Boosts Kennedy Clubs on West Coast," *Roswell* (N.Mex.) *Record,* October 9, 1960; "Vote or Suffer Consequences, Sen. Chavez Tells S.B. Group," *San Bernardino Sun,* October 9, 1960; and "Chavez Says Rich Get Richer under GOP," *Fresno Bee,* October 6, 1960.

31. Quoted in "Chavez Says Rich Get Richer under GOP," *Fresno Bee,* October 6, 1960.

32. Ibid., and "Chavez Criticizes GOP's Policy on Latin America," *Corpus Christi Caller,* October, 1960 (day of publication unavailable).

33. "Chavez Criticizes GOP's Policy on Latin America."

34. Ibid.

35. "Chavez Says Rich Get Richer."

36. For an in-depth study of the Tucson middle class up until World War II, see Sheridan, *Los Tucsonenses.*

37. Ibid., 249–55; also, see Oscar Martínez, "Hispanics in Arizona," in *Arizona at Seventy-five,* ed. B. Luey and N. J. Stone, 87–122; David L. Torres, "Dynamics behind the Formation of a Business Class: Tucson's Hispanic Business Elite," *Hispanic Journal of Behavioral Sciences* 12 (1990): 25–49; and David L. Torres and Melissa Amado, "The Quest for Power: Hispanic Collective Action in Frontier, Arizona," *Perspectives in Mexican American Studies* 3 (1992): 73–94.

38. For information on the Alianza Hispano-Americana, see Kaye Briegel, "Alianza Hispano-Americana, 1894–1965: A Mexican American Fraternal Society" (Ph.D. diss., University of Southern California, 1974); Sheridan, *Los Tucsonenses,* 111–13; and Olivia Arrieta, "The Alianza Hispano Americana in Arizona and New Mexico: The Development and Maintenance of a Multifunctional Ethnic Organization," in *Renato Rosaldo Lecture Series Monograph* 7 (1991): 55–82. For information on the International Union of Mine, Mill, and Smelter Workers, see D. H. Dinwoodie, "The Rise of the Mine-Mill Union in Southwestern Copper," in *American Labor in the Southwest: The First One Hundred Years,* ed. James C. Foster, 46–56; Vernon H. Jensen, *Nonferrous Metals Industry Unionism, 1932–1954;* and M. T. García, *Mexican Americans,* 175–98.

39. Portillo interview.

40. Roybal interview, August 19, 1997. See also,"Arizona Viva Kennedy Officers, Board Members Listed by Leader," *Phoenix Republic,* October 5, 1960.

41. Peña interview. There was a semblance of a state organization. Tony Bonilla would be designated as the state chair, but the structure was rather loose. See minutes of the Viva Kennedy Club, October 3, 1960, García Papers. Also, see Tony Bonilla letters to club presidents in Sinton, Houston, Corpus Christi, Bishop, Alice, and Mathis, all of which (except Houston) were located in South Texas. These letters are in the García Papers.

42. Open letter from Hector P. García, Henry B. González, Roberto Ornelas, and Albert Peña, Jr. to Texas voters (undated), García Papers.

43. Ibid.

44. Ibid.

45. See Tony Bonilla, letter to Cleotilde García, October 21, 1960, thanking her for hosting a reception in her home for state senator González. Another letter from Bonilla, dated October 31, 1960, thanks her for hosting U.S. senator Chávez. Also, see "Chavez Criticizes GOP's Policy on Latin America," which mentions a private reception for Senator Chávez in Cleotilde García's home.

46. See minutes of the Texas state organizers of the Viva Kennedy Club, October 3, 1960, García Papers.

47. The Civic Action Committee was founded by Houston reformers, some of whom were connected to local LULAC and G.I. Forum chapters. Its bulletin would be one of the periodicals that sought to publicize major political events such as González's run for governor and the Viva Kennedy campaign.

48. "Kennedy Calls National Conference on Constitutional Rights Oct. 11–12," *Campaign Bulletin* (National Democratic Party), October 1, 1960, 1.

CHAPTER 5

1. The Viva Kennedy posters stood out in numerous pictures of Kennedy campaign parades and rallies. See chap. 4, note 19.

2. See Hector P. García, letter to Carlos McCormick, November 16, 1960; and José Alvarado, letter to García, December 19, 1960, both in García Papers.

3. "Mexicans Pleased by Election of Kennedy," *Kansas City Star,* November 21, 1960.

4. Ibid. For general view of the election results, see "As Votes Kept Coming In—Here's What Really Happened," *U.S. News & World Report* (November 28, 1960): 69–70.

5. "Viva Kennedy Clubs Deliver Biggest Texas Demo Gains," *The Press,* November 9, 1960, 1; also, "Valley Counties Solid for Demos," *Corpus Christi Times,* November 10, 1960; and "Kennedy Wins Starr by Heavy Majority," and "Jim Wells Goes Strongly Demo, Two Boxes Out," both in the *Corpus Christi Caller,* November 9, 1960. For the impact of the religious issue, see "Religion Helped, Not Hurt Kennedy," *Texas Observer* (November 11, 1960): 1.

6. Quoted in article in *Spokesman Review* (November 11, 1960) (no page number available), García Papers.

7. García, letter to Albert Peña, Jr., November 11, 1960, García Papers.

8. "Mexicans Pleased by Election of Kennedy."

9. "Forumeers and Sen. Kennedy Ride into White House on Mexican Burro."

10. Manuel Avila, letter to José Alvarado, October 14, 1960, García Papers.

11. "El Señor José Alvarado invitado de honor a la toma de posesion del Señor Presidente John F. Kennedy," *El Anunciador* (Chicago, Ill.), January 14, 1960. This is a reprint of the letter of invitation to attend the inauguration.

12. "State to Fare Well, Sen. Chavez Asserts," *Albuquerque Tribune,* November 10, 1960.

13. Ralph Estrada, "Ethnic Equity and Political Progress," *Alianza,* September, 1961, 6.

14. García, letter to President-elect John F. Kennedy, January 11, 1961, García Papers.

15. Carlos McCormick, letter to García, January 14, 1961, García Papers.

16. Ibid.; also, see Flores, letter to García, February 4, 1961, García Papers.

17. See García, letter to Phillip Leon, February 4, 1961, explaining procedures on how to apply for government work. Also, see García, letter to McCormick, December 19, 1961, in which García submits the names of two individuals who want to work in Washington, D.C. Neither individual's résumé indicates relevant experience.

18. See "Sen. Chavez Charges of Spanish American Snub Brings Some Appointments," *Forum News Bulletin,* March, 1961; García letter to McCormick, February 18, 1961; "Tell News at Presidential Press Parley Expect Other Forumeers to Be Named," *Forum News Bulletin,* March, 1961. Also, see "Latinos en Varios Puestos Oficiales," *La Prensa* (San Antonio, Tex.), February 14, 1961.

19. "High Job Offered Latin American," *Forum News Bulletin,* February 18, 1961.

20. "Sen. Chavez Charges of Spanish American Snub."

21. Ibid. Also, see José Alvarado, cable to Dennis Chávez, January 16, 1961, García Papers.

22. García, letter to Vicente Ximenez, March 10, 1961, García Papers.

23. Roybal quoted in "Kennedy Patronage, Latin American Policies under Fire," *Congressional Quarterly* (January 23, 1961); and "Viva Kennedy Leaders in Revolt," *Valley Morning Star,* June 28, 1961.

24. This was Reynaldo Garza. More will be said about him in this chapter.

25. "Telles Appointed," *Forum News Bulletin,* March, 1961, 6.

26. "Kennedy Patronage . . . under Fire."

27. Ibid.

28. "Periodical Tells of Revolt by Spanish-Americans, Hit JFK Patronage and Latin Policies," *Forum News Bulletin,* July, 1961, 2; "Viva Kennedy Leaders in Revolt."

29. García, letter to Avila, July 22, 1961, García Papers.

30. Ibid.

31. "Los Viva-Kennedy Clubs y las Promesas Incumplidas de La Presente Administración," *El Quijote,* September 15, 1961.

32. Ibid.

33. "Editorial," *Forum News Bulletin,* July, 1961, 5.

34. Ibid.

35. See V. G. Roel, letter to Carlos McCormick, January 24, 1962, García Papers.

36. For an in-depth view of Reynaldo Garza's rise to become a federal judge, see Louise Ann Fisch, *All Rise: Reynaldo G. Garza, the First Mexican American Federal Judge.*

37. García, letter to John F. Kennedy, November 18, 1960.

38. See "Suggested draft letter from Hector García, Henry B. González, Albert Peña, and Mayor Raymond Telles to Sen. John F. Kennedy," 1960, García Papers.

39. Ibid.

40. Ibid.

41. "Battle Boils Over Latin American as U.S. Judge," *Corpus Christi Caller,* January 14, 1961.

42. See biographical sheet titled, "Qualifications of Judge E. D. Salinas," dated January 2, 1961, García Papers.

43. Ibid.

44. Ibid.; see also Ed Idar, Jr., letter to García, October 26, 1959, García Papers.

45. Ibid. Also, see Salinas, letter to García, April 16, 1959, in which he expresses confidence in being appointed to the federal bench by the Republican administration. Another letter to García from Salinas adds more information on the positive support. Unfortunately, the letter is undated but can be found in scrapbook 52-70 in the García Papers.

46. Salinas, letter to García, October 28, 1959, García Papers.

47. See memo from Ed Idar, Jr., to All State Officers, Directors, and Local Groups, January 14, 1960. Idar, the state G.I. Forum executive secretary, informed the aforementioned of the resolution adopted by the organization's board of directors on January 10, 1960. For a view of the national letter-writing campaign, see form letters to Rep. Sidney Yates (Illinois), Sen. Hubert H. Humphrey (Minnesota), Sen. Paul H. Douglas (Illinois), and to Lawrence F. O'Brien, Special Assistant to the President. All are in the García Papers.

48. See "Judge Salinas Urges U.S. Gov. Note Presence of This Country's 12 Million Latin Americans; Ask Their Use," *Forum News Bulletin,* August, 1960.

49. For an in-depth discussion of the rising opposition to Salinas, see "Confidential Memorandum," December 19, 1960. Written by Idar, this memorandum details the maneuvering by local politicians as well as Vice-President-elect Johnson and Senator Yarborough to block Salinas's appointment. Also, see Ed Idar, Jr., "Epilogue," January 14, 1961, a report that gives a day-by-day account of Salinas's failure to get the appointment. Both documents are in the García Papers. Another document of value is an undated cable from Idar to Robert F. Kennedy that details Yarborough's efforts to promote another Mexican American judge whom Idar describes as an "excellent man" but with "relatively little experience."

50. For a mention of the possible opposition in Salinas's hometown, see Salinas, letter to García, January 7, 1961, and another [undated] Salinas letter to García titled "Personal Corresp.," García Papers. Both letters dismissed the opposition but do not close the door on the potential for problems in the solid support from his home region.

51. See Oscar C. Dancy (Cameron County, Texas, judge), letter to Peña, June 7, 1963, García Papers.

52. Ralph Yarborough, letter to García, March 11, 1960, García Papers.

53. See Idar, "Confidential Memorandum," 3–5.

54. See Idar, "Epilogue," 14.

55. Lyndon B. Johnson, letter to García, March 11, 1960, García Papers.

56. Idar, "Epilogue," 12–13.

57. Ibid.

58. Ibid.

59. Ibid., 16.

60. Ibid.

61. See Salinas, letter to García, January 7, 1961, in which he tells the G.I. Forum leader that Reynaldo Garza had told him he was not making a bid for the job. Garza told Salinas that his friends and supporters were pushing him to do so because of his friendship with Johnson and Yarborough.

62. See Roybal, Idar, and Peña interviews. All three men reiterated this point.

63. See "Frontiersmen (J.g.): Do They All Want to Be President?" *Newsweek* (March 9, 1962): 80, for a discussion of the types of mid-level staffer appointees Kennedy surrounded himself with. Also, see Joan Morrison and Robert K. Morrison, *From Camelot to Kent State: The Sixties Experience in the Words of Those Who Lived It.*

CHAPTER 6

1. See McCormick, letter to García, March 16, 1961, García Papers.

2. "Viva Clubs Now Permanent, Choose Mexican Americans for Political Action Name," *Forum News Bulletin,* March, 1961. Also, see "Viva Kennedy Clubs Meet to Form National Political Group," *Forum News Bulletin,* April, 1961.

3. These entrenched political organizations and politicians were holdovers from the days when prominent Mexican ranching families held power or they were families who had allied themselves with new Anglo American groups that challenged the old ranching and farming interests. Neither group, however, offered much to the poor of the Valley. See M. T. García, *Mexican Americans,* 28–29, and also his *The Making of a Mexican American Mayor,* 19–20. These pages talk about the father of Viva Kennedy leader Raymond L. Telles, when he was, for all purposes, a barrio politico. Also, J. Gilberto Quezada, *Border Boss: Manuel B. Bravo and Zapata County,* tells the story of one of the most important Mexican American bosses in South Texas.

4. M. T. García, *Mexican Americans,* 40–42.

5. For one view of the political divisions and ambiguities, see Ralph C. Guzmán, "Politics and Policies of the Mexican American Community," in *California Politics and Policies,* ed. Eugene Divorin and Arthur Misner, 350–85. For a much older but still perceptive view of Mexican American political behavior, see O. Douglas Week, "The Texas-Mexican and the Politics of South Texas," *American Political Science Review* 24 (August, 1930): 607–27.

6. See "Narrative Report of National Political Leadership Conference," March 26, 1961, 2, in García Papers. Also, "Viva Kennedy Clubs Meet to Form National Political Group," *Forum News Bulletin,* April, 1961.

7. "Narrative Report of National Political Leadership Conference," 3.

8. Ibid.

9. Ibid., 3–6.

10. Ibid., 6.

11. Ibid., 7.

12. Ibid., 4–7.

13. See Acuña, *Occupied America,* for a view of the variant history among the states most populated by Mexican Americans. Also, see Fernando Peñalosa, "Toward an Operational Definition of the Mexican American," *Aztlán* 1 (spring 1970): 1–12. See also Richard Griswold del Castillo and Arnoldo De León, *North to Aztlán: A History of Mexican Americans in the United States.*

14. I heard Carlos Guerra say this in a rally in San Antonio, Tex., in the summer of 1972.

15. See Anaya's "Aztlán: A Homeland without Boundaries," in *Aztlán: Essays on the Chicano Homeland,* ed. Rudolfo Anaya and Francisco Lomeli, 230–41.

16. "Narrative Report of National Political Leadership Conference," 7. See also Kenneth Burt's booklet, "The History of the Mexican American Political Association and Chicano Politics in California," issued by MAPA in 1982. The acronym would eventually become PASSO, but I have chosen to use PASO because most of the leaders did so until at least 1964, when this particular story ends.

17. See "Political Association of Spanish Speaking Organizations (PASO) Board Meeting Held April 28th and 29th, 1961," 1, García Papers. The list of those in attendance does not include González, Peña, Chávez, and Montoya, though it lists Roybal as being absent. See also "Las Vegas, Nevada," dated April, 1961, García Papers (a news release/official minutes document detailing what happened in the meeting in Las Vegas), and a flyer from García to "All members of the Board of Directors of the Political Association of Spanish Speaking Organizations of the U.S.," April 6, 1961, García Papers.

18. Ibid.

19. Ibid., 3–8.

20. Ibid., 4–7.

21. Ibid., 8. See also García, letter to Paul Arranza, February 27, 1961, in which García asks a G.I. Forum leader about the use of the descriptor "Mexican American" and whether to recruit Cubans and Puerto Ricans to PASO.

22. Ibid., 4, 9, 18–20.

23. See García, letter to Carlos McCormick, March 15, 1962, García Papers, in which García tells McCormick of a new organization in Arizona—the American Co-Ordinating Council on Political Education—headed by Eugene Marín, a member of the national PASO group.

24. "PASO Board Meeting," 22–24.

25. Both González and Roybal were preparing for congressional campaigns, Chávez was ill, and Montoya was preparing to replace Chávez in the U.S. Senate.

26. García, letter to McCormick, March 15, 1962, García Papers.

27. See note 26 for the only letter this author found that criticized a reform leader from another state. Another letter from García, this one to Roybal, May 20, 1961, reveals García's frustration over California MAPA's unwillingness to join PASO but also his refusal to condemn the action.

28. See "PASO Takes First Gigantic Step Towards Its Grass Roots Movement and Local Organization," an open letter from García to national PASO membership, July 10, 1961, García Papers.

29. At the Victoria meeting of what was then called MAPA , some participants talked of permanently maintaining the Viva Kennedy Clubs, but that was seen as unfeasible because the name implied a temporary organization. See letters from Tony Bonilla to Viva Kennedy Club officers of several communities in South Texas, dated November 10, 1960, García Papers.

30. "PASO Takes First Gigantic Step," 1.

31. Ibid.

32. "Mexican Americans' Balance of Power Dramatically Illustrated," *Forum News Bulletin,* June, 1961, 1. Also, in same issue, see "Dr. García's Support Could Have Given Win."

33. Idar, telephone interview with author, February 4, 1997.

34. Ibid.

35. George I. Sánchez, letter to Idar, January 25, 1962, García Papers.

36. See Idar, letter to Ronnie Dugger, January 25, 1962, 1–2.

37. Ibid., 2.

38. See "Two Men Who Filled a Vacuum," *Texas Observer* (February 25, 1961): 5, for Dugger's endorsement of Maverick over González.

39. Idar, letter to Dugger, 2–3.

40. See George I. Sánchez, "The American of Mexican Descent," *Chicago Jewish Forum,* 20 (Winter 1961– 62): 120 –24.

41. Ibid., 124.

42. See "Political Interests of Latins United," *Texas Observer* (September 15, 1961) for the quote on Messkill's suggestion that this "doctrine is racism in reverse."

43. Peña, quoted in ibid.

44. Sánchez, quoted in ibid.

45. Ibid.

46. See the Idar-composed "Convention Memorandum," January 19, 1962, 2, sent out to "All Members and Prospective Members of PASO," García Papers.

47. Peña, quoted in "Latin Group Split on Endorsement," *Texas Observer* (February 16, 1962): 1.

48. Sánchez had also received a letter from García, dated February 7, 1962, which assured him that no commitments had been made to any candidate. García's letter is in the George I. Sánchez Papers in the Benson Latin American Collection, General Libraries, University of Texas at Austin. For Idar's quote, see his "Convention Memorandum."

49. Peña interview.

50. Idar interview. See Sánchez, letter to Idar, January 29, 1962, in Sánchez Papers. In the letter, Sánchez also blasts LBJ's candidate, John Connally, whom he assumes had the inside track for a PASO endorsement.

51. "Convention Memorandum," 1.

52. Idar interview. See also "Latin Group Split on Endorsement," 2.

53. Sánchez, letter to Idar, January 29, 1962.

54. Thurman and Proctor quoted in "Latin Group Split on Endorsement," 1.

55. Idar interview.

56. Ibid.

57. "Latin Group Split on Endorsement," 1–2.

58. Ibid.

59. Sánchez, quoted in ibid.

60. Yarborough and Sánchez, quoted in ibid.

61. Quoted in ibid.

62. Idar interview.

63. Quoted in Cuellar, "A Social and Political History of the Mexican American Population," 49.

64. Sánchez, quoted in "Latin Group Split on Endorsement," 2.

65. See Sánchez, letter to Gregorio E. Coronado, February 17, 1962, Box 37, Sánchez Papers.

66. "Latin Group Split on Endorsement," 1. PASO also endorsed Jarrod Secrest for lieutenant governor, Tom Reavley for attorney general, and Woodrow W. Bean for congressman-at-large (a temporary position in Texas to exist until all redistricting was completed). Unfortunately for PASO, none of them won the election.

67. Cuellar, "A Social and Political History of the Mexican American Population," 49. In Idar's own county, the pro-Yarborough forces would refuse to support the convention's decision. See Idar, letter to García, February 22, 1963, García Papers.

68. See Leo J. Leo, letter to García, February 27, 1962, García Papers. Also see George I. Sánchez, letters to Gregorio E. Coronado, February 17, 1962, and to García, March 6, 1962, also in García Papers. Both letters reveal Sánchez's disbelief at the PASO endorsement of Daniel.

69. See Idar, letter to "Dear Friend," May 2, 1962, García Papers.

70. See Sánchez, letter to Idar, May 16, 1962, García Papers. The author was unable to find a copy of Idar's reply to Sánchez.

71. "Political Summons in Bexar," *Texas Observer* (October 5, 1962): 1.

72. Ibid.; see also, "Sleeping Giant," *Texas Observer* (June 1, 1962): 3.

73. "Political Summons in Bexar," 1; see also, "PASO Withdraws," *Texas Observer* (October 12, 1962): 1.

74. "Political Summons in Bexar," 1; see also, "PASO Withdraws," 1.

75. Quoted in "Political Summons in Bexar," 2.

76. Ibid.; see also, "PASO Withdraws," 1–2.

77. Quoted in "Political Summons in Bexar," 2.

78. Ibid.

79. Ibid.

80. "Political Summons in Bexar," 2.

81. Quoted in "Latins and Votes," *Texas Observer* (January 19, 1962): 1, 3.

82. Ibid., 2.

83. Cuellar,"A Social and Political History of the Mexican American Population," 49.

84. For the story of Crystal City, see Julian Samora, Joe Bernal, and Albert Peña, *Gunpowder Justice: A Reassessment of the Texas Rangers*, 110–14; John Staples Shockley, *Chicano Revolt in a Texas Town*, 24–41; and Cuellar,"A Social and Political History of the Mexican American Population," 55–62. Possibly the best work done on Crystal City is Armando Navarro's *The Cristal Experiment: A Chicano Struggle for Community Control*.

85. Ibid., esp. Navarro, 33–36.

86. Ibid.

87. Quoted in Cuellar, "A Social and Political History of the Mexican American Population," 59.

88. "What Is PASO?" undated pamphlet in García Papers.

89. Quoted in "Not a Single Spanish Surname . . . ," *Texas Observer* (August 23, 1963): 5.

90. Ibid.

91. For an excellent discussion of the Crystal City controversy among PASO members, see "The Struggle for PASO," *Texas Observer* (June 14, 1963): 3–6.

92. García quoted in Cuellar,"A Social and Political History of the Mexican American Population," 61.

93. Quoted in "PASO Official Accuses Anglos of Injecting Race Issue in Valley," *Valley Evening Monitor* (Harlingen, Tex.), May 24, 1963, 3-A.

94. Quoted in Paul Thompson column, "Hector's Ache," *San Antonio Express*, June 17, 1963. Also, see Mrs. Amador A. Aguilar, letter to García, June 17, 1963, which expresses some members' opposition to their Forum chapter giving Ray Shafer the plaque. The letter is in the García Papers.

95. See García, letter to Roel, July 13, 1963, García Papers.

96. "The Struggle for PASO," 5.

97. Garcia, quoted in ibid. For Bonilla's quote, see "Teamsters and Peña Continue to Roll," *La Verdad*, June 14, 1963, 1.

98. Peña and Fuentes, quoted in "The Struggle for PASO," 5.

99. Ibid.

100. Peña interview.

101. Sánchez, letter to Father John A. Wagner, April 12, 1962, Sánchez Papers.

102. Hector García, quoted in Thompson, "Hector's Ache"; see also "The Struggle for PASO," 5–6.

103. Ibid.

104. William Bonilla, quoted in "The Struggle for PASO," 5.

105. Ibid.

106. The Corpus Christi PASO chapter would, in fact, vote for Peña as chairman, leaving García to declare that he would work with the PASO chapters outside of Texas. See "The Struggle for PASO," 6.

107. See "Crystal City Mayor Rejects LULAC Bid," and "New Hidalgo Unit Head Says Group Not Anti-PASO," *Corpus Christi Caller,* June 14, 1963.
108. García, letter to Virgilio G. Roel, July 13, 1963, García Papers.
109. García, letter to Robert F. Kennedy, June 13, 1963, García Papers.
110. Quoted in "Texas Latins Bid for Better Lot with Ballots," *Fort Worth Star-Telegram,* April 15, 1964.
111. Ibid.
112. *Fort Worth Star-Telegram,* April 15, 1964.
113. Leo, quoted in ibid.
114. Alan Lessoff, personal communication with the author, spring 1998.
115. Quoted in *Fort Worth Star-Telegram,* April 15, 1964.

CHAPTER 7

1. Idar interview, February 4, 1997.
2. García, letter to Virgilio G. Roel, July 13, 1963.
3. Ibid.
4. See Idar, letter to R. P. Sánchez, June 18, 1963, García Papers.
5. There were many political figures in Texas who feared González because of his ability to undermine their political careers. In an interview with the author, Ed Idar, Jr. spoke of González's need to be seen as the only Mexican American leader in San Antonio. Chicano activists found out about the congressman's wrath when they sought to organize in his home town. See I. M. García, *United We Win,* 27–29. For the best treatment of González's intolerance of opposition, see Ronnie Dugger, "Gonzalez of San Antonio—Part 5—The Politics of Fratricide," *Texas Observer* (December 12, 1980).
6. See letter to "Angel"—presumably José Angel Gutiérrez, founder of La Raza Unida Party of Texas—by an unknown author, dated March 15, 1970, Albert Peña Papers, Special Collections and Archives Department, University of Texas at San Antonio Library. This letter contains the complete text of a speech given by Henry B. González in which he stated that "I was not then nor am I now an ethnic candidate."
7. See Benjamin Márquez, *LULAC: The Evolution of a Mexican American Political Organization,* 64, 73, 86–94, for a discussion of the Bonilla influence in LULAC.
8. Peña participated in numerous political organizations beyond PASO, and Fuentes would even run for lieutenant governor. See Ronnie Dugger, "San Antonio Liberalism: Piecing It Together," *Texas Observer* (May 27, 1966): 1–5, for a discussion of some of Peña's political activities in his hometown. See also "Albert Fuentes Makes His Case," *Texas Observer* (February 21, 1964), for Fuentes's run for the lieutenant governor post.
9. See Christine Marín, *A Spokesman of the Mexican American Movement: Rodolfo "Corky" Gonzales and the Fight for Chicano Liberation, 1966–1972,* 12.
10. See keynote address by the Honorable Albert Peña, Jr. at the Annual P.A.S.O. State Convention, September 27, 1970, at the Driscoll Hotel in Corpus Christi (Peña

Papers). This address is a ten-page document in which Peña states, "I have made no commitments to campaign for anyone else in this November election except for La Raza Unida Party."

11. Quoted in Cuellar, "A Social and Political History of the Mexican American Population," 61.

12. Idar interview.

13. See Sánchez, *Forgotten People,* for his attempt to integrate New Mexico's Mexican American population into the national historical narrative.

14. Kennedy would never be a divisive issue among Mexican American reformers. They might vacillate between feeling good about him or criticizing him for his policies, but there is no record to this author's knowledge of fighting over him or his policies.

15. For a good discussion of *cacique* politics, albeit in Mexico, see Claudio Lomitz-Alder, *Exits from the Labyrinth: Culture and Ideology in the Mexican National Space.*

16. Idar interview.

17. See Barrera, letter to García, January 2, 1961, García Papers.

18. See discussion of dues for PASO members in the minutes of the PASO board meeting held in Las Vegas, Nevada, on April 28–29, 1961, 17–18, 22–24, García Papers. The delegates seemed stuck between one dollar, which was too little in their estimation, and two dollars, which was too much.

19. See Louise Stanford, "Mathis since the Revolution," *Texas Observer* (August 23, 1968): 12–14. This article discusses a group of PASO-type reformers who gain control of a small South Texas town. It covers their difficulties in governing when confronted by an Anglo American minority which accuses them of radicalism and racism in reverse. Lacking both resources and a consistent ideology, they come into conflict with each other and are eventually defeated.

20. See "Political Summons in Bexar," *Texas Observer* (October 5, 1962): 1, for an example of a disdainful critique of the PASO leadership and its strategies. Also, see the handwritten letter from Luella Louther to García, dated April 30, 1970, García Papers, which ridicules Mexican American reformers for wanting what they did not deserve and for continually fighting among themselves. Another more subtle criticism can be seen in a June 7, 1963, letter from Oscar C. Dancy (county judge of Cameron County for more than forty years) to Peña, also in García Papers. Cameron County, at the southern tip of Texas, was predominantly Mexican American but had been governed by Anglo Americans since the Texas Revolution. In the letter Dancy expresses his dislike of unions and emphasizes the "good" relations between the races. Mexican Americans simply had to support the Democratic administrations in Texas and Washington, D.C.

21. PASO retained its middle-class focus and did little to provide programs or activities for young people, while the Chicano Movement activists targeted young people for recruitment. José Angel Gutiérrez, one of the leaders of the Chicano Movement in Texas, did establish a PASO chapter at Texas A&I University in Kingsville but had

to fight the state organization to get memberships for persons younger than eighteen. See José Angel Gutiérrez, interview with the author, Independence, Ore., September 13, 1985 (tape in possession of the author).

22. For a discussion of middle-class reformers' hostility to the Chicano Movement, see I. M. García, *Chicanismo*, 128–29, 140–43, and "El rechazo de Aztlán." The latter deals with the eventual conflict between Mexican American reformers and Chicano activists in a small community in South Texas.

23. Ibid.

24. See "Mexican Americans Will Strive On . . . ," December 17, 1970, PASO file folder, Box 77, Peña Papers. The article quotes John Alaniz reading off the names of Mathis, Beeville, La Jolla, Alamo, and Crystal City as places where PASO had helped organize Mexican Americans. After the Crystal City debacle, PASO leaders were more private about their local organizing efforts.

25. See García, letter to President Kennedy, April 29, 1961, for an example of this reverential treatment.

26. See "Hispanic Leaders Will Work on Clinton Campaign," United Press International copy, September 17, 1992, reprinted in the *Forum News Bulletin*.

27. See Santillan and Subervi-Vélez, "Latino Participation in Republican Party Politics in California," 285–319.

28. Griswold del Castillo and De León, *North to Aztlán*, 155–57.

29. See "Statement by Vicente T. Ximenez," undated news release by the Inter-Agency Committee on Mexican American Affairs, García Papers. Also, see I. M. García, *United We Win*, 20; and Acuña, *Occupied America*, 331–32.

30. Márquez, *LULAC*, 15–38; and M. T. García, *Mexican Americans*, 25–61.

31. Gómez-Quiñones, *Chicano Politics*, 103.

32. See resolution in minutes of the PASO board meeting on April 28–29, 1961, in Las Vegas, Nevada. The PASO leaders pledged support for Kennedy's policy toward Cuba and his Alliance for Progress program for Latin America.

33. I. M. García, *United We Win*, 37–50.

34. Marín, *A Spokesman of the Mexican American Movement*, 2.

35. See undated *Bulletin* of the Civic Action Committee, Houston Metropolitan Research Center of the Houston Public Library.

36. Ignacio M. García, "Backwards from Aztlán: Politics in the Age of Hispanics," in *Chicanas and Chicanos in Contemporary Society*, ed. Roberto M. De Anda, 191–204.

37. Ibid.

38. For a discussion of the intent of Chicano studies, of which Chicano history is an important part, see Ignacio M. García, "Juncture in the Road: Chicano Studies since 'El Plan de Santa Barbara,'" in *Chicanas/Chicanos at the Crossroads*, ed. David Maciel and Isidro D. Ortíz, esp. 194–95. See also I. M. García, *Chicanismo*, 43–67.

39. García, "Juncture in the Road," 198.

40. For Peña's own assessment of why he lost, see two untitled speeches, one dated June, 1974, and the other June 5, 1974, in Box 77, Peña Papers.

Bibliography

COLLECTED MATERIALS

Civic Action Committee. *Bulletin* and archives. Houston Metropolitan Research
    Center, Houston Public Library.

García, Dr. Hector P. Papers. Special Collections and Archives, Bell Library, Texas
    A&M University–Corpus Christi.

Peña, Albert. Papers. Special Collections and Archives Department, University of
    Texas at San Antonio Library.

Sánchez, George I. Papers. Benson Latin American Collection, General Libraries,
    University of Texas at Austin.

BOOKS

Acuña, Rodolfo. *Occupied America: A History of Chicanos.* 2d ed. New York: Harper &
    Row, 1981.

Allsup, Carl. *The American G.I. Forum: Origins and Evolution.* Austin: University of
    Texas Press, 1982.

Anaya, Rudolfo A., and Francisco Lomeli. *Aztlán: Essays on the Chicano Homeland.* Albuquerque: University of New Mexico Press, 1991.

Anders, Evans. *Boss Rule in South Texas.* Austin: University of Texas Press, 1982.

Arellano, Anselmo F., and Julian Josue, eds. *Arthur L. Campa and the Coronado Cuatro Centennial.* Las Vegas, N.Mex.: Editorial Telerana, 1980.

Bell, Daniel. *The End of Ideology: On the Exhaustion of Political Ideas in the Fifties.* Glencoe, Ill.: Free Press, 1960.

Bogardus, Emory. *The Mexican in the United States.* Los Angeles: Arno Press, 1934.

Castañeda, Carlos. *Our Catholic Heritage of Texas, 1519–1936.* 7 vols. Austin, Tex.: Von Boeckmann–Jones, 1936–58.

Cooney, John. *The American Pope: The Life and Times of Cardinal Spellman.* New York: Times Books, 1984.

Crosby, Donald F. *God, Church, and the Flag: Senator Joseph R. McCarthy and the Catholic Church, 1950–1957.* Chapel Hill: University of North Carolina Press, 1978.

Dolan, Jay P., and Allan Figueroa Deck, eds. *Hispanic Catholic Culture in the U.S.: Issues and Concerns.* Notre Dame, Ind.: University of Notre Dame Press, 1994.

Fisch, Louise Ann. *All Rise: Reynaldo G. Garza, the First Mexican American Federal Judge.* College Station: Texas A&M University Press, 1996.

Foley, Douglas E., Clarice Mota, Donald E. Post, and Ignacio Lozano. *From Peones to Politicos: Ethnic Relations in a South Texas Town, 1900–1977.* Austin: Center for Mexican American Studies, University of Texas, 1977.

Fones-Wolf, Elizabeth A. *Selling Free Enterprise: The Business Assault on Labor and Liberalism, 1945–1960.* Chicago: University of Illinois Press, 1994.

Foster, James C., ed. *American Labor in the Southwest: The First One Hundred Years.* Tucson: University of Arizona Press, 1982.

Galarza, Ernesto. *Barrio Boy.* New York: Ballantine, 1972.

———. *Strangers in Our Fields.* Washington, D.C.: Joint United States–Mexico Trade Union Committee, 1956.

Gamio, Manuel. *The Mexican Immigrant, His Life Story.* Chicago: University of Chicago Press, 1931.

García, Ignacio M. *Chicanismo: The Forging of a Militant Ethos among Mexican Americans.* Tucson: University of Arizona Press, 1997.

———. *United We Win: The Rise and Fall of La Raza Unida Party.* Tucson: Mexican American Studies and Research Center, 1989.

García, Mario T. *The Making of a Mexican American Mayor.* El Paso: Texas Western Press, 1997.

———. *Memories of Chicano History: The Life and Narrative of Bert Corona.* Berkeley: University of California Press, 1994.

———. *Mexican Americans: Leadership, Ideology, and Identity, 1930–1960.* New Haven: Yale University Press, 1989.

Garcia, Richard A. *Rise of the Mexican American Middle Class: San Antonio, 1929–1941.* College Station: Texas A&M University Press, 1991.

Gómez-Quiñones, Juan. *Chicano Politics: Reality and Promise, 1940–1990*.
Albuquerque: University of New Mexico Press, 1990.

——. *Roots of Chicano Politics, 1600–1940*. Albuquerque: University of New
Mexico Press, 1994.

Grebler, Leo, Joan W. Moore, and Ralph C. Guzmán. *The Mexican American People:
The Nation's Second Largest Minority*. New York: Free Press, 1970.

Griswold del Castillo, Richard, and Arnoldo De León. *North to Aztlán: A History
of Mexican Americans in the United States*. New York: Twayne Publishers,
1996.

Griswold del Castillo, Richard, and Richard A. Garcia. *César Chávez: A Triumph of
Spirit*. Norman: University of Oklahoma Press, 1996.

Gutiérrez, Felix F., and Jorge Reina Schement. *Spanish-Language Radio in the
Southwestern United States*. Austin: Center for Mexican American Studies,
University of Texas, 1979.

Guzmán, Ralph C. *The Political Socialization of the Mexican American People*. New
York: Arno Press, 1976.

Jensen, Vernon H. *Nonferrous Metals Industry Unionism, 1932–1954*. Ithaca, N.Y.: ILR
Press, 1954.

Keller, Gary D., ed. *Chicano Cinema: Research, Reviews, and Resources*. Binghamton,
N.Y.: Bilingual Review, 1985.

Lomitz-Alder, Claudio. *Exits from the Labyrinth: Culture and Ideology in Mexican
National Space*. Berkeley: University of California Press, 1992.

Madsen, William. *Mexican Americans of South Texas*. New York: Holt, Rinehart and
Winston, 1964.

Marín, Christine. *A Spokesman of the Mexican American Movement: Rodolfo "Corky"
Gonzales and the Fight for Chicano Liberation, 1966–1972*. San Francisco: R&E
Associates, 1977.

Márquez, Benjamin. *LULAC: The Evolution of a Mexican American Political
Organization*. Austin: University of Texas Press, 1993.

Martínez, Oscar J. *Troublesome Border*. Tucson: University of Arizona Press, 1988.

Matusow, Allen J. *The Unraveling of America: A History of Liberalism in the Sixties*.
New York: Harper & Row, 1984.

Memorial Address Delivered in Congress. Washington, D.C.: U.S. Government
Printing Office, 1963.

Miller, Tom. *On the Border: Portraits of America's Southwestern Frontier*. New York:
Harper & Row, 1981.

Morín, Raúl. *Among the Valiant: Mexican Americans in World War II and Korea*. Los
Angeles: Borden, 1963.

Morrison, Joan, and Robert K. Morrison. *From Camelot to Kent State: The Sixties
Experience in the Words of Those Who Lived It*. New York: Times Books, 1987.

Muñoz, Carlos, Jr. *Youth, Identity, Power: The Chicano Movement*. London: Verso,
1989.

Munro, Edmonson S. *Los Manitos: A Study of Institutional Values.* New Orleans: Middle American Research Institute, 1957.

Navarro, Armando. *The Cristal Experiment: A Chicano Struggle for Community Control.* Madison: University of Wisconsin Press, 1998.

Noriega, Chon A., ed. *Chicanos and Film: Essays on Chicano Representation and Resistance.* New York: Garland Publishers, 1992.

Quezada, J. Gilberto. *Border Boss: Manuel B. Bravo and Zapata County.* College Station: Texas A&M University Press, 1999.

Riding, Alan. *Distant Neighbors: A Portrait of the Mexicans.* New York: Alfred A. Knopf, 1985.

Rocard, Marcienne. *The Children of the Sun.* Tucson: University of Arizona Press, 1989.

Rodriguez, Richard. *Hunger of Memory: The Education of Richard Rodriguez.* New York: Bantam Books, 1982.

Ruiz, Vicki L. *Cannery Women, Cannery Lives: Mexican Women, Unionization, and the California Food Processing Industry.* Albuquerque: University of New Mexico Press, 1987.

Samora, Julian, ed. *La Raza/Forgotten Americans.* Notre Dame, Ind.: University of Notre Dame Press, 1966.

Samora, Julian, Joe Bernal, and Albert Peña. *Gunpowder Justice: A Reassessment of the Texas Rangers.* Notre Dame, Ind.: University of Notre Dame Press, 1979.

Sánchez, George I. *Forgotten People: A Study of New Mexicans.* Albuquerque: University of New Mexico Press, 1940.

San Miguel, Guadalupe. *"Let All of Them Take Heed": Mexican Americans and the Campaign for Educational Equality in Texas, 1910–1981.* Austin: University of Texas Press, 1987.

Sheridan, Thomas E. *Los Tucsonenses: The Mexican Community in Tucson, 1854–1941.* Tucson: University of Arizona Press, 1986.

Shockley, John Staples. *Chicano Revolt in a Texas Town.* Notre Dame, Ind.: University of Notre Dame Press, 1974.

Smith, Michael. *The Mexicans of Oklahoma.* Norman: University of Oklahoma Press, 1980.

Taylor, Paul S. *An American-Mexican Frontier: Nueces County, Texas.* Chapel Hill: University of North Carolina Press, 1934.

Tuck, Ruth. *Not with the Fist.* New York: Harcourt, Brace, 1946.

Vigil, Maurilio E. *Joseph Montoya, Democratic Senator from New Mexico.* Washington, D.C.: Grossman Publishers, 1972.

———. *Los Patrones: Profiles of Hispanic Political Leaders in New Mexico History.* Washington, D.C.: University Press of America, 1980.

Waxman, Chaim I., ed. *The End of Ideology Debate.* New York: Funk & Wagnalls, 1968.

Whitfield, Stephen J. *The Culture of the Cold War (The American Moment).* 2d ed. Baltimore: John Hopkins University Press, 1996.

Yuhas, Cassian, ed. *The Catholic Church and American Culture.* Mahwah, N.J.: Paulist Press, 1990.

Zamora, Emilio. *The World of the Mexican Worker in Texas.* College Station: Texas A&M University Press, 1993.

ARTICLES, DISSERTATIONS, AND THESES

"Albert Fuentes Makes His Case." *Texas Observer* (February 21, 1964).

Alvarez, Rodolfo. "The Psycho-Historical and Socioeconomic Development of the Chicano Community in the United States." *Social Science Quarterly* 53 (March, 1973): 920–42.

Anaya, Rudolfo. "Aztlán: A Homeland without Boundaries." In *Aztlán: Essays on the Chicano Homeland,* edited by Rudolfo Anaya and Francisco Lomeli, pp. 230–41. Albuquerque: University of New Mexico Press, 1989.

"Announce Viva Kennedy Club in Cal City." *Advertiser* (East Chicago, Ind.), October 27, 1960.

"Anyone Can Be Organization Man in Current Campaign." *Herald-Telegram* (Chippewa Falls, Wisc.), October 3, 1960.

Apodaca, María Linda. "They Kept the Home Fires Burning: Mexican American Women and Social Change." Ph.D. dissertation, University of California, Irvine, 1994.

"Arizona Viva Kennedy Officers, Board Members Listed by Leader." *Phoenix Republic,* October 5, 1960.

Arrieta, Olivia. "The Alianza Hispano Americana in Arizona and New Mexico: The Development and Maintenance of a Multifunctional Ethnic Organization." *Renato Rosaldo Lecture Series Monograph* 7 (1991): 55–82.

"As Votes Kept Coming In—Here's What Really Happened." *U.S. News & World Report* (November 28, 1960): 69–70.

"Back Democrats." *Hammond (Ind.) Times,* October 16, 1960.

Barrett, Donald N. "Demographic Characteristics." In *La Raza/Forgotten Americans,* edited by Julian Samora, pp. 159–200. Notre Dame, Ind.: University of Notre Dame Press, 1966).

"Battle Boils Over Latin American as U.S. Judge." *Corpus Christi Caller,* January 14, 1961.

Betten, Neil. "From Discrimination to Repatriation: Mexican Life in Gary, Indiana, during the Great Depression." *Pacific Historical Review* 42 (1973).

"Better Civilizations." *Life* (December 28, 1959).

"Both Sides of the Catholic Issue." *U.S. News & World Report* (September 26, 1960): 74–81.

Briegel, Kaye. "Alianza Hispano-Americana, 1894–1965: A Mexican American Fraternal Society." Ph.D. dissertation, University of Southern California, 1974.

Burt, Kenneth. "The History of MAPA and Chicano Politics in California." Issued by the Mexican American Political Association, 1982. Pamphlet.

Camarrillo, Albert M. "The G.I. Generation." *Aztlán* 2 (fall, 1971).

"Carlos McCormick Named Coordinator of National Viva Kennedy Clubs." *Forum News Bulletin,* August, 1960.

Castañeda, Carlos E. "Why I Chose History." *The Americas* (April, 1952).

"A Catholic for President?" *The New Republic* (November 18, 1957): 10–13.

"Catholics on the Court." *The New Republic* (September 20, 1960): 13–15.

"Chavez Boosts Kennedy Clubs on West Coast." *Roswell (N.Mex.) Record,* October 9, 1960.

"Chavez Criticizes GOP's Policy on Latin America." *Corpus Christi Caller,* October, 1960.

"Chavez Says Rich Get Richer under GOP." *Fresno Bee,* October 6, 1960.

"Crystal City Mayor Rejects LULAC Bid." *Corpus Christi Caller,* June 14, 1963.

Cuellar, Robert A. "A Social and Political History of the Mexican American Population in Texas, 1929–1963." Master's thesis, Texas State University, Denton, 1969.

Dinwoodie, D. H. "The Rise of the Mine-Mill Union in Southwestern Copper." In *American Labor in the Southwest: The First One Hundred Years,* edited by James C. Foster, pp. 46–56. Tucson: University of Arizona Press, 1982.

"Dr. Garcia's Support Could Have Given Win." *Forum News Bulletin,* June, 1961, 1.

Dugger, Ronnie. "Gonzalez of San Antonio—Part 5—the Politics of Fratricide." *Texas Observer* (December 12, 1980).

———. "San Antonio Liberalism: Piecing It Together." *Texas Observer* (May 27, 1966): 1–5.

———. "Who Lay Unnamed." *Texas Observer* (February 14, 1958): 1.

"Editorial." *El Grito* 1 (1967): 4.

"Editorial." *Forum News Bulletin,* July, 1961, 5.

"El Señor José Alvarado invitado de honor a la toma de posesion del Señor Presidente John F. Kennedy." *El Anunciador* (Chicago, Ill.), January 14, 1960.

Estrada, Ralph. "Ethnic Equity and Political Progress." *Alianza,* September, 1961, 6.

"Forumeers and Sen. Kennedy Rise into White House on the Mexican Burro." *Forum News Bulletin,* December, 1960, 1.

"Forumeers Participate as Individuals in 'Viva Clubs.'" *Forum News Bulletin,* October, 1960.

"Frontiersmen (J.g.): Do They All Want to Be President?" *Newsweek* (March 9, 1962): 80.

García, Ignacio M. "Backwards from Aztlán: Politics in the Age of Hispanics." In *Chicanas and Chicanos in Contemporary Society,* edited by Roberto M. De Anda, pp. 191–204. Boston: Allyn and Bacon, 1995.

———. "El rechazo de Aztlán: la contrapolitica de los hispánicos en Robstown, Texas." *NACCS Journal* (summer, 1999).

———. "Juncture in the Road: Chicano Studies since 'El Plan de Santa Barbara.'" In

Chicanas/Chicanos at the Crossroads, edited by David Maciel and Isidro D. Ortíz. Tucson: University of Arizona Press, 1996.

García, Juan R. "Hollywood and the West: Mexican Images in American Film." In *Old Southwest, New Southwest,* edited by Judy Nolte Lensink. Tucson: Tucson Public Library, 1987.

Garcia, Richard. "The Mexican American Mind: A Product of the 1930s." In *History, Culture, and Society: Chicano Studies in the 1980s.* N.p.: National Association for Chicano Studies, 1983.

"The G.I. Generation." *Aztlán* 2 (fall, 1971).

Glazer, Mike. "LA CSO History." Los Angeles Community Service Organization, 1965. Pamphlet.

"González." *Texas Observer* (May 30, 1958): 1.

González, Henry B. "Poll Tax Primer: The Behead Tax." *Texas Observer* (October 18, 1963).

González-Gutiérrez, Elizabeth. "The Education and Public Career of María C. Urquides: A Case Study of a Mexican American Community Leader." Ph.D. dissertation, University of Arizona, Tucson, 1986.

Graham, Robert Somerville. "Spanish-Language Radio in Northern Colorado." *American Speech* (October, 1962).

Griffith, Beatrice W. "Mexican Americans Enter L.A. Politics." *The Mirror,* May 6, 1949.

———. "Viva Roybal—Viva America." *Common Ground* 10 (August, 1949): 61–70.

Gutiérrez, David G. "Ethnicity, Ideology, and Political Development: Mexican Immigration as a Political Issue in the Chicano Community." Ph.D. dissertation, Stanford University, 1988.

Gutiérrez, José Angel. "Chicanos and Mexicans under Surveillance: 1940–1980." *Renato Rosaldo Lecture Series Monograph* (spring, 1986): 29–58.

Guzmán, Ralph C. "The Function of Anglo-American Racism in the Political Development of Chicanos." *California Historical Quarterly* 50, no. 1 (1971): 321–37.

———. "Politics and Policies of the Mexican American Community." In *California Politics and Policies,* edited by Eugene Divorin and Arthur Misner, pp. 350–85. Los Angeles: Addison-Wesley, 1960.

Hall, Martin. "Roybal's Candidacy and What It Means." *Frontier* (June, 1949).

"Henry Barbosa González: Mexican American Political and Governmental Leader, Lawyer." In *Notable Latino Americans,* edited by Matt S. Meier. Westport, Conn.: Greenwood Press, 1997.

"High Job Offered Latin American." *Forum News Bulletin,* February 18, 1961.

"Hispanic Leaders Will Work on Clinton Campaign." *United Press International,* September 17, 1992.

"How America Feels as We Enter the Soaring Sixties." *Look* (January 5, 1960).

"Informes al Pueblo." *Latin Times,* October 29, 1960.

"Jackie Talks to Latins." *Riverside Press,* October 13, 1960.

"Jim Wells Goes Strongly Demo, Two Boxes Out." *Corpus Christi Caller,*
November 9, 1960.

"Judge Salinas Urges U.S. Gov. Note Presence of This Country's 12 Million Latin
Americans; Ask Their Use." *Forum News Bulletin,* August, 1960.

"Kennedy es Nuestro Lider." *Latin Times,* October 29, 1960, 1.

"Kennedy Patronage, Latin American Policies under Fire." *Congressional Quarterly*
(January 23, 1961).

"Kennedy's Liberal Promises." *Time* (September 19, 1960): 23.

"Kennedy's Promises for the Future." *U.S. News & World Report* (November 21,
1960): 42.

"The Kennedy Story." *U.S. News & World Report* (November 21, 1960): 46–55.

"Kennedy Wins Starr by Heavy Majority." *Corpus Christi Caller,* November 9, 1960.

"Latin Americans Organize Viva Kennedy Committee." *Dallas News,* October 5,
1960.

"Latin Group Split on Endorsement." *Texas Observer* (February 16, 1962): 1.

"Latinos en Varios Puestos Oficiales." *La Prensa* (San Antonio, Tex.), February 14,
1961.

"Latins and Votes." *Texas Observer* (January 19, 1962): 1, 3.

"Let Juan Do It for You." *Desert Magazine* 19 (July, 1956): 27–28.

"Los Viva-Kennedy Clubs y las Promesas Incumplidas de la Presente
Administración." *El Quijote,* September 15, 1961.

Martínez, Arthur D. "Los de Dodge City, Kansas: A Mexican American Community
at the Heartland of the U.S." *Journal of the West* 24 (1985).

Martínez, John R. "Leadership and Politics." In *La Raza/Forgotten Americans,* edited
by Julian Samora, pp. 47–62. Notre Dame, Ind.: University of Notre Dame Press,
1966.

Martínez, Oscar. "Hispanics in Arizona." In *Arizona at Seventy-five,* edited by
B. Luey and N. J. Stone, pp. 87–122. Tucson: Arizona State University Public
History Program and History Society, 1987.

"Mexican Americans' Balance of Power Dramatically Illustrated." *Forum News
Bulletin,* June, 1961, 1.

"Mexicans Pleased by Election of Kennedy." *Kansas City Star,* November 21, 1960.

Monsiváis, Carlos. "La Utopia Indocumentada: La Cultura Mexicana de los
Noventas." *Renato Rosaldo Lecture Series Monograph* 9 (1993): 51–60.

"Name Two Local Spanish Speaking Men for Kennedy." *Calumet (Ind.) News,*
October 12, 1960.

"New Hidalgo Unit Head Says Group Not Anti-PASO." *Corpus Christi Caller,*
June 14, 1963.

"New Mexico Dems Head Drive to Corral Spanish Vote." *Flagstaff Sun,* October 12,
1960.

"New Mexico Race Is Rated Toss-up." *New York Times,* September 19, 1960.

"Not a Single Spanish Surname . . ." *Texas Observer* (August 23, 1963): 5.

"The Only Way I Want to Win." *Texas Observer* (July 4, 1959): 5.

"PASO Official Accuses Anglos of Injecting Race Issue in Valley." *Valley Evening Monitor* (Harlingen, Tex.), May 24, 1963, 3-A.

"PASO Withdraws." *Texas Observer* (October 12, 1962): 1.

"Peña Is Not in LBJ's Club." *Texas Observer* (December 15, 1959).

Peñalosa, Fernando. "Toward an Operational Definition of the Mexican American." *Aztlán* 1 (spring, 1970): 1–12.

"Periodical Tells of Revolt by Spanish-Americans, Hit JFK Patronage and Latin Policies." *Forum News Bulletin,* July, 1961, 2.

"A Pessimistic View." *Texas Observer* (December, 1960).

"Political Interests of Latins United." *Texas Observer* (September 15, 1961).

"Political Summons in Bexar." *Texas Observer* (October 5, 1962): 1.

"Record Registration in East Chicago." *Latin Times,* October 22, 1960.

"Religion Helped, Not Hurt Kennedy." *Texas Observer* (November 11, 1960): 1.

Reyna, Jóse R. "Readings in Southwestern Folklore." *Perspectives in Mexican American Studies* 1 (1988).

"Robstown Latin Replies to Anglo." *Texas Observer* (August 1, 1959): 3.

Rodríguez, Eugene, Jr. "Henry B. González: A Political Profile." Master's thesis, St. Mary's University, San Antonio, 1965.

Romano, Octavio. "The Anthropology and Sociology of the Mexican American: The Distortion of Mexican American History." *El Grito* (1968).

Ruiz, Vicki L. "'Star Struck': Acculturation, Adolescence, and the Mexican American Woman, 1920–1950." In *Building with Our Hands: New Directions in Chicana Studies,* edited by Adela de la Torre and Beatríz M. Pesquera, pp. 109–29. Berkeley: University of California Press, 1993.

Sánchez, George I. "The American of Mexican Descent." *Chicago Jewish Forum* 20 (winter, 1961–62): 120–24.

———. "Bilingualism and Mental Measure: A Word of Caution." *Journal of Applied Psychology* 18 (December, 1934).

———. "History, Culture and Education." In *La Raza/Forgotten Americans,* edited by Julian Samora, pp. 1–26. Notre Dame, Ind.: University of Notre Dame Press, 1966.

Santillan, Richard. "Latino Politics in the Midwestern United States." In *Latinos and the Political System,* edited by F. Chris García. Notre Dame, Ind.: University of Notre Dame Press, 1988.

Santillan, Richard, and Carlos Muñoz, Jr. "Latinos and the Democratic Party." In *The Democrats Must Lead: The Case for a Progressive Democratic Party,* edited by James MacGregor Burns, William Crotty, Lois Lovelace Duke, and Lawrence D. Longley, pp. 173–84. San Francisco: Oxford University Press, 1992.

Santillan, Richard, and Federico A. Subervi-Vélez. "Latino Participation in Republican Party Politics in California." In *Racial and Ethnic Politics in California,* edited by Byran O. Jackson and Michael B. Preston, pp. 285–319. Berkeley, Calif.: Institute of Governmental Studies Press, 1991.

"Senator Henry Gonzalez to Speak." *Latin Times,* October 22, 1960.

"Senator Joins G.I. Forum." *Forum News Bulletin,* May, 1960.

"Senator Kennedy Sends Warm Message to G.I. Forum in Los Angeles." *Forum News Bulletin,* September, 1959.

"Sen. Chavez Charges of Spanish American Snub Brings Some Appointments." *Forum News Bulletin,* March, 1961.

Simmons, Ozzie G. "The Mutual Images and Expectations of Anglo-Americans and Mexican Americans." *Daedalus* (spring, 1961): 286–99.

"Sleeping Giant." *Texas Observer* (June 1, 1962): 3.

"Southern California Puzzles Experts." *New York Times,* September 20, 1960.

Stanford, Louise. "Mathis since the Revolution." *Texas Observer* (August 23, 1968): 12–14.

"State to Fare Well, Sen. Chavez Asserts." *Albuquerque Tribune,* November 10, 1960.

"The Struggle for P.A.S.O." *Texas Observer* (June 14, 1963): 3–6.

"Teamsters and Peña Continue to Roll." *La Verdad,* June 14, 1963, 1.

"Telles Appointed." *Forum News Bulletin,* March, 1961, 6.

"Tell News at Presidential Press Parley Expect Other Forumeers to Be Named." *Forum News Bulletin,* March, 1961.

"Texas Latins Bid for Better Lot with Ballots." *Fort Worth Star-Telegram,* April 15, 1964.

"This Is John Fitzgerald Kennedy." *Newsweek* (June 23, 1958): 29–34.

Thompson, Paul. "Hector's Ache." *San Antonio Express,* June 17, 1963.

Torres, David L. "Dynamics behind the Formation of a Business Class: Tucson's Hispanic Business Elite." *Hispanic Journal of Behavioral Sciences* 12 (1990): 25–49.

Torres, David L., and Melissa Amado. "The Quest for Power: Hispanic Collective Action in Frontier Arizona." *Perspectives in Mexican American Studies* 3 (1992): 73–94.

"TV Talks Spur Kennedy and Nixon Activity." *Chicago Daily Tribune,* September 28, 1960.

"Two Men Who Filled a Vacuum." *Texas Observer* (February 25, 1961): 5.

Underwood, Kathleen. "Process and Politics: Multiracial Electoral Coalition Building and Representation in Los Angeles Ninth District, 1949–1962." Ph.D. dissertation, University of California, San Diego, 1992.

Valdes, Dennis Nodín. "El pueblo mexicano en Detroit y Michigan: A Social History." Ph.D. dissertation, Wayne State University, 1982.

"Valley Counties Solid for Demos." *Corpus Christi Times,* November 10, 1960.

"Viva Clubs Now Permanent, Choose Mexican Americans for Political Action Name." *Forum News Bulletin,* March, 1961.

"Viva Kennedy Club." *Latin Times,* October 15, 1960.

"Viva Kennedy Club Is Planned." *Corpus Christi Caller,* September 23, 1960.

"Viva Kennedy Clubs Deliver Biggest Texas Demo Gains." *The Press,* November 9, 1960, 1.

"Viva Kennedy Clubs Host Senator Gonzalez." *Latin Times,* October 29, 1960, 7.

"Viva Kennedy Clubs Meet to Form National Political Group." *Forum News Bulletin,* April, 1961.

"Viva Kennedy Leaders in Revolt." *Valley Morning Star,* June 28, 1961.

"Viva Kennedy Movement in East Chicago." *Latin Times,* October 1, 1960, 1.

"Viva Kennedy Quarters Opened in East Chicago." *Hammond Times,* October 9, 1960.

"Vote or Suffer Consequences, Sen. Chavez Tells S.B. Group." *San Bernardino Sun,* October 9, 1960.

"Voting Drive for Latins Criticized." *Texas Observer* (November, 1955).

Week, O. Douglas. "The Texas-Mexican and the Politics of South Texas." *American Political Science Review* 24 (August, 1930): 607–27.

Weshler, Louis, and John Gallagher. "Viva Kennedy." In *Cases in American National Politics and Government,* edited by Rocco J. Tresolini and Richard T. Frost. Englewood Cliffs, N.J.: Prentice Hall, 1966.

Index

American G.I. Forum (*continued*)
171; saw need for political role, 36; successful at integrating women, 51; supplied most club leadership, 54; Wichita convention of, 45; wooed by Kennedy staff, 45

Americanism, 7; in the barrio, 26; emphasized, 19; learned in school, 24

American Society, 6, 10, 17; critical of, 20; frustration with, 35; fundamentally good, 27, 37; gaining benefits of, 28; Mexican American middle class in, 36; not allowed collective rise, 9

Anaya, Rudolfo, 127

Anglo Americans, 7, 14, 18; lacked faith in Mexican Americans, 62; lifestyle changes of, 27; more insensitivity by, 121; persuasion of, 70; prejudiced boards of, 80; prejudices of, 40, 61; retrenchment by, 64; sympathetic, 21; used as allies, 156; writers, 19

anti-communism, 18, 19, 35, 38

assimilation, 21, 24–25, 38

Avila, Manuel, Jr., 106, 107, 111

Aztlán, 84, 103

barrio, 5, 17, 18, 20, 21, 70; Americanism within, 27; forces of acculturation in, 24, 26; lever-pulling in, 99; Mexican candidates in, 30; new reformer in, 35; no need to remain in, 38; politics in the, 124; suburbanization of, 84

Bay of Pigs, 110–11

Bexar County Democratic Coalition, 142

Bexar County Democratic Party, 72

Bonilla, Tony, 100, 101

Bonilla, William, 100, 153, 155

border, 18, 26, 40

bracero program, 36, 39

Camelot, 18, 13; Mexican American version of, 83–84; not the one envisioned, 180; proved flawed, 174

Campa, Arthur L., 22, 67

Cañamar, Charles, 88

Carrion, Arturo Moráles, 109

Casso, Ramiro, 51, 137

Castañeda, Carlos, 22, 28, 35; wrote complementary history, 75, 176

Castro, Raul, 98, 169

Catholicism: downplayed, 58, 59; promoted conformity, 18; selling point for Kennedy, 55

Catholic Youth Organization, 18

Chávez, César, 46, 175

Chávez, Dennis, 11, 30, 31, 43, 63; asks colleagues for appointment support, 108; assures constituency, 107; background of, 65–66; chides Yarborough, 119; criticizes Kennedy Administration, 109–10; honorary chair of clubs, 54; initially supports LBJ, 57; knew Kennedy, 44; meets with Gonzalez and Roybal, 44; no-show at PASO, 128; one man crusade of, 95–97; only significant Demo leader, 121; prominence of, 93; supporter of New Deal, 56; visits Midwest, 89

Chicano activists, 28, 77, 99, 169

Chicano Movement, 10, 103, 105, 163, 168–69, 172, 175; groups within sought uniformity, 60; post-era of, 69

Citizens for Kennedy-Johnson clubs, 51

Civic Action Committee, 29, 101

civic participation, 25, 28

civil rights: for blacks, 14; conflict over, 41; in Democratic party platform, 39; Henry B. Gonzalez's record on, 31

Cold War, 56; impact on Mexican Americans, 16; nations preoccupation with, 38; red-baiting of, 17; television during, 22; tempers politics, 32

Communism, 8, 14; in developing countries, 57; fears of, 38; growing in Latin America, 46; saving the U.S. from, 40

Community Service Organization, 70, 93, 175

conformity, 14, 17, 18

Congressional Hispanic Caucus, 176

Congress of Spanish Speaking Organizations, 56

Connally, John, 120; attacked by PASO, 151; at Paso convention, 137, 139; wins election, 144–46

conservatives, 42, 91, 149

constitutional rights, replaces notion of Mexicanness, 15

Cornejo, Juan, 149

Corona, Bert, 27

Corpus Christi, 29, 36, 132, 158; Chávez in, 96–97; Mexican American leaders meet in, 54

Crystal City: fiasco, 164; PASO campaign in, 147–50; PASO conflict over, 151–56

Cubans, 92

Daniel, Price, 137, 139–44

De Anda, Jimmy, 119

de la Garza, Adolfo, 51

Democratic Party, 5, 7, 32; attacked by García, 37; consequences to, 114; endorsed Salinas, 115; among Midwest Latinos, 89, 91; more sensitive at national level, 56; most Mexican Americans belonged to, 55; national convention of, 33–45; "our Party," 100; PASO committed to, 151; recent commitments of, 87; represented at PASO meeting, 139; seen as hindrance to Viva Kennedy, 49; in

Texas, 42; threatened by PASO leaders, 132

Depression, the, 13; discrimination, 6; emphasized through vulgarity, 20; increases union activity, 16; not a Mexican American issue, 41; programs during, 68; rampant, 16

Dugger, Ronnie, 135

Eisenhower, Dwight D., 34, 86, 95, 99, 110, 114, 115, 116

election outcome, 105–106

electoral arena, 6, 30, 31, 62, 70, 86

El Quijote, 111

Estrada, Ralph, 57, 130

ethnic identification, 15, 48, 58, 70, 163, 175

Falcón, Moses, 148

federal courts, 37

federal government, 17, 37, 39; attitude toward migrants, 39; could make things happen, 86; homefront attitude of, 69; indifference of, 134; intervention of, 80; involvement in migrant issues, 46; romanticized view of, 38

Flores, Juan A., 108

Forum Bulletin, 48, 53, 109, 112, 132

fourteenth amendment, 6, 24

Fuentes, Albert, 145; PASO executive secretary, 150; seeks PASO leadership, 154–55; supports teamsters, 153–56; testifies in congress, 150–51; used PASO as forum, 163

Galarza, Ernesto, 27, 28

García, Cleotilde, 100

García, Hector P., 11, 28; accepts Garza's appointment, 120; accuses Democrats of close-mindedness, 111; angry over

García, Hector P. (*continued*)
appointments, 125–26; attacked for Daniel endorsement, 142; background of, 63–64, 72–73; blames war casualties on segregation, 29; at civil rights conference, 57; committed to LBJ, 43; congratulates Peña, 106; criticizes schisms, 131; discloses frustration over appointment, 110; documents plight of migrants, 39; doesn't return to PASO, 160; endorses Daniel, 139–40; gives personal assurance, 102; had specific agenda, 35; involved in veterans' issues, 36; laments prejudice, 146; letters to club members, 53; named national co-chair, 54, 98; quick temper, 156; remained in the barrio, 178–79; sent to Jamaica, 109, 112; sought Anglo American sympathy, 41; threatens to quit Democrats, 114; urges Salinas appointment, 113; views on teamsters, 153–55; writes to National Democrats, 36–41; wrote flyers, 99; wrote Kennedy about appointments, 108

García, Mario T., 5–6, 79

García, Martín, 149, 152, 154, 164

Garza, Reynaldo G., 112, 119

G.I. Bill, 17, 24

Gonzales, Rodolfo, "Corky," 163, 175

González, Henry B., 11–12, 30, 31, 43; background of, 64–65, 71–72; celebrity in Midwest, 89–90; conflict with Daniel, 140; distanced himself from PASO, 156, 161–62; emphasizes Kennedy's liberalism, 102; meets with Roybal, 44; met Kennedy, 44; most successful politician, 172; named national co-chair, 54; not endorsed by liberals, 133; no-show at PASO meetings, 130; offered ambassadorship, 109; practical crusade, 61; remained a Kennedy Democrat, 179; runs for senate, 131–32; Sánchez disappointed with, 135; wins congressional seat, 146

González-Mireles, Jovita, 27

Gutiérrez, José Angel, 9, 175

Guzmán, Ralph, 93

Hidalgo County, 50–51, 52, 155

Hispanic Generation, 8, 169, 176–78

Idar, Ed, Jr.: chastises liberals, 133–34; criticizes Yarborough, 118–19; defends Daniel endorsement, 143; describes Forum as naive, 48; enlisted in Kennedy campaign, 48; founder of local Viva Kennedy Club, 50–51; glad PASO dead, 161; knew little of national group, 59; laments reformers' inexperience, 167; not a radical, 164; predicament of, 137; prolific writer, 162; rejects Sánchez reconciliation, 144; supports Daniel, 139–41; writes convention call, 136; writes Kennedy, 52

International Union of Mine, Mill and Smelter Workers, 17, 97

Johnson, Jake, 146

Johnson, Lyndon Baines, 34; commits to civil rights plank, 41; resists Salinas appointment, 117–18; seeks to influence PASO, 155; supports Connally, 137; vacates seat, 131

Kennedy, Jacqueline, 59

Kennedy, John F., 3–5; anointed leader of party, 102; barely knew club leaders, 57; becomes member of Forum, 45; club image of, 55; death immortalizes him, 156; different from other Democrats, 53; emulating style of, 172; fights communism, 57; gave hope,

with Yarborough, 119; only leader of PASO, 162; political style of, 72; re-elected PASO leader, 155; remained the *caudillo*, 168; represented Political orientation, 42; responds to editorial, regroups, 145–46; selected MAPA chair, 124; sought more voter revolts, 150; at state convention, 136–42; state director of clubs, 98; still committed, 179; takes exception to discrimination charge, 135; too Americanized, 163

political appointments, 6–7, 10, 38, 39, 40; Anglo American, 111; few Latinos contacted for, 107; forum calls for, 46; no commitment on, 48; lack of, 120–23; principles called for, 79; to represent U.S., 83

Political Association of Spanish-speaking Organizations (PASO), 127–30; beyond integration, 164; campaign debacle of, 147; conflict over Crystal City, 151–55; convention split in, 142; demise of, 156; embolden by victory, 151; favored coalition, 135; involvement in Crystal City of, 147–50; jumps into senate race, 131; last effort of, 157–59; limited vision, 165–69; promotes itself, 134; ridiculed by media, 145; split becomes permanent, 160; state convention of, 136–42; structural weakness in, 143; unable to make in-roads, 146

politics of accommodation, 10, 173–74

Portillo, Ernesto, 98

postwar years, 13–18; ethnocentricity of, 19

poverty prevalent in leave, 13, 15; contradiction of, 25; a factor in barrio, 21; had ended for liberals, 14; push people to communism, 57

Proctor, Les, 138

Puerto Ricans, 90, 92, 106, 109, 110, 111–12

racism, 20, 21

Republicans: attacked by Chávez, 95; attacked by García, 37; efforts among Mexican Americans, 34; at PASO convention, 139; possible support of, 110; urged to recruit Mexican Americans, 48

rhetoric of reform, in English, 14–15, 20–21

Richey, John, 20

Rio Grande Valley, 117, 124, 137, 152, 157

Rockefeller, Nelson A., 110

Roel, V. G., 112, 119, 153, 161

Roosevelt, Franklin D., 56, 57, 68, 86, 96, 102

Roybal, Edward R., 27, 28, 30; appointed state director, 54; considered for appointments, 109; criticizes administration, 110; elected to city council, 31; founded Hispanic Caucus, 179; incensed over appointments, 125; meets with González, 44; in Midwest, 89–90; 1940's candidacy of, 93; no-show, 128, 130; promoted Kennedy's liberalism, 102; relationship with Kennedy, 95; represented particular generation, 67, 69–70; successful politician, 172; supported Kennedy, 43; travels across nation, 94

Rubi, Frank, 54

Rucoba, Richard, 54, 88

Ruiz, Vicki L., 24, 26

Salinas, E. D., 112, 114, 123; positive about appointment, 115; opposition arises to, 117; fails to get appointment, 119–20

San Antonio, 42